# Living
# with
# My
# Century

*For Clodagh and for Mireia and John*

# Living with My Century

# Eda Sagarra

THE LILLIPUT PRESS
DUBLIN

First published 2022 by
THE LILLIPUT PRESS
62–63 Sitric Road, Arbour Hill
Dublin 7, Ireland
www.lilliputpress.ie

Paperback ISBN 9781843518358

A CIP record for this title is available from The British Library.

10 9 8 7 6 5 4 3 2 1

The Lilliput Press gratefully acknowledges the financial
support of the Arts Council/An Chomhairle Ealaíon.

Set in 12pt on 16pt Garamond by iota (www.iota-books.ie)
Printed in Kerry by Walsh Colour Print

# Contents

*Illustrations between pages 146 and 147.*

# *Acknowledgments*

I would like to thank all who read the manuscript critically and made helpful comments: my sister Clodagh and my nieces, Syra and Moira Forshaw, my cousins, Eoin O'Brien and Ronan Lyons, my colleagues in Trinity, especially Daragh Downes and Frank Barry, together with Gisela Holfter (University of Limerick) and Finola Kennedy, and my golfing friends who kept me at it: May Redmond and Anne Valentine.

And thank you too to my publisher, Antony Farrell of The Lilliput Press, to my sage editor, Djinn von Noorden and to Julitta Clancy and her daughter Elizabeth for the index.

# *Author's Note*

This memoir was written in my eighty-seventh and eighty-eighth years during the Covid-19 lockdowns of 2020/21, when the country and much of the world was in a state of suspended animation. During the first three or four months of the virus, we old people (a term I still think as only applying to other people) were not allowed go outside our homes. Nor even to engage in conversation with those kind family members and neighbours who took on the chore of doing my shopping. I have lived almost all my life surrounded by people and I love to talk. How was I to fill the long days ahead?

What about a memoir? I had tried to write one when I turned fifty, but the results had long been confined to the wastepaper basket. Then I recalled a conversation in 2018 with my German friend Wolfgang Frühwald (1935–2019): 'write as though you were just telling a story'. And so, every day from late March 2020 onwards between 5 and 6 am, I would sit up in bed with a large pot of tea beside me and start reminiscing. After a brief breakfast and a surreptitious trot seven times up and down the pavement outside the house before the neighbours were awake,[*] it was up to the laptop in my study at the top of the house to start writing for a couple of hours.

At ten it was time to take a break, listen to mass broadcast on TV and put in the rest of the morning attacking the masses of yellow celandine invading the overgrown back garden (the weather in the first lockdown was wonderful). Trying to bin each of the ten or so little nodules attached to those hundreds of celandine roots, which if left would choke every other growing thing, was a great distraction. So, after a brief post-prandial siesta (I am Spanish, or rather Catalan, by marriage), it would be back to the desk till six in the evening in time to get dinner with the shopping dropped outside my hall door – no one, but no one, was allowed in or near. You could only talk to people at due distance across the railings – and I am getting deaf.

Living in this new isolated world after my gregarious life was very strange. In normal times I would be out most of the day, walking or playing golf, dropping in for a cup of tea with friends or visiting those who were sick or housebound, or at work down in the College or other libraries. Now I could only read about what was happening in the outside world in the newspapers or on Irish and English TV and try to imagine what it must be like to live permanently alone without family or cooped up in a two-roomed flat with small children who had nowhere to play, or in packed tenements where people got on each other's nerves.

After a few weeks being confined to barracks, I began to live in two worlds, in my 'barracks' but also, and increasingly, immersed in the world of my past, which in an odd way, became ever more vivid as the lonely weeks passed. The very fact that normal social as well as economic life was at a standstill defamiliarizes the present and awakens us to an awareness of all sorts of things and freedoms we had always taken for granted. Perhaps remembering past times and more particularly people in my past and recalling them in a story would give me some perspective on what was happening right now?

This book is written in a time of restriction that is, mercifully and thanks to the vaccines, perhaps no more than a pandemic-enforced hiatus.

---

[*] That is, just about one kilometre.

Much of the book is, however, written *about* a time when restrictions were the norm. The Ireland of the decades I was born and grew up in – the 1930s, 40s and 50s – was as different from the Ireland of today as you could imagine. Younger people today who read of the restrictions to which women were subject in that time will find it difficult to comprehend why our generation and the one that followed ours didn't challenge the system. But probably the greatest contrast between the Ireland of then and now (at least pre-Covid) was the room for manoeuvre – or rather the absence of it. Today most people are mobile. The Ireland when I was young was in almost every respect a static, hierarchical and paternalist society, one in which the accident of your birth would generally determine your whole life.

In my late teens, I read a book that made me realize for the first time how much history is encapsulated in a single life: Mary Carbery's *The Farm by Lough Gur* (1937).[*] It tells the story of the daughter of a 'strong' farmer in Limerick, Mary (Sissie) O'Brien, as told in her mid-eighties to and recorded by her young companion Mary Carbery. Apart from Sissie's vivid recall of the personalities, customs and manners of post-Famine Ireland in the 1860s and 70s, a particular fascination of Mary Fogarty's story lies in showing the extraordinarily long reach into the past a good memory and a habit of observing people can give. I don't have a Mary Carbery to listen to my memories, so I've had to write them down myself. Of course, memory plays tricks on us. I have never believed a writer (there may be exceptions) who 'so accurately' remembers things that have happened to her or him at two or three years of age. I imagine many of my own earliest 'memories' were shaped by what I was later told by adults.

As a child I kept a diary, but mine was a nature diary, a record of birds or wildflowers I had seen that day. It was written in spidery writing, one page for a whole month, as paper was a scarce commodity in and after the war years 1939–45. My subsequent diaries, kept intermittently over my adult life, provided an uneven record of events, thoughts and

[*] *The Farm by Lough Gur.* London: Longmans and Green, 1937, re-issued Dublin: Lilliput Press, 2010 and 2018.

feelings, serving as an occasional useful memory prompt in writing the present account. Much more graphic in recalling the past at a given point are letters. Clodagh and I wrote weekly letters home from boarding school and our parents, especially my father Kevin O'Shiel, were great letter-writers. Unfortunately, most got lost in the various house moves. However, my correspondence with my Manchester friend Tony (A.O.J.) Cockshut and his wife, the children's author Gillian Avery, has survived. The correspondence, which extends over half a century, began in a desultory way when they moved to Oxford in the mid-1960s. Gill's and my letters, written at intervals until shortly before she went into care in 2016, are characteristically full of 'non-events', which she always managed to make amusing and worthwhile. His are much more serious, mainly about politics, history and religion – he was an early convert to Catholicism from public school in Winchester and would become our daughter Mireia's godfather. A few years after we moved to Ireland in the late 1970s the correspondence became weekly. At the time I would have preferred a more leisurely exchange, such as with Gill, but Tony was strong-willed and peremptory in his demand for a reply within the week to his every missive. When we visited them once or twice a year, we would take a year of the correspondence and read each other's letters aloud. It was astonishing how immediate and how vivid was my then recall of events, personalities and impressions long since buried in memory, which these sessions evoked.*

When, most unwillingly, we first-year students at University College Dublin in 1951 attended the obligatory classes in logic, one of the first things we learnt was that one must never generalize from the particular. Yet every autobiographer nurtures the belief that their life is in a special way representative of the times she or he has lived through. And so it is, but only of the limited sector of society in which that individual lived

---

* I still write and send my weekly missive to Tony, who at ninety-four has lost his sight and is slowly dying, full of fortitude, visited regularly by his friends at Oxford. His daughter sends regular updates on his condition and she re-directs my letters to his carers who read them to him. After our deaths, the archivist of Tony's Oxford College, Hertford, has agreed to accept our correspondence of almost 3000 letters (c. 1500 from each) for the use of future historians.

and worked. My mother's Cork family was thoroughly matriarchal and our father, like many fathers with daughters but no sons, was in effect if not in name a feminist. Moreover, I was fortunate to find myself in a profession, at least in Britain and later in Trinity College, where gender discrimination was a good deal less marked than it was for most Irish women in the workplace.

This book, then, is written in the belief that, while no life is amply representative, every person's experience is a unique reflection of the times through which they have lived. As such, each of us has a story worth recording for those who come after us.

Thus begins, on the far side of double vaccination against the coronavirus, my own long reach into the distant past.

*Dublin, August 2021*

# — ONE —

## *The 1930s: Who I am and where I came from*

FAMILY

My elder sister Clodagh and I were the relatively uncommon mixture of Irish counties, our father from Tyrone in Ulster and our mother from Cork, the largest and most southerly county of the province of Munster. In Ireland we all have our stereotypical associations of the character of each county, of Tyrone people as being frugal and (to outsiders surprisingly) proud of their rugged landscape,* while Corkonians are regarded as having an irritating sense of superiority, documented in their alleged fondness for a white map of Ireland with only Cork in red, the rest being marked 'not Cork'. At the time of his marriage to our future mother Kevin O'Shiel at thirty-eight was thirteen years older than his wife. In the secretive manner of Irish families in those days, we were never told about his first marriage nor of his two sons, our stepbrothers, who had died at birth, the second costing his mother her life. And when as a child I came across a large cigarette box inscribed in Irish '*Do Caoimhghín Ó Siadhail le linn a phósta …*

---

\* See the 1962 guidebook: *Tyrone Among the Bushes*, published by the Tyrone Association.

*22 Mí Lúghnasa, ó n-a Chó-ofigigh 1922*\* and shared my exciting discovery with Clodagh, it never dawned on either of us to speak about it to our parents. We only discovered about our deceased half-brothers sixty years later during a visit to our father's sister, Syra.

In common with most Irish families, we were descended on both sides from small farmers (my mother would insist, 'medium farmers'). The O'Shiels were a long-established Ulster family, hereditary physicians to the princely Ulster O'Neill family. They had changed their name to Shields in penal times, having had their 'profitable lands' confiscated in the 1660s for being 'on the wrong side'. Kevin's father, the mild-mannered Francis Shields, had been apprenticed by his eldest brother to a local solicitor, a characteristic step at that time among the slightly better-off farming classes concerned with upward social mobility. Francis' mother, Elizabeth (Mitty) Roantree (1864–1932), granddaughter of a butcher and daughter of a primary school teacher and later inspector of schools, was evidently made of stern stuff. She was certainly much more socially ambitious than her husband – to her son Kevin's frequent embarrassment. When she announced to her husband and their then teenage children that she was going to apply for membership of the local tennis club only to be told that she wouldn't succeed: 'There are no Catholics in Omagh Tennis Club', she simply said, 'There will be when we are members.' And Mother was always right. She didn't wholly approve of Kevin's choice of second wife, who evidently didn't take her mother-in-law's pre-wedding advice to buy a 'good serge suit for Sundays'. Instead, she like her four sisters preferred to make her own (fashionable) clothes and loved, as my father did, fancy hats and high-heeled shoes to show off her shapely legs. We never knew our northern grandmother, but my impression of her is indelibly shaped by my first encounter with her authentic voice in the form of her will. I suppose the desire to exercise influence on the living beyond the grave is part of human nature, but never a good idea: Working on my father's biography in the National Archives in 2004,

---

\* The inscription reads: 'To Kevin O'Shiel … 22 August 1922 from his colleagues' (in the Provisional Free State government of 1921–2). Ironically, his marriage took place the morning after his friend Michael Collins' assassination.

I checked our various ancestors' wills and encountered the following: 'I divide my possessions between my son Frank and my daughter Syra. To my eldest son, Kevin O'Shiel, I leave the sum of £150 which is more than the value of all the presents he gave me in his lifetime.'

The fertile townlands of Imovalley farmed by the Smiddy 'tribe' from East Cork, whose men were as small in stature as in their holdings, were worlds removed from the stony ground of eastern Tyrone tilled by my O'Shiel ancestors. Cecil's paternal grandfather William Smiddy was probably the first of his family to realize the potential of his own holding and moved to the outskirts of Cork city in the late 1870s. Cecil's maternal grandfather, Cornelius O'Connell, had gone into the timber business and could afford to send his only surviving daughter Lilian, born in 1879, to Paris for a year to train as a painter. His money was well spent. Several professionally executed portraits and studies of still-life in oils and water-colours adorn the walls of Lilian's descendants. She married Willam Smiddy's eldest son Timothy in 1900, who was employed by his father-in-law in the family business, but unfortunately abandoned her art after her marriage, probably following the birth of four children in five years. Cornelius O'Connell died in 1904 but when his widow Mary followed three years later, she left the family business to her youngest son, aged twenty-two, disinheriting his elder brother and making no mention of Lilian or her grandchildren, whose father was now out of a job. Women's power is often termed 'soft power', but clearly, as suggested by these two female ancestors, Mary O'Connell *née* Crowley and Elizabeth O'Shiel *née* Roantree, 'softness' could on occasion be toxic.

For decades I liked to pride myself on our typical 'Irish peasant' origins. Closeness to the land, as my father so often told me, was a feature of the Irish psyche, and as a young adult after years of being made to feel different following four teenage years in an English boarding school and in all more than twenty years living abroad, I continued to identify myself and our family with 'the broad mass of the Irish people'. It was only when confronted with the historian Roy Foster's description of my biography of Kevin O'Shiel (2013) as an uncommon document on an upper middle-class northern Catholic family, and more particularly when I read Tony Farmar's study of middle-class Ireland from the late nineteenth to the mid-twentieth century,[*] that I was forced to face the fact: ours *were* privileged lives. For, despite its financially straitened circumstances and narrow tax base, where a mere 60,000 citizens were liable for income tax, the Irish Free State (1922–48) paid its senior civil servants handsomely. At the time of my birth in 1933 my father as Land Commissioner had a salary of some £800 a year and my mother could afford to employ two country girls, Josie as housemaid and Dolly to look after us as small children. Josie wore a navy cap and uniform in the morning, pale brown and cream in the afternoon; Dolly, whom we idolized (and who together with Josie for years was prayed for each night), wore a dark blue dress with a large white apron except when taking us to the park for our daily walk. Though they had free 'bed and board' and 'the mistress' supplied their uniforms, they would have been paid for a six-and-a half-day working week a wage of no more than sixty or seventy pounds a year. This they would put towards their 'dowry'; Dolly in due course got married from our house.

When in 1970 the pioneering Thekla Beere began her two-year research as newly appointed chairman of the Commission on the Status of Women (1970), she was, as she later explained in her understated manner to an interviewer, 'surprised by what we found'.[†] People of her world, she said, had little or no conception of the harsh lives of 'the broad mass of the Irish people', more particularly of women. If they were married, many women were worn out at the age of forty by multiple births, if single, generally forced to spend their lives as unpaid labourers on the family holding. Domestic service in 1930s and 1940s Ireland was one of the few options for single women in Ireland whose parents could not afford to pay for secondary education (the preserve of the 'privileged few'). It was a lottery as to whether one's employer treated her servants as human beings;[‡] if not, the employee had little redress

---

[*] Farmar, Tony. *Privileged Lives: a social history of middle-class Ireland 1882–1989.* Dublin: A&A Farmar, 2010.

[†] Quoted in Bryson (2009, 62).

[‡] For an eloquent literary example of inhumane treatment by her 'respectable' employer,

4

since her ability to change jobs in the hope of better conditions was entirely dependent on the 'maid's reference'. 'When reading a reference always look for what isn't there,' my grandmother would advise, and this was at least as true in terms of insight into the character of the employer as for those seeking work.

## CATHOLIC IRELAND

To my generation and to the following one, 'Catholic Ireland' was self-evidently the context of our world. Most Irish families had relations in female or male religious orders or among the diocesan clergy. We were no different. A sizeable percentage of any final-year school class in mid-twentieth-century Ireland would 'enter'; relatively few before the 1970s would 'drop out' before their final profession as nuns, monks or priests, not least on account of 'the shame' this would bring upon their families and community. All but one of 'ours' stayed the course. On our mother's side was a great-uncle, Brother Aloysius, who spent seventy years as a Christian Brother, more than half as headmaster of the Richmond, later known as O'Connell School(s). Of the nuns I can only recall Great-aunt Nora, probably because our aunt Muriel hated going to see her as a young child, 'as she always had a bit of cabbage stuck between her front teeth'. On our paternal grandparents' side of the family, we had one (Jesuit) priest, Fr Daniel Shields, a pillar of conservative values who served many years as chaplain to one of the Guards Regiments in Britain. Three of our Roantree grandmother's sisters became nuns in different orders. None of our own aunts or uncles or their children entered religion, probably reflecting the greater career opportunities by then available for middle-class Irish Catholics. For the proliferation of priests and nuns in mid-nineteenth-century Ireland had been a relatively recent phenomenon. At the time of the Union (1801)

who liked to demonstrate her piety and social status by entertaining the parish priest to handsome dinners in their 'Kingstown' (i.e. Dún Laoghaire) home, see the figure of the cook in James Plunkett's *Strumpet City* (1969), cast off in old age after decades of faithful service into the workhouse.

there had been a mere eleven convents or houses for women religious on the island; a century later these numbered 358 and thirty-five respectively. An essential element was socio-economic. Career opportunities in Ireland both for women and men in nineteenth-century Ireland were narrowly circumscribed, and the religious life offered a 'career'. The convent provided a place where the Catholic middle classes, growing in numbers and prosperity from the 1860s onwards, could 'place' their unmarried daughters, some of whom would train as teachers and nurses. To be head of a prosperous convent was one of the few careers between about 1870 and the early 1950s where gifted and ambitious Irishwomen could find an outlet for their abilities. 'Soft power' in the hands of those who know how to exercise it is a force to be reckoned with and 'Reverend Mother' could wield considerable local authority. In 1886 James Shields, our grandfather's eldest brother and heir to the family farm, decided aged forty-four that he needed to get married 'to ensure the succession'. Accordingly, he appeared for his appointment with the Superior of Loreto Convent Omagh and made his wishes clear. His chosen bride would be of a good local family, healthy and young. 'Mother' had three candidates to hand, all in their mid to late teens, and his choice fell on Margaret McElhinney, in due course our dear great-aunt Maggie, daughter of a local merchant. She, a quarter of a century younger than her husband, now became mistress of our ancestral farmhouse, grandly named Altmore House, with its ever-open front door to the hall where chickens roamed in and out.

Of my father's three maternal aunts who became nuns, only one achieved the status of 'Reverend Mother'. This was Aunt Syra (1862–1952), eldest of her nine siblings and evidently favourite sister of my northern grandmother (1864–1932). Both had been educated in Normandy by the religious of Christian Education,* which Syra joined on finishing school.† The order had been founded by one Fr Lafosse after the French

---

\* I still have her well-thumbed French prayer book on my desk; my own aunt Syra (named after her) told me her mother always spoke French to her at home in Omagh once she had started learning French in Farnborough.

† How great-grandfather Daniel Roantree (1824–1898) managed to send his two eldest

6

Revolution of 1789; chained to a fellow priest, he had survived one of the notorious death marches organized by the French revolutionaries of the 1790s as part of their effort to exterminate the clergy, symbol of the hated *ancien régime*. Great-aunt Syra was indeed a formidable phenomenon. She and two other members of her Norman convent were sent in the year 1900 to 'help convert England', by establishing a boarding school for Catholic girls in Salisbury. The school later transferred to Farnborough, near the British military garrison at Aldershot, to provide suitable boarding school education *inter alia* to the daughters of officers who might be sent for service abroad. Farnborough was the home of the exiled and extremely pious Spanish-born Empress Eugénie Montijo, widow of Emperor Napoleon III. Soon Mother Roantree was a regular visitor to tea in the ex-Empress's residence, the palatial Farnborough Hill, originally built in the 1860s for the London publisher Thomas Longman. When the empress died in 1920 Mother Roantree managed to secure the impressive mansion for her ever-expanding convent school. Her Fénelon-inspired educational philosophy laid much stress on the development of critical powers – how else were English Catholics, still the object of much public prejudice, to compete with their peers in the 'real' world?

When I came back to Farnborough as a secondary schoolgirl, I used to visit her after lunch in her cell, where, then in her eighties, she was permanently confined to bed, with a lay sister known as 'the Tug' to look after her every need. At the end of the visit, I would stand up to go so as not to be late for class, whereupon she would admonish me grandly with: 'when I visited the Empress, I always waited until she dismissed me'.* Her cell window high in the north wall of the convent chapel looking straight down on the altar was inspired by the Spanish king Philip II's bedroom in his former palace of El Escorial. Under her direction the convent had prospered to the extent that she could have the

---

daughters to a Norman convent, I have no idea. For a somewhat idealized but representative portrait of French-speaking Belgian and Irish convents see Kate O'Brien's novel *The Land of Spices* (1941).

* As Queen Elizabeth does in the Netflix series, *The Crown*.

large and severely neo-Gothic convent chapel built in 1920, designed not by some diocesan Catholic builder but by the Anglican architect Adrian Gilbert Scott, whom she personally engaged and who had worked with his brother Giles on Liverpool's cathedral and on the current House of Commons. She once told me that Scott had said to her on his final visit to the now completed chapel: 'I suppose, Mother, you'll now fill it with your pious statues?' 'I wouldn't dream of it. I'm low church,' she told me she had assured him. And apart from the simple Stations of the Cross along the walls, there was but one austere statue of the Virgin Mary in the Lady chapel. Our order, she would remind me regularly, aimed to teach us to think for ourselves: '*Nous ne sommes pas les soeurs de l'instruction catholique,*' she would add mischievously, enjoying a dig at her 'less enlightened' religious sisters, '*nous sommes les dames de l'éducation chrétienne*' (we are not the sisters of Catholic instruction, we are the ladies of Christian education). When she died the *Aldershot Military Gazette* dedicated a substantial obituary to her, declaring her to have been 'erect as a guardsman' and 'the best type of regimental officer'. Aunt Syra's younger sisters, the equitable Ursuline Mathilda (Aunt Tilly) and the rather intense Sister of Charity Elizabeth (Aunt Nancy) were educated in Ireland and entered Irish religious orders. Perhaps, after setting up three of his sons as medical doctors (uncles James of Dún Laoghaire, Joe of Newbridge, and Dan in Bray), money was getting tighter for great-grandfather Daniel Roantree. For all so-called choir nuns needed a 'dowry' to be accepted into their order, the amount varying according to the standing and wealth of the convent. Girls who felt they had a vocation, and no dowry, became lay sisters, effectively unpaid domestic labourers but with the advantage of bed and board for life.

Religious ritual became a central part of our life. In September 1938 the whole family embarked on the *Princess Maud* at Dún Laoghaire (which the Roantree cousins still insisted on referring to as the much grander sounding 'Kingstown') to travel to our new school at Farnborough Hill. Here Clodagh, now aged seven, would follow the tradition of our Ulster family and make her First Communion there. And Aunt Syra further decreed, 'Eda might as well go along as well.'

To my parents my age was not an issue: 'She's a bit young but the young understand love.' How right they were.

I can still see myself clutching my one-armed teddy bear climbing up as far as I was allowed on the ship bringing us to Holyhead from Dublin so that 'he could see the view'. I don't remember any classes or school rooms at Farnborough apart from what we called Signorina's lair, where a white-haired Italian lady was responsible for mending, her room full of wonderful materials and heaps of torn sheets and clothes. My bed in the big dormitory was beside that of the nun who supervised us ten little girls at night. As there were no other children of my age in the school, I probably spent the term 'helping' Signorina, who like her fellow countrymen idolized small children and whom I loved passionately in return. But the absolute highlight of 1938 was our First Communion on 8 December, a day subsequently celebrated by the family every year in a much-loved ritual. To this day it is marked by exchange of telephone calls or emails between Clodagh and me. My mother, aunt Muriel and godfather Vincent Kelly came over for the occasion (and no doubt to enjoy a trip to the London shows). Besides the excitement of someone spilling tomato soup on Muriel's check suit, there was so much to remember and relish in later years. There were our fine muslin Communion dresses and little satin petticoats with real lace on the hem, made by my mother, which we would later endlessly dress up in as long as we could squeeze into them; there was the beautiful chapel early in the morning lit by candlelight followed by breakfast in the mysterious nuns' dining room with a whole boiled egg for myself. We had been prepared over weeks by an old Jesuit, Fr Aloysius Roche, author of a lovely prayer book in verse used by generations of small children. He had continually told us over the previous weeks not to be afraid, as God loved us, but I for one was not convinced that He wouldn't be cross. When it came to the dreaded moment of First Confession in the little room off the chapel, Fr Roche asked me if I would like to sit on his knee. The rug on his lap looked most inviting but I felt far too guilty to accept and remained behind the little grille to confess my awful sins.

And the sins? I was a confirmed thief. The other seven-year-olds in our dormitory would regularly lose their baby teeth and the tooth fairy would leave them a silver sixpence on the windowsill overnight. I had no hope of earning one as my teeth seemed stuck in my mouth, and as I always woke early, I would slip out of bed to 'inspect' the windowsill and if luck was on my side add the sixpence to my collection. Eventually of course I was caught, sent supperless to bed, to revel in the luxury of victimhood. And do it again when I thought I could get away with it. I had had the three conditions to get absolution from my sins firmly lodged in my little mind as part of our preparation for the Sacrament of Confession: full knowledge, full consent and firm purpose of amendment. (The last proved a problem for me.)

Many years after, twenty-two to be exact, my husband asked me, 'Did your parents not love you to send you off to boarding school from the nursery?' As a Spaniard he couldn't figure out how on earth families could part with their young children. Surely it must do lasting damage. I certainly didn't feel that way.

As an adolescent I always looked back on late 1938 as marking a new stage in my life. While they moved to a new house, my parents decided to send me for several weeks to stay with my grandfather in Omagh in the care of his eccentric but splendid housekeeper Bridget. Bridget had come from a small farm to Highfield as housekeeper when my grandmother died in 1932 and would stay till his death seventeen years later, nursing him in his last illness. We children were fascinated by the fact that she lived entirely on tea and brown bread and butter, never sharing the fatty roasts and the dreaded sago puddings my grandfather liked. Bridget was a woman of strong views, her pet dislike being the Murnaghan family – Mr Murnaghan (known later as 'young George' to distinguish him from his father 'old George')* was our grandfather's partner in his solicitors' firm Shields and Murnaghan in John St Omagh (still in business, though

---

* It became confusing as in time 'young George' had a son, also George, who had in time had another George, who I believe had another George …

no longer with 'Shields'); her prejudices regarded them as 'uppish' and in no way the equal of her beloved master. The problem was that I simply loved going to tea with the Murnaghans, not just because Joan, the tenth and youngest in the family, was my playmate, but because Mrs Murnaghan was such a lovely motherly person, a wonderful stepmother to the eight children of her deceased sister and dear mother of Joan and her elder brother Kevin (named after my father). And because tea was far more lavish and tastier than at Highfield and it was so much more fun being with all Joan's big brothers and sisters who teased us and took us hazelnut-picking.

Highfield was a one-storey house set back from Omagh's Crevenagh Road. I remember going up the few stairs to the attic bedroom with my candle (there was no electricity). My bedroom overlooked the potato fields and from the window Granddaddy would shoot pigeons. Shelves were stacked with old *National Geographic Magazine*s, a later source of wonder. Now and again we visited Bridget's small family farm on her day off where I was allowed to feed the hens and look for eggs. Other pictures in my mind were of rides with my grandfather in his pony and trap when he went out to visit clients in the countryside or when I was allowed to 'help' him with his tomato plants and accompany him to inspect his potatoes and Jerusalem artichokes in the large vegetable garden. And then there was that never-to-be-forgotten occasion on a hot summer's day when I persuaded Joan Murnaghan that we should abandon our dresses and run around the terraced front garden in our knickers. Nothing escaped the sharp eyes of Omagh's upright citizens! The 'scandal' was even reported to my grandfather in his office, and I squirmed at his gentle but stern reprimand. For our grandfather, unlike his allegedly quick-tempered spouse, was a most easy-going man with a dry sense of humour, measured in all his ways, and his censure carried weight.

The next memory I can date precisely: it was 3 September 1939, the day the Second World War broke out. I was playing in the garden at Cherrywood and the bandage on my cut knee had slipped so I got Padraig, the gardener, to fix it. I'm not sure what he did but the result was blood poisoning, a serious matter in those pre-antibiotic days. For weeks I was made to stay in bed, forced to lie on my front because the whole back of my right leg was covered with great big green-headed boils. The treatment involved a yellowish paste called antiphlogistine, administered twice daily. To keep it all in place and protect the bedclothes, the infected parts were covered by dark green waterproof sheets, which had to be ripped off before each fresh application, breaking the barely formed 'crust'. It was painful and horrible, and I remember feeling infinitely ill-used when my endless bleatings of 'come up and talk to me!' went largely ignored, apart from mealtimes and at night. Eventually the boils healed but not long after that an outbreak of smallpox called for vaccination. I can still recall the thrill when our family doctor drew an inky line across my thigh with his fountain pen to indicate where the needles should go in. I don't know what went wrong but I suffered a dreadful reaction. It again involved endless bed rest and nothing to do but lie there and brood on my wrongs. That too eventually passed, and I could at last join Clodagh at her new school in Bray, some three or four miles away but accessible by bus from the end of Cherrywood Road or from Shankhill railway station a mile or so over the hill. No question in those days of being driven to school. In any case very soon private cars were taken off the road as the war cut off petrol supplies in Ireland for all but the army, the police, the fire brigade and a few doctors, plus of course the more influential politicians;* our little Austin took up its position on wooden stands in one of the stables for the next five years.

Miss Brayden's small school near the Bray railway station in the summer of 1939 was utter bliss, not least because you had to climb up and down a great big metal bridge over the railway line to get there. A big thrill was the workbook, a copy book with a pale blue cover in which you were allowed to write – something I had always been in trouble for doing up to then. (You wrote in pencil because that could be rubbed out and the workbook then used by the next class.) At six I

---

* Thus Minister Seán McEntee and his wife Margaret, *née* Ryan, could buy up our Brittas bungalow where we spent the summer, as without petrol we had no way of getting there.

was ostentatiously reading and leaving around my father's history books to get attention, proudly reciting the dates of English kings and queens from a red history of Britain (no Fenian heroes here) and being shushed as a show-off. Our joy in Miss Brayden's was alas brief. Public transport was becoming increasingly problematic on account of the war, so my parents sent us as weekly boarders to Loreto Convent Bray. I remember being brought up on the first night to our dormitory to see our beds surrounded by curtains, no towels to dry your hands on, cold water and no heating except in the dining room and the huge hall, which held six different classes. Within weeks we all had chilblains, exacerbated by our rush to warm our freezing hands on one of the few available radiators. Soon we had chilblains on our toes as well, red and raw and itchy. Discipline was strict, not to say harsh and sometimes unforgiving. One day eight-year-old Clodagh, normally a model child, 'gave cheek' to a teacher. She was summoned by Mother Mercedes and forced to walk from one end of the long hall up on to the stage, between the six now silent classes, to be slapped on her hands with a wooden ruler and 'shamed' in sight of the whole junior school. One evening a new arrival, aged six, was sitting unhappily at my table with a plate of egg, potatoes and peas in front of her. As any sensible child might she turned her fork around to scoop up her peas and was scolded by the table nun for 'bad manners': you pick up peas one by one. She was made to stand up for the whole meal and then sent to bed with no supper.

Far worse was the daily ritual in our dormitory. A homesick little friend of mine wet her bed each night. Every morning she was made to stand up at the dormitory door holding the wet sheet in her little hands, so that we and the girls from the neighbouring dormitories could see her as they filed down past our door to breakfast. How to explain such wanton cruelty to small, homesick children? Four or five years later, my father, who never commented on school or teachers, gave me an explanation that in retrospect made some sense to me. When I was about eleven, I suddenly started not wanting to go to school. Our French teacher Mother C., tall and gaunt, had started slapping us hard if we couldn't recite our irregular verbs on demand. I failed to give her the preterite tense of the French verb *naître* (to be born) and got a wallop on my fingers. (I have never once been called upon to say '*je naquis*' – but I have never forgotten it.) My father explained that Mother C. was the only daughter of a prominent Dublin surgeon's large family. Her mother had died. She was unlikely to attract a marriage partner and the surgeon's prospective new wife had made it a condition of marriage that the daughter be got out of the house. The local convent was the answer. Yes, I agreed, she must be miserable, but why take it out on us?

Fortunately, in 1941 Clodagh and I got infested with nits in Bray. When the nits refused to yield to the awful weekend scraping of our scabby skulls by the fine-tooth comb, and when they hatched and lice were added to the mix, we were removed from Bray and sent as day girls in October to the newly opened Loreto Foxrock, where all sorts of delights awaited us. Principal among them were for Clodagh her two lifelong friends, Dorothy Purcell, now Stafford-Johnson, and Helen Briscoe who inhabited the enormous Brennanstown House in Carrickmines alone with her South African ex-goldminer father and statuesque mother. For me it was my two great friends Maryanne MacDonald (1933–2019) and Fionnuala (Fin) Murphy (1932–2018), daughters of ESB (Electricity Supply Board) engineers, both of whom had been centrally involved in the Shannon rural electrification scheme of 1927. And there were many more. We survivors still meet regularly almost eighty years later, no longer to climb trees but to play bridge and reminisce: Helen Darcy, Marjorie Byrne, now Beattie, the beautiful Cynnia McCaffrey (*née* Costello, sister of Paul, the designer). At Foxrock there was hockey and then hockey matches, there were the big grounds with trees to climb and play hide-and-seek in, there was Sister Louis Gonzaga, our brilliant teacher of maths and Irish, soon our favourite subjects, until she went 'off to the missions' and, as so many of my and subsequent generations experienced, her successors hadn't an idea how to teach that beautiful language. For me the star was Mother Edmund, hardly taller than us and who had never darkened the door of a university but who taught history in a way that determined me, aged eight, that I would be a historian and nothing else. For two decades I never lost sight of this goal. That I didn't manage to realize it belongs to the social and cultural history of Irish women and to a later chapter of these memoirs.

Clodagh and I were temperamentally and in character and interests so different that we virtually never, as far as I can recall, played together. She was careful with her things and tidy in appearance, where I was messy, treating her belongings as my own and no number of protests from her or reprimands from our mother inhibited my borrowing her books, often to be returned with jammy fingerprints. At all events I remember being much on my own, reading any storybook I could get hold of, writing up my daily nature diary, and with that complete self-absorption of the child, being very conscious of each 'stage' in life I was inhabiting. Numbers had colours in my mind, green and yellow ones for 'favourite' ages – five, seven and nine. To be seven was, I felt, to have left small childhood behind me. Nine was a wonderful age, but ten something to be dreaded. I remember counting and relishing the days in July and August before my tenth birthday and wishing they could last for ever.

# TWO

# *The 1940s: School*

## CHERRYWOOD HOUSE

In late 1938 my parents made the felicitous decision to live in the country. My mother had grown up in Cobh and Cork city, my father in Omagh, but he had remained at heart a countryman. Cherrywood House, attached to our neighbours' Cherrywood Lodge, had been built in the Bride's Glen valley in 1736, a beautiful, twelve-roomed Georgian house with nearly an acre of mature garden. The house mouldered gently, riddled with dry rot and in urgent need of repair, which our benign landlord could never afford to address as the rent was only £2 per week. We children didn't notice, and it didn't seem to bother our father too much that each morning, when he took his leather shoes out of the damp hall cupboard to go to work, he had first to clean off their covering coat of greenish blue verdigris. There was no heating apart from the hall and kitchen and the spluttering fire (with damp turf) in the study where the family sat in the evenings except on Sundays. In winter it took at least two hours to get warm enough in our cold beds to fall asleep, unless childhood illnesses or a sharp frost prompted our mother to give us one of those heavy ceramic bed-warmers against which small toes got unmercifully stubbed. Early bed was *de rigueur* for us children. One of my abiding memories is of the distinctive sounds of each downstairs door as I lay in bed: the heavy hall door, the doors to the study, the drawing room and the dining room with its little half-circular corridor running into it from the hall, the old cottage-type door leading to the kitchen. Their quiet sounds would be regularly punctuated by the *tum-tum* of the diesel train crossing the great viaduct over Cherrywood Road en route between the city and Bray. The house was full of mice, with rats in the stables; we had no cats as my mother was allergic to them. Our two Scots terriers, the overbred Kim and Sam, were useless, Kim afraid even of the chaffinches who would swoop down to share his dinner and Sam who was too lazy to notice. Clodagh, no nature-lover and ever practical, devised her own method of dealing with the mice. She would put some cornflakes in an empty box in our bedroom fire-place, and as soon as she heard the scrabbling, would seize the box, cover it with a book and rush out to the yard where a cement-leveller was kept handy to decapitate the wretched beasts as they emerged. I, guilty by association, watched and did nothing to stop the slaughter.

But it was the setting of Cherrywood in its valley – now buried under Soviet-style industrial 'development' – that became and has remained the locus of my imagination. Still today when I read of a country house, a stream, an old garden or a country lane in a novel, as, say, in *The Mill on the Floss*, an image of these once-familiar surroundings presents itself and has to be adapted to the fictional reality of that world.

Coming up the half mile from the main road at Loughlinstown village now on the N11 highway, a big rusty gate on the right-hand side of Cherrywood Road led to a neglected driveway. Just inside on the left was a huge climbable chestnut tree with a long protruding branch ideal for hanging upside down on, with or without a book, and scaring visitors. Best of all, but on the right-hand side of the drive were the twelve- to fifteen-feet-high sturdy laurel trees, cut in the exact shape of Cherrywood House and Lodge: you could climb up at one end and negotiate your way right across to the other. My friends and I would spend whole afternoons up there, only reluctantly coming down for our tea of milk and bread and jam or orange Galtee cheese. The driveway ran parallel to the road, separated from it on the left-hand side by a rather rank piece of ground where the septic tank was located, covered probably intentionally with strong-smelling wild garlic. Up at the corner of the house stood a gigantic redwood sequoia tree, further along from which was a former tennis court, now a neglected lawn on to which the windows of the dining and drawing rooms on the south side of the house faced. My father's favourite spot was just under one of the dining-room windows, with his tea-cup-marked paperback copy of Chekhov's stories or a Turgenev novel plus one or two nature books invariably beside his chair. To the right of the drive was the main garden, which must have been laid out on the south-facing slope by generations of great gardeners. The house itself, its porch added later, faced east looking out on to a large stretch of gravel and a rock garden and a lawn edged to the east and south by rickety pergolas covered in roses in summer. Beyond, the garden was divided into three sections by three parallel paths. The top and middle thirds had fruit bushes, with vegetables beyond, tended once a week by Padraig the gardener; the bottom section had three apple trees and beyond were the many potato ridges and masses of rhubarb. Tall trees at the end, bounded at the entrance by our laurel tree house, hid a lane beyond which was a high-walled orchard owned by a neighbour, which we could peep into but were not allowed to enter.

At the back of the house and sheltered by a steep hill to the north was a large yard with various outhouses and the two-storey broken-down stables, the top storey occasionally used by a neighbouring farmer to store his hay. They were full of swallows' and house martins' nests in summer, attracted no doubt by the swarms of midges, which got into your hair and itched unmercifully at night. My mother was a keen gardener, in summer the place was full of flowers, fruit and vegetables. I would lie by day under the raspberry bushes on the carpet of speedwell and stuff myself till I was covered in hives, and in summer nights slip out of bed to stock up on apples for leisurely later consumption.

My father, like his father before him, was a nature-lover and amateur ornithologist. An early photo in our family album shows him pointing out a wildflower to my four-year-old sister (who wasn't particularly interested). It wasn't till I was seven that he started teaching me the names of the wildflowers on our walks, graduating eventually to birds when he felt I could identify with his help most of what we had come across in *A Flower Book for the Pocket.*[*] Sometimes before going to bed on a summer evening he would take us out to the sequoia tree and make scratching noises on the bark as if he were a cat. Immediately the three or four roosting tree creepers would start up and fly away in alarm. Saturdays from then on were deemed birdwatching days and our 'bible', the small, battered volume of *The Observer's Book of British Birds,*[†] always accompanied us on our walks. When I was about eleven my father made me and my school friend Fin members of the Dublin Naturalists Field Club, accompanying us for the first year. Afterwards, under the stern eye of elderly members, the stout-booted Miss Brunner, the impossibly lean Mr Brunker, the ancient Colonel Scroope or even Ireland's greatest field naturalist, Mr Lloyd Praeger,[‡] we bussed each Saturday afternoon to the lanes, fields and woods past Bray, Enniskerry and Greystones, up the Dublin mountains, or across to the Bull Island in North Dublin to watch waders, ducks and geese. The Field Club members extended our knowledge to less common birds, advising us when and where rarities such as the shore lark, snow bunting or Arctic geese were to be found, and familiarized us with the songs and habitat of individual species; all the sort of things which learnt as a child are never forgotten. For hours we would tramp, later joined by a young boy in wellingtons far too big for him, Christopher Moriarty. Fin was the fortunate possessor of first-class field glasses, a present to her electrical engineering father P.G. Murphy when he left Siemens in Berlin to come back to the ESB, eventually as chief engineer. My father bought binoculars from Thomas Gill's, one of the long-established shops in that once most elegant of Dublin streets, Dame Street (pre-pandemic a heavily polluted thoroughfare

---

[*] Macgregor Skene. Oxford: OUP 1937.

[†] S. Vere Benson. London and New York: Frederick Warne & Co. Ltd, 1937.

[‡] Author of the 1937 classical study of Irish botany, geography, geology: *The Way That I Went.*

clogged with buses and rushing pedestrians tethered to their mobiles). Later Fin and I each acquired a telescope for watching distant shore-birds. Whenever Fin, who lived in Blackrock some six miles away, came back to stay, we would pool our knowledge and gradually became quite expert, especially after my father bought us the five-volume standard work on birds, Witherby's *British Birds.*[*] Every evening I would record the names of all the birds seen in my nature diary. (Three-quarters of a century later I can still identify most common birds as they flash by and if loud enough by their call or song.)

Equally scarce, though we didn't appreciate it, was running water.[†] In the mid-1940s, if some 48 per cent of Irish households had an indoor water supply, only 9 per cent of rural households had that luxury – and almost half of these still depended on the nearest well, which could be fields away. Fetching water was, as it still is in many parts of the world, 'women's work'. We did notice one of the village pumps on Cherrywood Road as we walked to and from the bus stop, and sometimes saw an elderly neighbour from one of the cottages bent over her heavy bucket. It never dawned on us to offer to help – help would probably have been refused as 'not proper'. When after the war petrol was available again and we had our car back on the road, my mother would stop to give anyone she saw from the cottages a lift to Sunday mass. Afterwards we children would complain of the way they smelt – the sweetish smell of unwashed poverty, had we realized it – and be regularly ticked off for snobbery. It did not occur to us to find it strange that our maid slept in the smallest room in the house, nor that she was expected to work six-and-a-half days a week, to get lunch before having her afternoon off on Sundays and to be back by 10 pm. Once, when our young maid was getting over a bout of diphtheria (rife in our poverty-stricken Loughlinstown village), we were allowed to visit her in St Colmcille's, the ex-workhouse hospital. I do remember our being shocked at the wretched conditions

* H.F. Witherby et al. *Handbook of British Birds.* 5 vols., London: H.F. and G. Witherby, 1943.

† See Mary E. Daly. '"Turn on the Tap": The State, Irish Women & Running Water' in Valiulis & O'Dowd (1997), 206–19.

of the ward where she had been isolated for weeks, far from home, with just a coverlet over her, no sheet nor pillowcase on the bolster in a bed in which I imagine others had slept before her. We missed her when she was discharged home and never took to her successor Lily, a Dubliner, in stature almost a dwarf. Lily got on well with our mother and stayed with us for six years. At night I would find her sitting at the kitchen stove reading her way through the *Children's Encyclopedia*, no doubt in the hope of bettering herself. At the very least her reading awakened her political awareness. She would spend her free afternoon with her aunt and one morning, after all those years with us, she decided she had had enough. 'Me aunt,' (pronounced 'ant'), she informed my mother in Clodagh's and my presence, 'me aunt says, it's too far out, the money isn't enough and I'm goin' on Monday.' And she went.

The only time I do recall being shocked out of my comfortable self was on one of our annual visits to town on 8 December, the Marian church feast of the Immaculate Conception and the anniversary of our First Communion. Every year from 1939 until we went to boarding school at fourteen, my godfather Vincent Kelly would collect us at the bus stop in Merrion Square, take us to mass in St Andrew's Church on Westland Row where we had been baptized. (Most middle-class babies were born in city nursing homes in those days and baptized within a week.) From there we would walk up to his club, the United Services Club on Stephen's Green, where an old waiter in crumpled white tie and tails would ritually tie a large white serviette around our necks and serve us our porridge like grown-ups. One Christmas in the early 1940s my mother needed to do a message off Gardiner Street, once the hub of upper-class social life and at the time the worst of Dublin's notorious slums. As we passed a yard full of children, I saw a tiny toddler just about able to walk with nothing but a vest on him, his little nappy-less bottom, quite literally, blue with the cold. Hardly surprising that infant mortality was rife among the Dublin poor.

On account of his northern background, education and our neighbourhood, at least half of my father's close friends were Jewish, Church of Ireland or Presbyterian. With many of his Catholic friends and colleagues he was an active member of the Society of St Vincent de Paul, which involved weekly visits by the members to local families in need of financial help. He enjoyed the work, as he was tactful and always able to enter other people's worlds however different their circumstances were from his own. I remember one case he eventually passed on to me when I was a student, and we were living in the Dublin suburb of Donnybrook. Miss Curran, born as she liked to tell him as a lady 'with a Protestant mother', was crippled with arthritis. She was 'rescued' from pitiful poverty in her damp cottage on the banks of the Dodder near Ballsbridge, only to be immured in the unfortunately named Royal Hospital for the Incurables (now the incomparable Royal Hospital). Here she was bedridden, confined to a coffin-like cubicle with scarcely space for the bed and a visitor's chair, the rough wood floor covered with splinters, waited on by slatternly women (I saw them in action). My father spoke with admiration of how she had kept her pride. 'Had I been a Protestant I would now be in a home for gentlefolk instead of here among common people,' she would remind him each time. To me she would say that she always kept up standards in the midst of squalor by insisting on warm water to wash her face at night 'to open the pores', followed by cold water to close them, and finally an application of a few drops of violet essence to offset the surrounding smell. My father always dressed in suit and tie when he went on his weekly visit to stress her status as a lady. On one occasion he nearly came a cropper when she sought solace in him at what she saw as the appalling collapse in professional standards on the part of the hospital doctor. 'You won't believe it, Mr Commissioner, but the doctor – you will not credit it – has been recently seen coming out of a *common public house*!' 'I hid my blushes,' he told us afterwards – as a 'regular' of the same local hostelry.

When my friends came to stay, we would climb trees and play in the river, taking a picnic of jam sandwiches to one of the small islands or to venture further afield, maybe up to the Ballycorus lead mines and the lake there, where once another visiting friend fell through the ice in her new bright green coat. It evidently never dawned on our parents to check that we were safe or when Clodagh and I and our friends cycled the two miles to the sea at Corbawn Lane in Shankhill to swim out as far as we felt like. Nor when I wandered off on my own as I did most days after school through neighbouring fields and woods in search of plant- and birdlife. At weekends my friends came with clean clothes on Saturdays and returned home on Sunday with packets of rinsed-out garments, grubby from sliding down the steep embankment on the far side of the viaduct or falling into our stream, or even clad in my spare clothes. This could be a problem once clothes rationing came in around 1942, as material to make them was now on coupons and I had been reduced to a single spare pair. On one occasion, when my spare was in the wash, I climbed over a gate with iron uprights. Alas, the crotch of said knickers wrapped itself around one of the uprights and the only way I could get free was to wriggle as hard as I could till the fabric finally gave way. I knew I would be in deepest hot water with my mother, so I secreted the tattered garment in a chest of drawers in an unused bedroom, removing it to the next hiding place as, with Mammy hard on my heels and under instructions to find the 'missing' object, I looked for it in vain. Naturally, I was found out, but I don't remember the sanctions. I can only recall my mother smacking me once, under extreme provocation and then not hard, though I still remember the shock. Discipline was her sphere in my father's view, even when he reported feeling shamed by having observed my eight- or nine-year-old-self 'brawling like a common urchin with local boys' at the Foxrock bus stop outside the convent. He would have been absolutely horrified at the idea of a father slapping a girl.

Monday mornings and most other mornings would see a gaggle of us classmates arrive early to school, to play 'witches and fairies', an endless game which involved one half climbing trees in the nuns' garden, descending with shrieks to chase and 'kidnap' the other half, the 'fairies', and then in summer fill up with their gooseberries and anything else eatable that was going. We played it endlessly and with variations, as the grounds of Loreto Foxrock were at that time very extensive (when I joined in September 1941 there were only twenty-one pupils) and I can't imagine why we were not detected sooner. The 'good' girls in the class, or as we saw it the lazy ones, were sitting on their benches at the back of the class when we panted in at the last moment. They regarded the rest of us as 'swots' and formed a little clique of their own. I never did my homework until just before or during class (there were far more interesting things to be done outside school). It was a different matter when term reports came with the recurrent 'Homework very slapdash – Eda is extremely untidy in her work and appearance.' Decent exam marks cut no ice with either parent. On the other hand, a rare phrase in my report, 'Homework always done if still untidy', earned me a wonderful book: *A History of Britain.*\* There was no mention of Ireland apart from having been conquered by the Normans, but that didn't bother me then. I was immensely proud of it and resolved to turn over a whole new leaf – until, having boastfully passed it around an uninterested class, no doubt to show off my 'superior' brain, the clique 'borrowed' it and in revenge adorned poor Queen Mary with an inky crown.

These years between six and twelve were the war years, 1939–45, which, apart from a few shortages, hardly impinged on our lives. Apart from butter and sugar rationing we had all we needed to eat; our diet was simple but good quality, meat and fish, milk, porridge, homemade brown bread and jam. Tea, which like coffee we were not allowed to drink till our late teenage years, was a precious commodity for adults. Fortunately for them, when my parents undertook to look after Sheila Philips, Clodagh's close friend from pre-war Farnborough days, following her parents' departure in 1939 for India, their parting gift was a great chest of tea. Its contents, shared among family and friends, lasted almost till the end of what was known in Ireland as 'the Emergency'.† The press was particularly stringently censored in the Free State on account of our neutrality, so news of what was going on was sparse, though the BBC, to

---

\* By R.J. Unstead, author of so many books on British and other history that he became known in his day as 'Mr History'.

† i.e. the Second World War.

which our grandfather in Omagh listened for hours every day, offered rather more information on our regular visits up north. Not that we were interested, apart from pictures of Polish children queuing for food, which I recall in the context of 'Eat up your spinach, the poor little Polish children would love to be able to enjoy it.' For us, the war only meant marginal discomforts: the lack of paper to write my poems, and the wet turf, which made lighting the fire a major operation and only barely dispelled the cold of our damp house. (On one occasion we were taken to see the mountains of turf lining the whole of the main artery of the Phoenix Park to ensure that Dublin would not freeze.)

A highlight of those years was the wedding of our aunt Ita in July 1942 to Dr Harry O'Flanagan.* Clodagh and I were bridesmaids, very proud of ourselves in our purple, black and brown kilts, with pale blue blouses, all made by my mother. The bride had made her own outfit (no white weddings in those days with clothes rationing), 'a beige jumper suit, edged in petersham', as my grandmother wrote to her elder daughter in England. Work was hard to find in wartime Ireland and the newlyweds left for a GP practice in Accrington, then to a better job in the Rhondda valley. For a young doctor seeking experience, the tough Welsh mining community brought both much new life experience, but after several months and Ita's pregnancy, Harry joined the medical corps of the RAF and Ita returned to share a flat with her very demanding mother-in-law in Dublin where Brian was born. With mother-in-law interfering at every moment (socially ambitious, 'Mrs O' had left her warm-hearted grocer husband back in Roscrea), Ita became, in her sisters' phrase, 'a nervous wreck'. Cecil and Muriel conferred, with the result that mother and baby came to live with us for a year. The novelty soon wore off, and my little nose was out of joint as attention focused, I felt, exclusively on baby Brian.

The countryside in those days was a gregarious place and the grown-ups had a lively social life, evidently not much affected by the lack of cars. Everyone travelled on bicycles or on foot to each other's houses, to tea or to fork suppers on Sundays. Our neighbours in Shankhill were

---

* Later influential Registrar of the College of Surgeons.

frequent visitors, Tony and Eilish McDowell – whose eldest son, the economist Moore, I occasionally minded – Michael and Evelyn Tierney, and the architect Johnny Robinson from Dalkey and their families. Others included Alfred O'Rahilly, tiresome but loyal friend of my grandparents, and my godfather Vincent Kelly (a semi-permanent feature of our lives, who tried my father's endless patience);* more occasional ones included Michael Scott, who had served his time in Vincent's architect's office, and the diplomat Josephine McNeill, widow of James McNeill, former Governor General of the Irish Free State, at whose Governor General's residence in the Phoenix Park my parents had first met in 1929. And there were the lugubrious Joe Brennan and his amiable wife Evelyn, both from Cork, Tommy McLaughlin, architect of the Shannon Scheme, plus the innumerable lawyer friends, among them the formidable Mick Carson, who traded Masonic jokes with my father (whose first father-in-law had been an anticlerical Catholic Mason). I loved to see the house full of guests and be allowed to hand things round so I could listen to the talk, ears cocked. My parents always seemed to be going to weddings, christenings or funerals, including those of our Church of Ireland or Presbyterian neighbours. This was unusual at the time, as Catholics were forbidden by their church to endanger their faith by even entering a 'heretical' place of worship. As 'good' Catholics our parents always sought permission to do so, not from the local parish priest, who would have refused it, but from Jesuit friends (including my father's cousin Fr Dan Shields). The Jesuits put more emphasis on the cardinal virtue of charity.

My reaction to one casualty of the war showed up a characteristic lack of empathy with the outsider common among a closely knit group of children. Our neighbours in Cherrywood Lodge suffered the tragic loss of their only child Denis at the age of thirteen. He had been my playmate, and I remember the heart-breaking day I spent at his parents' request helping to sort and pack up his toys to give to charity. A year

---

* I can only once recall a momentary lapse, when he said: 'Vincent will take his own life one day.' 'What an awful thing to say,' one of us expostulated. 'Ah, but you remember Oscar Wilde's *Ballad of Reading Gaol*: "Each man kills the thing he loves."'

or so later they fostered a French orphan girl of my own age. As they were Presbyterians and she a Roman Catholic, she was sent to school to Foxrock convent, and I had to look after her. I hated every minute of my charge and with my friends tried various stratagems to palm her off on someone else. She would continually criticize life in Ireland and was clearly damaged by her experiences; neither she nor her foster parents got on and the poor unhappy child was eventually sent back to France.

In few aspects of daily life is the contrast greater between then and now than in the absence of modern media in our lives. In the 1930s, 40s and 50s Irish people devoured newspapers, most households like our own taking daily and evening papers, often in addition to one or more regional newspapers from their home county. The other staple element of every household above the poverty line was the battery wireless. We listened to the radio every weekend, our favourite being Joe Linnane's *Question Time* on a Sunday night. How did we children amuse ourselves in long winter evenings apart from reading or sewing? One of the few residues of Sabbatarianism in southern Ireland was the church's ban on sewing on Sundays (in Northern Ireland you couldn't even kick a ball around). Unlike most people in the country our parents didn't play cards, but when our grandmother came to stay it was snap, happy families, whist, rummy and, among ourselves, dominoes and tiddlywinks, and board games: Ludo, Snakes and Ladders, draughts. Later it was Monopoly and for me chess, taught me by my godfather. I probably would have played chess seriously but for the strange impact his passion for the game had on him. For some years Vincent Kelly played correspondence chess all over Europe and the USA, but became so addicted that, living on his own after the break-up of his marriage, he was playing up to twenty hours a day, forgetting to eat or sleep. He suffered a severe nervous breakdown and was confined for months to what was then known as St Patrick's asylum in Dublin's Kilmainham, recognizing no one. Once, when I was about fourteen, I went with my mother to visit him. He used regularly to bring her a bottle of Chanel No. 5 from his trips abroad,* and she hit on the idea that people recognize scents even

* Vincent Kelly, who designed all the modernist TB hospitals in Ireland, was the first

if they cannot recognize faces. She put some of the perfume on the kind of linen handkerchief he liked to wear and as soon as she placed it on his hand, he spoke her name. Eventually, following the harsh electric treatment of the time, he recovered to lead a relatively normal life again. But he and I never played chess again.


## FARNBOROUGH HILL ONCE MORE

In the autumn of 1947, when I was fourteen, it was decided to send me back to boarding school in Farnborough. Saying a miserable goodbye to Fin and Maryanne and my other Foxrock classmates I felt the fates mounted up against me as I joined almost half the class being sent for their last school years to various convents in England. My sister was already in her third year at Farnborough with her own network of friends; they included besides Sheila several members of the extensive wine merchant family, the Gilbeys from England, and the Gonzalez from England and Barbados. England was a foreign country to me, and it took a while to integrate. Clodagh, now aged sixteen, proved to be a consummate travel marshal. I was given crisp instructions from the start: first off the boat at Holyhead, first on the train and first on to the next one for Euston station at Crewe Junction, first off at Euston and run as fast as you could to get one of the few taxis to Waterloo station for the train to Farnborough. All this in the middle of the night or early morning; if we travelled the twelve-hour journey by night rather than by day, we went half price (£2 single fare until you were fifteen).* As the beginning of term coincided with the autumn equinox, the sea was invariably rough, and we would arrive around one in the morning on to the platform at Holyhead having been thoroughly seasick. There we Irish 'emigrants' were forced to queue endlessly, freezing in winter,

---

Irishman to be elected president of the British Institute of Architects (1935) and was in frequent demand as a guest speaker at home and abroad.

* To my infinite embarrassment, right until my seventeenth birthday when I was far too tall to pass for 'under fifteen', my mother still insisted I go half fare, resuscitating a cast-off old Farnborough blazer with my now long arms protruding far beyond the end of the sleeves.

to have our luggage taken apart for contraband. My first impressions of 'England' (as we Irish called the British) were not favourable. As my mother always sent the nuns butter, bacon and sausages we regularly and angrily saw these disappear into the maw of the British customs officers.

To begin with I could hardly understand what my new English companions were saying. Asked in my first week of term to make a list of those willing to play on hockey teams, I wrote down their names as I heard them and was aggrieved at their mocking laughter: Patricia 'Farla' (Fowler), Margaret 'Lore' (Law) etc. I took refuge in the splendid school library and picked out the volume of the recently published *Oxford Junior Encyclopedia* and read the article on Ireland, which began: 'In Ireland the family sits at mealtimes around the kitchen table with a large pot or bowl of milk in the centre. Each person has a spoon in their hand and potatoes on their plate which they dip in turn into the milk …' Furious, I returned to my desk in the classroom and spent the rest of the hour preparing a large poster and sticking it on the back flap of the desk, demonstratively left open so that I could translate the text for the curious. It read '*Cuimhnigh Luimnigh agus feall na Sasanach*' ('Remember [the siege of] Limerick and the treachery of the English.')* I was now a confirmed Irish nationalist and lost no time in challenging 'misguided' views.

Following my refusal in early November of that first term to contribute my shilling for our dormitory's wedding present to Princess Elizabeth when she married Prince Philip of Greece, I was sent to Coventry with nobody allowed to speak to me. I enjoyed my brief martyrdom of suffering for Ireland's sake, but Ireland and Ireland's woes were, as ever, not to be taken seriously by 'sensible' English people, and my classmates soon took no more notice of what they dismissed as my posturing. I sought solace with the sympathetic (and equally nationalistic) Irish lay sisters in the huge school kitchen, helping with the washing up, or buried myself in a satisfying diet of Douglas Hyde's *Songs*

---

* Following the siege in 1690 the invading English army promised safe passage if the Irish surrendered. They did and most were slaughtered as they emerged. Fortunately, our O'Shiel/ Shields ancestor who had taken part in the siege got away to France.

*of the Irish*, Lennox Robinson's edition of *A Golden Treasury of Irish Verse* and the poems of Francis Ledwidge. Nothing like poetry as balm for the bruised heart.

Shortly after I was taken out of circulation. Used to a good diet of home-cooked food, the post-war rationed food in England of margarine on sliced white pan, greasy horsemeat and overcooked cabbage and fish simply turned my adolescent stomach. I just ate my porridge and dry crusts of the bread and drank the watery milk, apparently losing a stone in a matter of weeks, though I was growing fast. When black warts began to appear on my face, I found myself banished to the infirmary: no sport, no visitors, and a diet of disgusting hot egg-flip morning and afternoon. How adolescents hate to be different. It was bad enough to be deprived of hockey but to be singled out for special treatment as Reverend Mother's great-niece was too much. The days and nights were endless until I asked for something to read. Our English mistress obliged with a dozen Dickens novels. Sam Weller, David Copperfield, Pip, Little Nell, Scrooge, Fagan and Mr Pecksniff in *Martin Chuzzlewit* filled the next weeks almost satisfactorily until it was time to go home for Christmas. When we arrived off the boat my mother took one look at me: 'You're staying at home next term.'

And what a term it proved to be. I was made to stay in bed till mid-morning, was indulged in every (reasonable) wish, even to the extent of being brought into town and given all of seven shillings and sixpence to spend as I wanted. In Woolworths my eye caught a display of the new-fangled biros, pens that, it seemed, never needed to be filled with ink nor ever made those nasty blots. These very ordinary biros cost two shillings and six pence each and I spent the whole sum on three of them, leaving no money for the books I had planned to buy. The expected reprimand never followed. After a few weeks of this idyllic life and to prevent my schoolwork falling behind I was sent to have lessons with a neighbour's daughter of my age, Maria Murrough-Barnard, together with one of her friends. I didn't learn anything apart from how other people lived. My new friends were Church of Ireland and wealthy: Maria's grandfather was D.E. Williams, owner of the whiskey liqueur firm known as Tullamore Dew, and her friend's father was a Slazenger, maker of the famous tennis rackets. A governess was in charge of their education, the local Church of Ireland school not being quite posh enough. Miss Honiton was elderly, diminutive and, as she repeatedly informed us, a 'King's Scholar' (whatever that meant), a type encountered in later years in Agatha Christie novels. Her command of maths was limited, so she preferred to concentrate on English, history of the British Empire minus Ireland, notably the kings and queens of England, plus 'religious knowledge'. Though I relished our 'theological' arguments, the other two were bored, so she deftly put 'religious education' on the long finger. Now it was my turn to be bored, as the intellectual diet would hardly have satisfied a nine-year-old. Morning 'lessons' were evidently designed simply to provide young ladies with conversation material for the drawing or ball room, with the rest of their lives spent outdoors on their ponies or later the hunt. Afternoons were much better, spent looking after Maria's passion, her hens. Several were potential champions and she taught me the seven criteria you needed to know to judge a thoroughbred hen. I was deeply impressed but found no further use for this element of my education.

I had started to read the newspapers and to get interested in politics. In the 1948 elections I tried to canvas for the Labour Party, merely on the grounds that it was the party with the smallest number of members and clearly needed all the support it could get. But it was an even smaller new party, *Clann na Talmhan*, which caught the voters' imagination after its leader, Joe Blowick, surprisingly unseated the Fianna Fáil party's TD in their traditional South Mayo stronghold. And Joe – ominously for us, though we didn't know it yet[*] – was made Minister for Lands and thus my father's boss in the new coalition government (1948–51), which had succeeded in bringing de Valera's sixteen-year reign to a sudden end.

---

[*] That Christmas Eve my father came home with the dreadful news for us teenagers that the new Minister was transferring the Land Commission from Dublin to his home constituency in Mayo. Fortunately, his cabinet colleagues intervened, and it never happened. But whenever I hear Blowick's name, I see my mother, sister and me on the bottom steps of the stairs in our flat, all three gripping the bannisters and looking aghast at my father standing in the entrance below.

By the end of that spring term, the novelty of my cosseted existence had begun to wear off and it was a relief to be back in boarding school after Easter. True, there were early obstacles to overcome. All new girls were sent to learn the correct posture and movement. I, alas, was the only one in my group who had had to take 'remedial classes' in curt-seying to 'Reverend Mother'. The early start to the day didn't bother me. The nun on duty would come into our dormitory on the stroke of 6.30 am, armed with a wooden window pole. '*Benedicamus Dominium*' (let us bless the Lord), she would intone going round to each bed in turn, to which we had to reply as we leapt on to the cold floor, '*Deo gratias*' (God be praised). Whoever didn't instantly leap out got a firm dig in the ribs with the pole. If you weren't going down to early mass (and the nuns never made an issue of this), you could crawl back into bed for another half hour, otherwise it was mass and bed-making followed by silent breakfast. It was hard for adolescent girls to adjust to these endless periods of obligatory silence, especially in the dormitory at night and for the half an hour after lunch when there was always so much to talk about. But the Farnborough nuns were great believers in '*mens sana in corpore sano*' i.e. that teenage girls' inclination to self-dramatization and even hysteria could be managed by making them stay quiet for set periods and also have the chance to run about for substantial parts of their day. We had games for three periods every day, one after break-fast, but only, as the headmistress Mother Horan so embarrassingly repeated to the assembled school, having first ensured that we would remain 'regular' for life by an obligatory visit to the lavatory. (Far more embarrassing to us adolescent girls was her insistence that we record our 'P' – the days we had our period – in a book kept for her inspection.)

In the afternoon and for the boarders in the evening we had more games: hockey, lacrosse and netball in winter, tennis, swimming and rounders in summer, with lots of inter-class competition for those who didn't 'make' the school teams. Inter-school team matches were played with both Catholic and state schools and here too the nuns' modern outlook was well in evidence. Clodagh's talent as a tennis player soon saw her join more senior girls on the school's A team. As she appeared downstairs clad in her new uniform (made by our mother), the games mistress, Mother Bickford, took one look at her modest knee-covering skirt and sent her straight back up to the dormitory: 'Take *at least* four inches off that tennis skirt – we can't have the other schools saying, "Here comes the convent!"' Mother Bickford had, we were told, 'seen action in the real world' and could take on anyone. We giggled as she tucked up the skirts of her nun's habit and, hockey stick aloft, strode in the direction of the peeping Toms, soldiers from the Aldershot barracks lurking in the undergrowth at the edge of our hockey field. When many years later the new PE teacher from Dublin, Yvonne Menton, told her that the school's swimming pool was inadequate for her gifted pupils, Mother Bickford went off to Aldershot, interviewed the relevant officer and obtained permission for the girls to use the army pool. The message, as far as Mother Roantree and her nuns were concerned, was that, after centuries of 'no popery' almost defining English life, their pupils should learn that Catholics in England need no longer keep a low profile. They were both entitled to and under obligation to play their full part in society and must be educated to do so. The school uniform, so distinct from the normal convent rig-out and designed by Reverend Mother herself, was part of that strategy, of what would nowadays be called the school's mission statement. It was not just to look nice but to stand out in a crowd and the girls should like wearing it. In place of ghastly gym tunics (so unflattering on lumpy adolescent figures), black stockings and horrid hats, our vivid green and purple striped blazers and reasonably short navy skirts, plus bright scarlet berets, were a good example of the medium being the message. And at Wembley Stadium in my last year when, to mark the new visibility of Catholic England on the centenary of the re-introduction of the centuries-long banned Catholic hierarchy in 1851, virtually every Catholic school in the country sent delegates to a massive open-air religious service, we Farnborough girls were easy to identify.

This new visibility and self-consciousness of the Catholic Church in England (as opposed to Britain)* was much helped by international

* In Scotland and Wales, and indeed in Liverpool, it was different; here traditional prejudice remained.

developments, notably the fall of Eastern Europe to Soviet Russia and the beginning of the Cold War and anti-Communist mania. As Catholics couldn't reasonably be suspected of being proto-Communists, increasing numbers from their ranks began to be recruited by the Foreign Office. Our teachers began to take our political education in hand. It started with daily broadcasts in 1949 of the Hungarian Cardinal Mindszenty's trial for 'treason' by the Soviets.* Schooled in Orwell's *Animal Farm* and his terrifying *1984*, which had just appeared, we had to listen to the radio every day for three weeks as the defendant – under the impact, we were informed, of a 'truth drug' called *actedron* – 'confessed' his disgusting crimes before the court, followed by his inevitable sentencing.

This time there was no stopping teenage hysteria. For several weeks none of us in our dormitory could sleep as we outlined to each other what concentration-camp life would be like, where, we were now so certain, all of us must end up as soon as the Russians came. It was only when large numbers fell asleep in class and our work showed alarming signs of neglect that the headmistress latched on to what was happening and put a stop to it. I still can't help feeling a shiver down my spine on the rare occasion I hear the name Mindszenty.

During my last school year 1950–1 we sixth formers had our own study-bedrooms in a special new wing of the school with several bathrooms. We revelled in the sense of trust and partnership as being co-responsible with the nuns for managing the younger pupils, a key element in Mother Roantree's educational philosophy. Farnborough girls should leave school equipped to take responsibility in whatever career they were called to. My ego was somewhat punctured when I discovered my nickname, coined by a cheeky lower-sixth-form madam, a small girl with dead straight blond hair and a fringe named Mary Holland: 'Goofy' did not at all accord with my new self-image. I never quite forgave Mary, not even when she went on to be one of Ireland's leading investigative journalists.

But there was no time to nurse wounded vanity. Besides schoolwork my games captainship took every available moment, from arranging

---

* József Mindszenty was the head of the Catholic church in Hungary, arrested following the 1948 Soviet invasion of Hungary and imposition of a Communist regime.

inter-school matches to helping coach younger pupils in hockey and lacrosse and chivvying the French and Spanish girls, who refused to see the point of sport, at least to take part. One of the French girls, a large awkward soul from a wealthy Normandy family, now became my special responsibility. Not only did Marie-Thérèse hate any form of physical exercise, she also, as one of the nuns told me in confidence, had a strict aversion to water: she simply did not wash herself. I had felt sorry for the lonely girl, who liked to talk French to me and didn't disparage my French accent.

Poor Marie-Thérèse developed an embarrassingly dog-like devotion to me, with the unintended consequence that our dormitory mistress gave me the delicate task of persuading her to take a bath and teaching her how to change her bedclothes. It took quite a bit of tact and moral blackmail. We teenagers were obsessed with washing ourselves. She had never taken a bath in her life: 'What will happen to my skin?' she cried in horror. Eventually she relented but wouldn't lock the bathroom door 'in case I drown' so I had to stand guard outside. As she retired to get dressed in the heavy but by now greyish corsets she lovingly stored under her eiderdown when in bed, I set about cleaning the thick black rim of dirt on the bath. When at the end of the year her parents came to collect her, I received a pressing invitation to come and stay in Normandy. For a whole week I, who was now normally perpetually hungry, found I could barely face the daily regime, which all the family tackled with gusto. It consisted of a six-course lunch followed at four o'clock by a sumptuous *goûter* of cream cakes and then some three hours later a seven-course dinner, all *haute cuisine*. Of bathrooms (apart from a lavatory) in that well-appointed villa – not a trace.

Most of my classmates were taking three A-level subjects, apart from a new girl, planning to do medicine, whose sheer intellectual brilliance dazzled us and to our grief quickly displaced myself and the other Irish girl, Monica O'Connor, at the top of the class. As I couldn't bear to part with any of my favourite subjects, history and French, which I hoped to study at university, nor English nor Latin, I took four, plus Irish to O-level, the last-named an entry requirement for University College

Dublin. Naturally there was no one to teach me Irish so I ingested (learnt by heart) the slim Christian Brothers' *First Irish Grammar* plus a sixteenth-century piece from Geoffrey Keating's *Dánta, Amhráin is Caointe*. This last was the set text for the University of London Matriculation exam, recognized as equivalent of the Leaving Certificate by the National University of Ireland for purposes of matriculation.

By another of those many strokes of luck in my life, we were offered the opportunity to take up an additional foreign language in the sixth form. I chose Spanish but during the summer vacation my grandfather, with characteristic prescience, told me to take German instead. It was July 1949, barely three months after the founding of the Federal Republic of Germany. 'This man Adenauer,' he said, referring to the newly appointed 73-year-old Christian Democratic chancellor, Konrad Adenauer, appointed chancellor after the recent elections, 'Adenauer may well make something of the new Germany,' he said. I shall be ever grateful for his advice. Our German teacher was an attractive young Austrian and our class of five took to the language straightaway. The German irregular verbs were child's play after their Irish counterpart.

To help us prepare for our French A-level orals, three of us were sent to spend the Easter holidays of 1951 in a sister convent in Laval, Normandy. What a culture shock it was! In Farnborough the food was pretty awful but in Laval we ate crisp baguettes and dined on freshly cooked local produce; on Sundays there was cider with lunch. In our sixth-form wing our individual study-bedrooms were bright and cheerful with four of us per bathroom. Laval's convent housed 300 boarders for whom there was one single wash basin, not, it appeared, overly used. Worse still, there were no sports at all. The only time we saw the sky above us was on the Thursday *promenade*, when a crocodile of soberly dressed girls marched under the eye of the accompanying nuns through the streets of Laval in silence! Imagine: apart from Thursday afternoons and on Sundays, we were strictly forbidden to talk to each other at any time in the entire week, neither by day nor at night in our dormitory, except to answer the teacher in class. Pent-up teenage emotions exploded without warning – we soon learnt what *crises de nerfs* (literally, crises of nerves) were all about. Back in Farnborough we had of course fought with one another, but always in words. Here, notably at night in the *dortoir*, out of sight of the nuns, we three would watch in horror as girls fell on each other over some trifling disagreement, tearing each other's hair and scratching their faces.

Classes were extremely formal affairs, but the academic level was impressive, particularly when it came to French language, literature and history. We 'English' girls were allowed out on Sunday afternoons on our own to walk downtown to savour our particular delight, a *religieuse* ('a nun'), an éclair made of two round balls of pastry with a 'veil' of scrumptious coffee or chocolate icing on top. On one occasion our class mistress told us she had arranged a special treat for us: we were to 'take tea' at the home of one of the aristocratic families, whose daughter was in our class. We must be on our very best behaviour. We looked forward to a mighty spread, ideally with lots of *rêligieuses*. What we got was one large loaf of bread and a dish of Norman butter: the aristocracy, we were later told, brought up their children simply. The daughters of the house waited for their parents to be seated, always addressing them in the polite form of *vous*, as in the bourgeois household of my future Catalan father-in-law I would also be required to do.

As an education for girls from mid-twentieth-century Ireland, Farnborough Hill was first class. Not all our mentors were equally inspiring, but all were well qualified, many of them Cambridge and Oxford graduates, and all clearly enjoyed what they did. Several were lay teachers, at least three who were not Catholics, appointed specifically to teach at sixth-form level. The high quality of the A-level syllabus was a constant challenge, and the pupil could choose her own 'special subject' among her favourite subjects. For me and my fellow students of history it was western monasticism with *The Monastic Order in England* by the Regius Professor of History at Cambridge, Dom David Knowles OSB, as our bible. The school offered us an interesting social reflection of the disparate origins of the non-Irish Catholic community in England, notably the Poles, daughters of the officers who had fled after the 1939 German invasion and who were now fighting in the British army, one of whom became head girl; her successor was the striking Jewish Rosemary Alexander, a convert to Catholicism, later Trinity College Dublin gold medallist in mathematics and later still Provincial of the Order. And then there was the Iberian and South American cohort, with whom Clodagh was especially friendly, prompting her to add Spanish to what would be her command of most Romance languages. Many of the girls from Europe and overseas seemed to my class to live on another plane from the rest of us: the Venezuelan girls told us that they went off at half term to London each with £35 spending money (my parents' annual school fees for me were £29) to stay in the Ritz, while one of the Spaniards from an Irish wild geese family but from 'darkest Madrid' (her grandfather had been General McMahon in Paris at the time of the 1871 Commune) expressed to us her amazement on learning that her Protestant classmates didn't actually have horns, as she had always been taught to believe.

One development I thought little of at the time, but which would play a major role in later life, was my mother's decision to make me a junior member of her golf club. It was in effect a sort of 'compensation' for the dreadful shock I had received when I came home to after that first eventful year at Farnborough in July 1948 and for which oddly neither of my parents had thought to prepare me. When we got off the boat we drove not to my beloved Cherrywood and the outdoor life but to a four-room top-floor flat in Dublin's Fitzwilliam Place, misery compounded by having to share a bedroom with my sister. What on earth was I to do with myself all those summer weeks so far from my friends in Foxrock till school began again in September? At first, I used to take the bike and go for long solitary rides up and down the nearby canal in the hope of getting to the countryside. Not a chance. Our flat looked down on Fitzwilliam Tennis Club where the courts were empty during the day. Clodagh spent most of her time there and soon acquired a partner, John O'Connor. But I was a useless tennis player. For a while I found an outlet in mean younger-sister-mode: I would lean out of the kitchen window and call out 'Clodagh loves John!' until my mother took a practical hand. She decided to have me learn to play golf.

The great thing about golf for mothers of tiresome teenage daughters is that it takes time, hours and hours in fact. After the first couple of lessons with the elderly professional, Mr Shannon, I could cycle the couple of miles to Milltown Golf Club and put in entire days there, just briefly coming back home for lunch. Eventually I was 'let out' to graduate to the rough, where as far as I can remember I spent the entire remainder of that summer, with the result that no rough, however thick, held terrors for me. In those days hardly any young people played golf at Milltown and certainly no girls. I must have been an odd sight, more particularly in the following year or so when I was allowed onto the course and would play eighteen or even thirty-six holes on my own. The following year, while I was planning to study history and French at University College Dublin after school, I found I liked German so much that I would continue with it as one of the two obligatory subsidiary subjects in first year. My future classmates would have had five years of German at school and I barely one and a half. Accordingly, my golf bag always contained Otto's *Deutsche Grammatik*. Every time I got into a bunker and failed to get out first time, out would come Otto. I would look round to see I wasn't holding anyone up and make myself learn six irregular verbs before proceeding. No doubt passing adult golfers thought, *That poor girl … poor Mrs O'Shiel.*

Over the next decades my mother and I played endless rounds together. I caddied for her at matches and went round with her to watch the professionals, our favourite being Harry Bradshaw, who would amble over to the pair of us to say hello no matter how serious the championship he happened to be playing in. We loved to watch Christy O'Connor's iron-play and later some of the British professionals when the O'Carroll's (later the Irish Open) began to attract major talent from across the water. Thanks to my godfather Vincent Kelly's unofficial status as secretary to the Irish Professional Golfers I even got to play a memorable round with him and Christy O'Connor in Sligo's Rosses Point. I also joined a coaching class with the legendary Henry Cotton, though in fact we Irish despised him as a bad sport for having accused Harry Bradshaw, honest as the day, of cheating in a major tournament.

This was probably the famous occasion when Harry's ball went into a broken stout bottle and with his wonderfully powerful wrists and easy swing, he smashed it out on to the green, perfectly admissible under the rules.

# — THREE —

## *The 1950s I: University*

I was now eighteen, grown up, and could realize my ambition to have a picture hat. This, I was sure, would distract attention from my chubby face and enhance what I thought one of my only two redeeming features, what women's magazines called my roses-and-cream complexion (plus freckles, alas), plus my relatively small waist, emphasized by wearing very tight belts. This, I hoped, might help redirect attention from my capacious hips and bust. Unfortunately picture hats went out that summer and my sister soon punctured my self-image by telling me I looked like an egg-timer.

My idealized image of university life proved equally disappointing. University College Dublin in Earlsfort Terrace was just around the corner from our flat at 5 Fitzwilliam Place, the reason for our move from the country to the city. Apart from the Science and Engineering Faculty in Merrion Street in what is now the Department of the Taoiseach, UCD was in a handsome art nouveau building, the current National Concert Hall. The interior hardly lived up to its exterior promise, the first floor a maze of look-alike rooms, the basement smelling nastily of carbolic soap and drains. Moreover, I didn't know anyone, having stayed on at school an extra year to do A Levels. My schoolfriends Maryanne and Fin were already embarked on their college careers, Maryanne in UCD Arts, Fin in an antediluvian physiotherapy 'academy' in Molesworth Street. I wandered round the corridors to try and find out where one was supposed to be – no student adviser in those days, no college tutorial system. One eventually gleaned the necessary information from other students, though most reacted warily to what was to them my 'English' accent. We first years had to take two main and two subsidiary subjects: Latin was obligatory, the other subsidiary subject would, I planned, be German. In addition, 'logic' was compulsory for arts students. Perhaps our first logic lecture can best exemplify to the modern reader the enormity of the ideological gap separating the Ireland of the early fifties from modern times. The professor, a Monsignor Horgan, was an imposing cleric on the elderly side. He concluded his peroration by addressing the large group of young men, women, nuns and clerical students with words to the effect of: 'You may go through college but fail despite your best efforts to gain a degree. But you will be far, far better off than if you had carried off all the prizes but having committed mortal sin you had endangered your immortal soul.' This I found puzzling. Why go to college in the first place?

Another oddity were the lecture arrangements: all the nuns, and there were loads of them, were seated at the front, the ones with the knitting 'chaperoning' their more academic sisters. Behind them to the right as you came in sat the serried black mass of the clerical students, who were not permitted to speak to girls, though they might answer them if addressed. To the left (no doubt befitting the gender nearest to the devil) were the girls, while the boys, the bad and the good, sat at the back. To the delight of the back rows and to the horror of those concerned, one of my new acquaintances from French class, the shapely Miriam O'Connell with her provocative pigtail, boldly ran up the steps and seated herself in the middle of the now blushing clerics. From then on, she relished her nickname, evidently given her by the clerical students, of 'Jezebel'.

I was eagerly anticipating my first French lecture, which would extend the wonderful world of French literature which our A-level studies of Racine, Molière, Balzac and other great French writers had opened to us. Alas, I had yet to encounter the effect of the stultifying modern language syllabus of the Irish Leaving Certificate. Worse still, the head of department, Professor Roche, and his second-in-command, Dr Cognon, relied on sarcasm as a favourite didactic tool. Our enthusiasm found no response, our accents were mocked, our best efforts ignored. In the German class of seven we six girls, all of whom apart from myself had French as their second main subject, nursed our grievances. In adversity friendships are formed. I found myself now part of an in-group; in due course we became determined to drop our beloved French in second year in favour of German. This was a risky decision for me as I failed the first-year exam but scraped through in the autumn re-sit thanks to a summer scholarship in Germany arranged by our professor, Miss Cunningham. (This failure later proved very useful when I had to console first-year students who had failed their German exam. I would open the interview with the unsuccessful candidate with: 'Tell no one, but I too failed my first-year German …')

Before embarking on that stage Professor Cunningham and I found we had a struggle on our hands to permit me to continue in German. There was a timetable clash with history, and the history staff were not prepared to allow me to miss any lectures in their department. The dean was a well-known medieval historian, Aubrey Gwynn; he was also an elderly member of the Jesuit order. In his office Miss Cunningham requested and I pleaded for special permission. But Fr Gwynn was adamant: *non posset*. Impossible. Whereupon I burst into tears of disappointment, Miss Cunningham followed suit but from rage at men and their obduracy. The over-six-foot tall, black be-gowned Dr Gwynn, towering over his petite colleague, raised his closed eyes to heaven and murmured: 'Dear God, I thank Thee for clerical celibacy.' Defeated, Miss Cunningham and I retired to lick our wounds. After Professor T.D. Williams's next history lecture, I asked his advice (he was a family connection, his mother, Angela Murnaghan was the sister of my grandfather's Omagh partner). In his customary ironic manner Williams said I could do the full history degree, known as VIIIB, which carried some cachet in the professional field, plus the half Arts degree in German. I would have to work very hard – he had not only done the same in his youth but two further degrees in law and in economics *and* had got a first in all four. As I frowned my disagreement he added: 'You're right, I forget that you are a woman.' He had engineered the right reaction in a student. 'That has nothing to do with it,' I replied and went off in a huff. I'd do it and show him. It was indeed hard work and left very little time for social life. Not that I had much and my few attempts at joining my sister at the College hops or dances were a humiliating failure. Clodagh with her violet eyes, dark hair and film-star eyebrows was a real beauty and never off the dance floor while I generally remained a wallflower.

I decided to try hockey. I had played in England for the Surrey county schools' team on the left wing and as I was a fast runner, the UCD hockey club welcomed me to play as centre-half on the College's first team. We had regular matches against the best, even playing against the Irish national women's hockey team.* Our uniform on the field consisted of thick orange Foxford woollen gym tunics, their broad pleats exaggerating one's natural curves, the thin black belt straining in my case to hold them in place. Black stockings were *de rigueur* for females. This was unfortunate for me as I was at nearly five foot ten inches in height tall and well built. In that pre-tights era, my mother was hard pressed to find black stockings big and long enough to pass muster: she eventually settled for buying two pairs, cutting the tops off one and sewing them to the tops of the second. Alas, in a heated match I lunged to tackle an opponent. There was a cracking sound, the seam broke and pink skin was exposed to the watching crowd: the moral police immediately ordered me off the field. It was not the failure of her subsequent valiant attempts to remedy the deficit which put a sudden end to my hockey career, but rather the new wide-angled camera lens employed by

---

* The Irish goalkeeper, Johnny Lambert, and the Irish centre forward, Joan O'Reilly, I would meet many years later as fellow members of Grange Golf Club.

the *Evening Herald*. Reporting on an important final against doughty opponents, which UCD had won with flying colours, a photograph of our team was displayed along the bottom of the entire back page of this widely read newspaper. As centre-half I was at the front, larger than life-size (not inconsiderable). As soon as I saw myself in it, I resolved never to appear in such unflattering garb again. I got rid of my hockey stick and never played again. The young suffer grievously over what seem to others mere trivialities. Later that year I was waiting at a bus stop after visiting my grandmother in Mount Merrion when I spied a weighing machine on the other side of the road (an optimist, I was always weighing myself, but always only to have my hopes dashed). As I stood on the scales, I opened a letter just received from the College: I had won a second-year scholarship worth £168. But my only concern was the arrow on the scale, there for all to see. I watched in horror as it rose to fourteen stone five pounds and burst into floods of tears. A kind passer-by came up to me and seeing the letter said: 'My dear, you have had bad news?' 'Yes, I have!' I sobbed. Life eventually thinned me down but years after, if I thought about the matter at all, I would always see myself as overweight.

Tuition in the UCD of the 1950s varied enormously. French was traditional, lectures to large numbers, language exercises and essays set and marked but never individually discussed. Quite the opposite was true of German, at least as far as submitted work was concerned. Our translation and grammar exercises and essays came back covered with red ink and admonishments for improvement. Our 'lecture' classes consisted solely of reading aloud classical plays of the German Enlightenment and hearing Professor Cunningham's comments. Our professor always took the heroine's parts; the Polish student, the only male, took over the hero's and the villain's while we six each had our turn in the minor roles.[*] As for the Arts departments of UCD, apart from history, archaeology

---

[*] As far as she was concerned, German literature stopped with the death of Friedrich Schiller, so that no text we studied post-dated 1805.

and one or two more, it could be said that what Professor Hugh Ryan of UCC had observed in a seminal essay in 1915 still applied to most Irish universities in the 1950s:

> The present system [of university education] based on the teaching of traditional knowledge, is suitable for a country the main industries of which are low grade, but it leaves almost entirely undeveloped, among the great mass of University graduates, the originality and initiative on which depend the future progress of Ireland in the industries best suited to the country.[*]

To go from German class to history lectures and tutorials was like transferring to another university. Desmond Williams, one of the finest Irish minds of his time, had studied at Peterhouse College Cambridge under Hugh Trevor-Roper,[†] followed by four years research in Berlin in the archives of the *Reichssicherheitshauptamt* (RSHA), the headquarters of the Nazi security service. He knew virtually everyone who was anybody in the German academic world and used his contacts shrewdly. More importantly for us, he recruited some of Peterhouse's most able young historians to the UCD history department: John Morrill (later LSE), Hugh Kearney (later Pittsburgh USA) and Jack Watt (later part of the founding group of Hull University historians), to join Maureen Wall, the department's only woman lecturer, and the professors of modern and medieval Irish history Robin Dudley Edwards, Fr Gwynn and the former infant prodigy, old before his time, Francis J. Byrne. Tuition was conducted in Oxbridge-style tutorials of two to three students. I was fortunate enough to be in Williams' group. Weekly essays presented and critiqued at the tutorial demanded an immense amount of reading, in some weeks several books in seven days: it was marvellous training and, most of the times, great fun. If fun was quite absent from our German training, we six students and a couple of those below us, notably Des Keogh, who like Lelia Doolan was destined to make his name on the stage, provided enough for ourselves. And then there was Goethe's *Faust*

---

[*] *Studies* 4 (1915), 337–50, here 350.

[†] Author of the celebrated *The Last Days of Hitler* (1948), but whose reputation was later damaged by his publicly expressed belief in the authenticity of the so-called Hitler Diaries.

(I and II). Then as now I am of the view that it is worth studying German simply to have encountered this greatest of German texts, companion of a lifetime.[*]

~

I spent the summers of 1952 and 1953 in Germany, the first thanks to William's contacts with two rather different German families in Marburg (in the Federal state of Hessen) followed by a four-week summer course at Tübingen university, arranged by Miss Cunningham. The young father of my first family was an unashamed advocate of Hitler's Germany, though he kept his views in-house. The second was spent mainly in a small *pension* with part of the day in the company of warm-hearted General Blumentritt and his wife in their few rooms. The remainder of their capacious villa had been requisitioned by the state to house some of the twelve million refugees from the East who had fled in 1945–6 from the Russians (sixteen million had left, four million had died on the trek). The genial general, whose Bavarian accent was almost impossible for me to understand, had served on the Russian front. Two of his Blumentritt cousins had been hanged following the failed assassination attempt against Hitler of 20 July 1944, as had a cousin of my penfriend Wendula von Wietersheim's father, who had served under the Paris leader of the plot, General von Stülpnagel. Despite my deficient German conversational powers, I enjoyed my first taste of German politics.

Back in Marburg in the summer of 1953 I spent a few days during the Federal elections with some new acquaintances in support of the Liberal Party (about which I knew nothing but 'liberal' sounded good). Our job: to paste Social Democrat posters with the flyer '*Von Moskau bezahlt*' (funded by Moscow). In this I was showing my lamentable ignorance, for I had no idea that many former Nazis had found a home

---

[*] Medievalists might beg to differ and insist on substituting the early thirteenth-century *Parsifal* for *Faust*. One devotee, the late Peter Johnson of Pembroke College Cambridge, allegedly knew the entire 50,000-line text by heart and if asked readily would cite any part.

in post-war Germany in one or other of the conservative or the 'liberal' parties, whereas the Social Democrats had been the only political party apart from the Communists to stand up to Hitler's determination in February 1933 to destroy the rule of law in Germany and had suffered accordingly. But in a sense, I was unconsciously recording contemporary sentiment among the citizens of the fragile young Federal Republic. Fear of Soviet Communism and hence of left-wing parties drove most German voters in the elections of 1949, 1953 and even 1957 to the right, more particularly to what they saw as the security of the Christian Democrats under the aloof but shrewdly pragmatic Konrad Adenauer. He had become the Federal Republic's first chancellor at seventy-three, reluctantly retiring fourteen years later. I never met him, though posters of his face with its curiously flat high cheekbones (the result of a car accident) were everywhere to be seen. Thanks to the DAAD, the German Academic Exchange Service, a group of us foreign students had been fortunate to be invited to Bonn during our summer course to meet the Republic's splendid first president, Theodor Heuss. Here indeed was the avuncular political figure post-Third Reich Germany so desperately needed. A prominent member of the old genuinely Liberal Party both under the Second Empire and the Weimar Republic, the Franconian Heuss enveloped each of our hands in his large warm *Patsche* (paw) and chatted and joked with us on that memorable day as if he had known us all our lives.

⁓

Back in UCD for our third and final year, I listened with envy to the accounts of my friends of their exploits during that fabulous *Sommersemester* at Tübingen: endless fun and friendships across Europe, lots of German culture and scarcely a word about lectures. By comparison I felt an utter swot. But swot was the reality of the next twelve months as the history department piled on the work and ever-lengthier German literary texts demanded to have essays written about them. One major disadvantage of taking the double degree was the prospect of the physically exhausting final exams in the autumn of 1954:* fifteen three-hour papers in a couple of weeks, ten in history and five in German, followed by three all-day sessions in Irish history. The first day of this typical Dudley Edwards pedagogical experiment was spent writing a long essay in exam conditions on an unseen topic; the second critiquing each other's work† and the third discussing the exercise. There were some eleven of us in the VIIIB finals class: two Poles, one Irishman (Tom Marmion), five clerical students, one nun, Sr Philip Anthony FCJ (half French, half Italian and wholly brilliant), one Belgian girl, Yvonne Marchand, later Morrell, and me. To round this endurance test off, our viva consisted of some three-quarters-of-an-hour's grilling by the extern (Michael Oakeshott of LSE), assisted by all the members of the history department. Desmond, as we now called him, was particularly irritating in not saying anything but peering round from behind the colleague seated in front of him; as he had a pronounced squint, you never know which eye was looking at you.

We survived physically and went our different ways. Professor Cunningham had secured me a DAAD annual scholarship to Freiburg, so off I set on the two-day journey via Liverpool, the Hoek of Holland and the Rhineland to the former Austrian territory of Breisgau. Freiburg is an ancient (1457) university in the beautiful cathedral city in the south-western Federal state of Baden (since 1952, to the undying resentment of the Badenese, now Baden-Württemberg). Here I planned to begin my training as a medieval historian of Germany via an MA in German literature to prepare for the competitive NUI Travelling Studentship examination in the autumn of 1955, which would fund my doctorate.

Alas for provincial naivety! My expectation of a tutorial system like the one in UCD met up with the reality of Germany's mass university system. Having secured my *Studienbuch*‡ after weeks of administrative

---

* Exams in UCD as in Trinity were still conducted in the autumn.

† This session went on long after supper time, but Dudley Edwards brushed aside repeated outraged phone-calls from Father and Mother Superiors.

‡ An official notebook, which would hold the record of all classes attended and seminars completed.

hassle I attended my first lecture. Nobody told you how the system worked, but eventually you put together your own study programme. I signed up for my first pro-seminar on Grillparzer on the advice of Professor Cunningham's predecessor, Professor Mary Macken,* hoping I would have the company of five or ten fellow students. Entering the classroom in good time I could hardly get a seat among the 150 or so already present. The history seminar with the medievalist Professor Gerd Tellenbach, whose fame as the authority on the famous quarrel between German empire and papacy under the eleventh-century Pope Gregory VII known as the Investiture Conflict, had directed my choice of Freiburg, was even more packed out. Worse still, the seminar in the Humboldtian sense of an exchange of knowledge and a meeting of fresh young minds with experienced researchers proved to be a mirage. For over an hour, one student who had had (invariably) his paper accepted for that date, read it out in a somnolent manner, followed by Tellenbach's comments and a few remarks from some of the old lags. After my colourful teachers in the UCD history department, almost all first-class communicators, the professor himself was dry as dust. The impression was not modified when, after queuing for a distant appointment at his *Sprechstunde* (literally 'speak hour') each week set aside for the purpose, I was eventually admitted to the august presence and told to expect a further five years of study for the doctorate.

Nor did the university offer much in the way of social life. College at home in Ireland was where you spent your day with your fellow students; not so here. In between classes students stood around in circles to discuss what they had just heard. You could join one and introduce yourself, after which you met each morning with most of the time in the quarter of an hour available being taken up with formal greet-ings: '*Guten Morgen, Fräulein O'Shiel*' '*Guten Morgen, Herr So-und-so / Fräulein So-und-so*' and obligatory handshake with each member of the circle followed as soon as the bell went with a repeat performance but this time as: '*Auf Wiedersehen, Fräulein O'Shiel*' etc. And we were

* First professor of German at UCD, a warm personality and popular colleague who was active in social justice and women's rights.

all only in our twenties. After classes everyone seemed to disappear home to their rooms to read and study. How to make proper contacts? There is a German phrase: *'Ein Deutscher Melancholie, zwei Deutsche ein Verein'* (one German, melancholy, two Germans a society). Accordingly, I looked round for a society (or two) to join and was directed to the *Katholischer Studentenverein* (Catholic Students Society) where I was welcomed as a new member. It was a large and formal organization, but I soon graduated from there to the smaller *Newman Verein*. The Newman Association proved to be a highly sociable if still pretty serious affair with lectures, slide shows, the occasional dance and, for me, the highlight of the summer, pilgrimages to local shrines on my ancient bicycle, named Rosinante after Don Quixote's horse, complete with *Butterbrot* (roll with butter) for a picnic with water from the local wells. We covered considerable distances, up to 40 km or more in the glorious Black Forest, though I occasionally encountered mild wonder or even disapproval from a few more earnest members for wearing on hot days the wide-skirted New Look summer dress my mother had made me, as she and I thought, just for such occasions: it was thoroughly modest in front but backless. Now and again one or two of the women students would remark on my 'courage' in wearing lipstick, the only one of our large group to do so. This was probably at least as much a hangover from Nazi puritanism as proper comportment for 'good Catholic' young women. The whole pilgrimage group of twenty to thirty got a great laugh on the day I infringed local custom after spying a line of cherry trees along the roadside laden down with delicious ripe black fruit and climbed up to get a handful. I had reckoned without the local farmer: my lovely dress was now covered with black tar from the bark, unnoticed in my greed, which proved almost impossible to wash off. The Newman Society also provided its members with a future countrywide network of contacts, which, given the extreme mobility of German society and Germany's culture of hospitality, would facilitate a newcomer's integration into the local community. In time I too would enjoy its benefits.

During my year in Freiburg, not yet a decade after the collapse of the Third Reich, none of the 'local' West German students mentioned politics, apart from some occasional expressions of resentment at what they saw as discrimination by their state. None of them, and many were desperately poor, got any form of grant, unless they held some rare award for outstanding academic distinction, whereas all the refugees got a basic living wage of DM 131 a month (£1 = DM 12.72). I made several friends among 'those from the East', notably the lively Silesians from the area which was now Poland, and others from the Catholic enclave of the Ermland in former East Prussia (also now Poland). To listen to them talk about their and their families' experiences in fleeing from the Soviets in 1945–6 was indeed a form of political education. Three of my closest, lifelong friendships came from that year in Freiburg: my Swabian friend Gertrud Härle (1927–2016) and her family, the then seminarian and Silesian refugee Wolfgang Nastainczyk (1932–2019) and Regina Mühlenweg (1934–2006) from Lake Constance, whom I first met in my Swedish evening class. Their lives encapsulated, directly or indirectly, much of the recent history of the former geopolitical entity known as Germany.

Regina was from Allensbach, eldest of seven children of one of the two founders of the Konstanz school of painting,* Fritz Mühlenweg, with his friend, the great Saxon Expressionist Otto Dix, whom I first met with his second wife, as he carved or rather tore apart the family Christmas goose.† Elizabeth, Regina's incomparable Austrian mother, always in great good humour – though suffering as all her children except Regina from a serious genetic kidney disorder – balanced masses of housework with her work as children's book illustrator to keep the family in funds. After the 1948 currency reform (*Währungsreform*) and before the founding of the Federal Republic a year later, when the Reichsmark was no longer accepted as currency and each citizen received DM 40, few people had funds to buy Fritz Mühlenweg's paintings. The burden of housework was

---

* The Allensbach Mühlenweg museum contains a representative collection of Fritz's and Elisabeth's work.

† Dix, known to us as 'Pappi Dix', allegedly tired of and divorced his first wife and married her sister; his striking portrait of 'Mammi Dix' can be seen in Essen's Folkwang Museum.

all the greater because neighbours would 'help' the *kinderreiche* family ('child-rich'—you could almost hear them sniff) by offloading their old clothes and half-rotten fruit and vegetables, which had to be 'processed' for what might be usable. I spent all but the summer university vacations at their home, my first job, when we were hardly in the door, being to attack the huge piles of ironing. Conversation in form and content was highly sophisticated, both parents being widely read in German, French, Latin and Greek literature and the house always full of the most interesting visitors. My German profited immensely as no one knew any English and Regina commanded a most recondite vocabulary. Fritz was widely travelled: he had accompanied the Swedish explorer Sven Hedin to the Far East where he spent some four years between 1927 and 1932 in China and Outer Mongolia, as part of both an international research team (plus 300 camels) and a secret German government mission to negotiate rights for the new Lufthansa. We never tired of listening to his stories, later written up as best-selling children's books. Elisabeth he had met when she was a student at the Vienna Art Academy, the same institution which had once rejected an eager young applicant, Adolf Stichelgruber, who later styled himself Hitler.* Frau Mühlenweg's family background was a sort of miniature history of the old Austrian Empire. Her grandparents included a Huguenot army officer from Galician Lemberg (later Polish Łvov, now Ukrainian Lviv), an Upper Austrian farmer and a Bohemian cook (Bohemian cooks were celebrated in former Austria), plus some French ancestry along the way. Wolfgang came from Neisse near Breslau (now Wrocław) in Silesia where his father had been classics master at the local *Gymnasium*. The Nastainczyks fled their home before the Russian army in January 1945 to Saxony, which in the summer of 1945 became part of the Soviet zone of occupation and in 1949 of the German Democratic Republic. They were forced to flee again, this time

---

* For years I wore her threadbare Dirndl, the Austrian traditional costume she had bought for thirty Austrian shillings in 1938. This had been her fee for producing a stylishly illustrated certificate of Hitler's honorary membership of the Academy, following the 1938 *Anschluss*, Austria's incorporation into Germany. This award had been accompanied by the craven apology on the part of the director of same academy for 'failing to recognize the genius' of the now Führer.

to West German Lower Saxony, when the East German regime dismissed his father, as a Catholic, from his school. Wolfgang decided to become a priest and came to take his theology degree in Freiburg. I first met him when he asked me at a Newman party to dance: imagine what they would have said back home? True, it was a very chaste affair, but sensibly the seminary authorities thought it important that those who would take a vow of celibacy had some idea of what they were doing. He later became a professor of pastoral theology at Regensburg, where in due course as dean of the faculty he recommended the appointment as professor of systematic theology one Josef Ratzinger, later Pope Benedict XVI.

The year at Freiburg included a memorable four-week trip to Egypt in the spring of 1955 organized by ASTA, the Students Union, at a cost of £30.* I travelled with thirty or so of my fellow Freiburg students, none of whom I knew, via Genoa to Naples, where we embarked for the five-day sea crossing in a small Turkish boat where no one spoke any language we could understand, – though we women in the group soon learnt that *Adamlar* was not the Turkish for 'ladies'. We had been instructed to bring our own food for the Mediterranean part; the Germans were all equipped with *Dauerwurst* (salami), hard cheese and sourdough bread. I bought lashings of lovely Italian cheeses and white bread at Naples; the next day the cheese had turned in the heat to whey, the bread would break your teeth. In desperation I ventured down to the kitchens of our third-class section with a drawing of a bowl of soup – not only did I get some, but from then on, the kindly Turks regularly passed me on the leavings of the over-fed passengers in first class. Our first night in the port of Alexandria saw us as dinner guests of the local police force, whose members kept on sending round a huge bottle of some apparently powerful spirit, urging us to drink; what the connection was with the ASTA president we didn't ask. Other highlights of the trip included a reluctant visit with our Cairo medical student hosts to the dissecting hall; in Cairo University every medical student has his own corpse to dissect, they proudly boasted – and we were shown all 165 (I had never

---

* I had wanted to go to Greece with the unexpected gift of a £30 award from my BA, but it cost £36: Egypt was second best.

seen a dead body before). We all slept in one great hall in iron bedsteads six feet off the ground: you wouldn't want to identify the various creatures on the ground below, cockroaches the best of the bunch. I saw my first scorpion but luckily no snakes. One of our days visiting Cairo's museum and the sights of the city happened to be St Patrick's Day. As I rode in a tram, I noticed a swarthy young Egyptian decorated with Irish flags and medals of the national saint; I asked him where he was going and he invited me along to an 'Irish party' in the Catholic church in Heliopolis, where I met the brother of our UCD history lecturer Maureen Wall, a White Father missionary stationed there. We went across the desert for twenty-two hours in a sand-filled train almost to the Sudanese border and then to the Valley of the Kings. The Aswan Dam was not yet finished, so along with all other famous sights we could visit the soon-to-be submerged temples of Karnak. By refraining from those luscious-looking strawberries, other fruit and vegetables and untreated water we managed to avoid the dreaded Egyptian tummy. Apart from the Icelander, who so gallantly forgave me for having a bar of chocolate in my pocket as we squeezed into a local taxi where the offending object melted into his white summer jacket, and a tall and very serious Prussian, I don't remember any of my companions. Back in Freiburg I was amused to be invited on a date by the Prussian who insisted on carrying my frilly handbag for me. 'A lady,' he instructed me, 'never carries anything when in the company of a gentleman.' Our acquaintance was short-lived.


ZURICH

In some senses Zurich University, to which I moved in the autumn term of 1955 to sit at the feet of the then luminary of German studies Professor Emil Staiger,* replicated my Freiburg student experience. The same hierarchical system, the same condescension by the professors, the elegant Staiger for literature and the rotund and peppery Professor

---

* Unfortunately, I failed to discover the baroque scholar Max Wehrli, a great teacher and personality, whose work, unlike Staiger's, has endured.

Hotzenköcherle for language and linguistics, the same formality among the students, exacerbated by the fact that we could not speak the local dialect. * The long winter semester from October 1954 to early March 1955 was at times so cold, with temperatures down to minus 24°C, that the hot-water bottle of our friend Karen once froze solid in her unheated room. Regina and I invited her, with our landlady's permission, to share one of our beds for the rest of the winter – not very satisfactory as the heavy down duvet was too short and narrow to cover two of us. The locals were friendly but generally anti-German and as I never spoke English included me in their prejudice. The first time Regina came to my room for tea the seven- and five-year-old daughters of my landlady peeped in and then rushed to their mother in the kitchen: '*Muetti*, our *Fräulein* has a *Saupreußin* in her room!' (They meant a German but used the term 'Prussian sow'.)

You could immediately distinguish the Swiss students from the Germans by their physical appearance: the Swiss men besuited and be-tied, the women in smart dresses, while the Germans were dressed in worn and much-mended garments, often hand-me-downs. A decade after the war the Federal Republic was still a poor country. Nor did the Swiss (partly because they spoke in dialect and most were ill-at-ease in 'High German') appear to want contact with the many students from Germany. We formed a group of our own, made jokes about their stand-offishness, socialized and went to the theatre together. One such occasion was the premiere of a satiric play by a young Swiss author called Friedrich Dürrenmatt: *Der Besuch der alten Dame* (*The Old Lady's Visit*), with the brilliant Berlin actress Thérèse Giese in the lead role. Everything about the staging and performance was magnificent.

---

* On my appointment to discuss my doctoral thesis project, Staiger was agreeable, his colleague anything but. 'You must reckon, Miss O'Shiel,' he pontificated, 'with at least four to five more years study before you can be competent in the [compulsory] Swiss-German language.' Years later, visiting my former Swiss flatmate Eva in the psychiatric unit of Zurich's university hospital, I discovered that these students rarely succeeded in presenting their doctorates in fewer than seven or more years of further graduate study – by which time, quite a number, like my friend Eva, were over thirty and often virtually unemployable.

However, the next day the local press voiced in no uncertain terms the outrage felt on behalf of Zurich and Switzerland at the savage caricature of their comfortable world. Next day we 'Germans', among them Antony Thorlby, later a colleague from Sussex University, invited the author, at the time only thirty-five years old but already as rotund as M. Michelin, to discuss his work with us. The ensuing intellectual treat was every bit as exciting as the performance, though firmly boycotted on grounds of 'national pride' by the Swiss students. It would be mainly British scholars, among them the Schröder professor of German at Cambridge, Leonard Forster, who in their research and teaching first established Dürrenmatt's international reputation.

Other concerns had meanwhile become more pressing. Life in Switzerland was extremely expensive, and though virtually all our money went on food and rent, I could never afford meat or fish that winter. In the previous five months I had spent all of £400 or half my NUI studentship. How was I to finish my PhD? A *Fasching* or carnival ball provided a sort of answer. I was dancing with a delightful Viennese who, having asked me my plans and sympathized with my financial worries, offered an original solution: there was nowhere, he said, cheaper than Vienna now that the Russians had departed the previous November. And besides, he added, everyone knows that the Central Cemetery in Vienna is half as big as Zurich and twice as much fun.

And so, in March 1956 I packed my belongings, said goodbye to Regina and my landlady and her girls and departed for Vienna, where I arrived at the *Westbahnhof* after the uncomfortable overnight train from Zurich just as dawn was breaking. The temperature was well below zero, snow everywhere and I was running a temperature, which soon developed into full-blown flu. My only interest was to find somewhere to lay my head. Eventually, having chanced during my search upon two altruistic American Quakers, I got an address in the Mozartgasse, a lane directly behind the cathedral. Ideal, you would think, and as regards location, it couldn't have been better, until having taken it straightaway I learnt that washing facilities consisted of a basin in the hall, in full view of the landlady's two adolescent sons. But by that time all I wanted was bed. The next day, with a roaring temperature, I ventured out to secure the ingredients for the Russian peasant soup recommended by my new American friends (two litres of water, half a kilo of cabbage, onions and potato. Boil it up, drink the lot and sweat it out). I drank as much as I could get down and endured a soaking-wet and generally horrible *Rosskur* (horse cure) for two nights and two days and, lo and behold, after forty-eight hours I was back to normal. I needed to deal with the unbeliev-able bureaucracy of registering as a student at Vienna University. Those familiar with the macabre satires of the Austro-Hungarian novelist Fritz Herzmanovsky-Orlando will have some notion of what I mean.

As a rule, charm is a concept rightly associated with the Austrian nation. But not with the university and other local bureaucracies I encountered over four semesters in their beautiful capital. If the head behind the window could make life difficult for you, it did: you got your stamp from one office and were sent to the next; they told you you had failed to read the small print and to come back with the 'other' stamp; you complied and did and got reprimanded for wasting their time. After fully five weeks of this carry-on, I got my student's card, which entitled me to get reduced fees if I passed the *Fleißprüfungen*\* at the end of the half-yearly semester. Normally foreign students paid three times as much as Austrians, which was fair enough as even with my small scholarship of the equivalent of £3 a week after having paid my rent of £1, I was much 'richer' than most of them. The best privi-lege of the student card was that you could attend any opera, concert or theatre – standing room only – for the princely sum of one Austrian shilling (72 shillings to the pound sterling in those days). One semester alone I went to sixty different performances, hearing great musicians such as the conductors Karl Böhm and Herbert von Karajan, the flau-tist Christian Rampal and German soprano Elisabeth Schwarzkopf in the *Großes Konzerthaus* and the Opera, plus all the great *Burgtheater*, *Volkstheater* and *Akademietheater* actors, including the inimitable Josef

---

\* A wonderful term meaning exams to prove your diligence, but ironic on account of the proximity in pronunciation of 'Fleiß' to 'Fleisch' – 'meat' but in this context 'fat' from too much sitting.

Meinrad playing Nestroy or the butler in Hugo von Hofmannsthal's *Der Schwierige* (*The Difficult Gentleman*). I attribute the early onset of varicose veins to endless hours standing listening to Wagner operas, notably *Tristan and Isolde*. I got scant sympathy from the cloakroom attendant when I complained of my aching legs after a six-hour session of the Maestro. 'Where is your score?' he asked contemptuously as he produced his own well-thumbed copy. He was probably paid a pittance for long hours of work, but the Viennese take their music seriously.

In Vienna you took two main subjects for your PhD, writing your thesis in one and submitting extended projects in the other. Having tasted the contrasting offerings of the professors of German, theatre studies and of history, I was more determined than ever to do my thesis in history. Heinrich Benedikt, the charming, elderly professor of modern European history, was enthusiastic and proposed a study of the historiography of the nineteenth-century Semmering railway, the first of its kind across the Austrian Alps. As a Jew he was one of the few members of the faculty not tainted by the recent past. Our professor of theatre studies, Heinz Kindermann, formerly professor of German, had been the editor of the rabidly xenophobic volume 100 of the long-established German text series *Deutsche Literatur in Entwicklungsreihen* and a diehard Nazi. In his volume *Political Poetry of the German Nation* (1938) he had included some of the most cringe-inducing elegies to Adolf. He accordingly lost his chair of German in 1945 but, as with so many others, was moved sideways with an equivalent salary and conditions. His successor in the Vienna chair of German, Moritz Enzinger, from many of his publications evidently only marginally less party loyal, had also lost his chair in 1945. He had been merely exiled to Innsbruck and duly returned to Vienna some years later. I sat in Enzinger's first lecture and listened open-mouthed to his preliminary remarks addressed to his audience, more than half of whom were women: '*Sie, junge Frauen,*' he declared, '*Sie täten besser, wenn Sie z'Haus blieben und stricken lernten.*' (You young women, you'd be better staying at home learning to knit.) I and a couple of other 'foreigners' were the only ones who never came back, though we had to take seminars with him. And yet in his early days he had pioneered the study of the Viennese comic theatre which was only 'rediscovered' as one of the highlights of Austrian culture a year or two after I had returned home.

Alas, that Christmas vacation Desmond Williams issued another piece of career-changing advice. 'Eda,' he said, 'who will want to employ you in Ireland as a specialist on an Alpine railway?' And then came the crunch line. 'If there is a man up for a job competing with you, he'll get it. Men do, that's how it is.' He paused, looking out of the window in his characteristic way, and added: 'There are no men in German studies.' I bit the bullet and turned up in Enzinger's office asking to be taken on as his doctoral student, to which he equally reluctantly agreed. He disliked foreign women and more particularly, tall foreign women. He was, to put it mildly, under-sized. On the three occasions I entered his office for my permitted tutorial I was careful to bend my knees so that I only topped him by a couple of inches. Seminar gossip would have it that his own wife was *very* large and *very* forceful. I don't think he ever actually read my thesis, a most positivistic piece of work on the *fin-de-siècle* poet Hugo von Hofmannsthal's reading. Another German lecturer was the delightful professor of dialectology Eberhard Kranzmayer from South Carinthia, who believed he spoke the purest High German but whose native dialect was for some weeks incomprehensible even to Austrians. His lectures, seminars and especially *Kundfahrten* – field excursions to experience the relevant dialects in the Austrian countryside – were feasts of intellectual and personal stimulus. The history professors included many of the luminaries of the Vienna history school, most notably Leo Santifaller and Alphons Lhotsky, with Hugo Hantsch, author of the standard history of Austria, and Heinrich Fichtenau.

To be in Vienna in the 1950s was to be on the fringes of the Iron Curtain. As soon as the Hungarian uprising broke out in October 1956, we students rushed to work in the refugee camps and heard at first-hand the experiences of our contemporaries on the other side of the curtain. Returning from a history department excursion on 4 November, we listened in horror to the noise of the Soviet tanks rolling into Budapest to crush the rising. Two of my new acquaintances had escaped from the prison where they had been confined for over a decade, under the Nazis and then under the Soviet puppet dictator. One of my Austrian mates in the camp, whom I watched in admiration as he sliced every piece of several large loaves precisely equal in size and weight, told me he had spent seven years in Siberia for being a student activist. After three years he was 'allowed' to work in the kitchen where, if he and his fellow prisoners cut some pieces too large and ran out, the ones at the end of the 17,000-person queue could actually perish from hunger.

Earlier that year I had made many friends from among the history students, cemented by a memorable ten-day excursion in my last year under the direction of professors Hantsch and Benedikt to north-east Italy as a former Austro-Hungarian province. We never had a minute to ourselves, between lectures and site visits, our European horizons being expanded by encounters with the artistic, architectural, political, social, linguistic, geographical and topographical character of the multi-national Empire, whose demise in 1918 had had such catastrophic consequences for Europe. We encountered such varied aspects of that history from, among others, the genius of Mantegna, to the strange proto-fascist figure of Gabriele D'Annunzio with his splendid Palladian villa near Verona and some of the decisive battlefields of Austrian wars. Professor Benedikt, born in 1886, was still drawing his pension in 1956 as a cavalry officer from his time on the Italian front in World War I where he fought at the battle of Isonzo and would continue to do so until his death in 1977. One memory provided me with a useful lesson for the future. Benedikt, warm-hearted but crafty, would frequently beg whatever group of students he happened to be with at lunchtime to keep him company – 'I hate eating alone,' he used to say. We of course couldn't dream of affording a restaurant meal and assured him we had already eaten, and then sat, mouths watering, as he ordered large quantities. And then: 'I can't possibly manage all this, but we can't waste it. Would you do me the favour of taking as much as you can?' The next time he tried the ploy when I was part of the group, I remonstrated. We had seen through the subterfuge, I added, which elicited the lesson: 'Apart from being a kindness on your part to an old and rich professor, just remember, if you are ever in later life in a position to help students, think of me.'

'Get out!' shouted Professor Kralik one dark November day in sergeant-major tone. 'Get out, Miss!' repeating it even louder as I hesitated at the end of my hour-long viva in Old High and Middle High German language and literature. I stumbled from his office feeling that this was it. Outside the door, handkerchief in hand to catch my tears, his assistant, the charming Dr Blanka Horaček, took one look and said: 'Don't worry, my dear. The Herr Professor has his gout day.' There remained the two-hour history viva (European with Professor Benedikt, Austrian with Professor Hantsch OSB), which I looked forward to even though you could be asked anything from the sixth-century Merovingians to the end of World War I.[*] Plus there was the much-dreaded *Philosophikum* for which I had little capacity and as the lectures had been supremely dull I learnt virtually nothing from them. All I can recall from the two history *vivas* was Professor Benedikt's response when, having asked me the name of William of Orange's principal general at the Battle of the Boyne I had mentioned the names of my Shields great-great-great-grandfather Daniel Shields and three of his sons, all but one of whom had fallen on the battlefield, he declared that 'a candidate should always be in a position to tell the examiner a fact of which he was unaware'.

I limped through the first philosophy exam, my meagre success, I am convinced, owing something to the fact that the pious Professor Gabriel had seen me at early morning mass in our local church. The second, a supreme and utterly absurd example of the now utterly stale yet still-dominant *Wiener Positivismus*, was psychology. It consisted solely of regurgitating half of Professor Rohracher's 600-page textbook. You had the choice between pages 1–300 or 300–600. Blessed with a good memory, I knew my half off by heart and was more than ready for 'the physiology of the eye'. But before I got to the actual exam I

---

[*] In the 1950s and for years to come neither universities nor schools in Austria taught the history of the two Republics (1918–38 and 1955 onwards) and certainly not the Nazi period (1938–45).

had evidently, like all the professor's doctoral candidates, to 'prove my character'. I was summoned for 8 am on a bitter November morning. Breakfast-less like everyone else there, and there were dozens of us, we awaited our turn. At precisely one o'clock his assistant announced: 'The Herr Professor has gone to lunch and won't be back today. Come back at eight tomorrow.' This time we at least came prepared, with breakfast behind us. Just before lunch I received the summons, regurgitated my piece and was congratulated on my 'excellent' performance and dismissed. There remained graduation day a few weeks later, just in time before the last money from my NUI studentship ran out. It was a complete anticlimax and a further demonstration of the sheer disloyalty of the university to its students. In our black suits we were conferred by the Faculty Dean 'as a job lot' in groups of ten or more and dismissed ten minutes later without further ceremony. I had no family there, fortunately for them. None of our subject teachers put in an appearance except dear Professor Kranzmayer from dialectology, together with our kind Lower Austrian history lecturers, the hunchbacked Dr Karl Lechner and the Cistercian monk from Heiligenkreuz who had nobly risked his abbot's ire on our visit there in order to let us into the *clausura* for a glimpse of the portrait of St Bernard greeting his Irish confrère Malachy. My name on the parchment unfortunately appeared in the Latin accusative as a Dutch cheese: *Edam O'Shiel ex Hiberniis partibus* (Eda O'Shiel from Ireland). As I reached the entrance door of the university onto the great central Vienna Ringstrasse, *Doktorrolle* (parchment) in hand, the porter, whom I had greeted politely each day for some two years, which he had acknowledged with scarcely a half-nod, bowed obsequiously with a loud '*Grüß Gott, Frau Doktor.*' Celebration was measured for lack of funds, but Regina and I happily shared a piece of spinach tart and one slice of delicious *Sachertorte* in the renowned Café Dehmel (now but a shadow of its former self) before collecting our bags and getting on to the train for our ten-hour journey to her home at Lake Constance en route for Christmas in Dublin and, presumably, unemployment.

# FOUR

# *The 1950s II: Emigration*

'*We were taught this history, you were sorta* [sic] *taught to hate England and then sent there.*'*

In the autumn of 1958, following graduation from the University of Vienna and having spent over three years as a student in Germany, Switzerland and Austria, I joined those hundreds of thousands of citizens of the Irish state forced to 'take the boat' and leave their country, in my case for almost the next two decades. After nearly seven years as a university student, I needed a permanent and ideally pensionable job and I needed it now. My father at sixty-seven was nearing retirement, suffering from heart problems. He could hardly expect to have to provide for his daughters indefinitely. On every one of my many visits home during my graduate years in continental Europe, my former history department at UCD would hold out the promise of a job. But when the newly self-confident 'Frau Dr' with PhD qualifications in

---

* Sharon Lambert. *Irish Women in Lancashire 1922–1960: their story.* Lancaster: University of Lancaster, 2001, 88.

both history and German language and literature presented herself early in 1958 to the authorities, no job was on the horizon. Once again in post-independence Ireland, myth and reality diverged. After graduation my sister and all my many women friends but two* had gone straight from college to teacher-training or secretarial college. From here they were 'placed' in offices and banks around the city, paid not according to their talents and with poor or no promotion prospects. The obvious choice for me, who couldn't and wouldn't learn to type (a grave error as it proved), was the civil service. Not of course in the hopes of following in my father or maternal grandfather's footsteps to a senior post at some future date. After all, I was only a woman. Faced with the expectation of being paid some two-thirds of what a man would earn for the same work and being forced to resign should I marry, I had opted with some reluctance and more trepidation for a career teaching history and therefore further study.

For the first few months in Dublin after returning from Vienna I had hoped to find something to allow me to stay where I wanted to live my life, in Ireland. In January 1958 I got temporary work at St Andrew's boys' school in Donnybrook (now Blackrock, Co. Dublin) teaching German and French (for which I had no qualification beyond A-level and first-year Arts French). I was to step into the shoes of the legendary Dr Scheyer, lawyer and refugee from Hitler's Third Reich and much-loved part-time lecturer at Trinity who had just died. Whether the school or the boys profited from my sojourn is more than doubtful. I taught German to ten-year-old beginners and enjoyed every minute of it. But I was hopeless at keeping discipline and it didn't take long for the boys to get the measure of me; they made me laugh with their constant interruptions: 'Miss, is it true that German girls are simply smashing?' etc. The headmaster, Mr Southgate, had assured me on appointment that he would deal with any problems – 'just send them to me' – which

---

* These were Lelia Doolan, among many other achievements the first woman artistic director of the Abbey Theatre and co-founder of the Irish Film Institute, and Mella Carroll, first female chairman of the Bar Council, judge of the High Court and of the Geneva-based International Labour Court.

I did, in batches of six. Having no brothers or male cousins of my own age it took a while for me to realize why the giggling returnees held their hands behind their back eliciting a delighted reception from the rest of the class: they had been beaten and it was all my fault! And they would now make my life a misery! Not a bit of it. Boys, it seemed, were not like girls. The victims even appeared to have acquired a certain status from the affair among their peers. For the rest of my time at St Andrew's chaos might reign on occasion in my German class but no one was ever sent again to the headmaster. Meanwhile my shortcomings as a teacher were becoming evident in my senior French class: my job was to prepare these fourteen- and fifteen-year-olds for their Intermediate Certificate or first state exam (today: Junior Cert.). In mitigation of my record, I have to say that I found the boys' knowledge of French grammar and idiom to be woefully deficient – nor did the French language feature among their priorities. The fact remained that the entire class failed their Intermediate French that June. Clearly, I was not cut out for a career as a schoolteacher. What next? I had been offered part-time work in June in the UCD archives 'Wild Geese Project', deciphering from often barely legible microfilms the names of Irishmen who had fought in the seventeenth- and eighteenth-century Habsburg armies. The pay, thirty pence an hour, was more than adequate for my needs. My sister and I were both living at home and our parents did not wish us to contribute to the household, so now I could devote much of my earnings to Russian conversation lessons with a poverty-stricken White Russian gentlewoman who lived in a beautiful, hopelessly damp little Georgian house off Eglinton Road in Donnybrook. Clodagh, meanwhile, with a first-class honours NUI degree in economics – one of the first Irish women, I believe, to achieve this, – proficient in shorthand and typing, fluent in French after her year at one of the *écoles normales* in Paris, was earning the princely sum of £2:50 a week (pensionable) as a shorthand typist in UCD's Academic Registry with little hope of advancement.

While I struggled in the evenings to read Pushkin's *A Captain's Daughter* in the expectation one day of having sufficient mastery to read his poetry in the original, my sister, more attractive than ever, was much occupied with which of her innumerable suitors should be her chosen one. She would regularly consult our grandmother on the matter, whose considered views would invariably end with the question, 'Is he for the long road?' Some clearly were, but she was spoilt for choice and I was often the unfortunate victim when she insisted that I play gooseberry. My role was to sit it out with the current ardent suitor in a visit to our house till he, furious with me, got the message and went home. I, being plump and awkward with young men, had few followers. One of them, Sam, whose family originally came from Cork, was a hand-me-down from Clodagh's surplus, a Trinity engineering student, great fun to be with and sharing my own outdoor interests. When he invited me to tea in College, to be off the premises by 6 pm according to the then Trinity regulations about women on campus, he assured me his 'wife' would be there too. He laughed when he saw the horror on my face: 'wife' in Trinity-speak meant his roommate.* Later I even got to the stage of being invited to meet his parents, who lived in Cheshire. Alas, we fell out over Suez (I as a former helper in the refugee camps after the 1956 Hungarian uprising, had witnessed how Britain's involvement in Suez had hampered the creation of an Anglo-European consensus to challenge the Soviets). Sam then emigrated to Australia, writing occasional newsy letters and eventually marrying a clearly delightful girl.

But it was hard to settle back home in my mid-twenties after the freedom of my graduate years, not least having to account to my mother for my movements. I missed my German and Austrian friends and their hospitable families and looked for contacts among the politically diverse Dublin German colony, notably in the Goethe Institute. I soon acquired in one of the masters at the German school a regular boyfriend. We didn't have a great deal in common apart from our love of the outdoor life, nor did he seem to fit in with our family, but he was very handsome – and German. Fairly soon things got difficult. In that summer of 1958, he and I would spend Saturdays walking the Dublin and Wicklow

---

* Where TCD students at the time might refer disparagingly to our alma mater as 'the hedge school in Earlsfort Terrace' we, feeling intellectually superior, would dismiss Trinity as 'just an extension of the British Empire for those not able to get to Oxbridge'.

hills, returning after dinner and dancing in the small hours to Ailesbury Drive, to find my weary mother sitting angrily in the kitchen waiting up for me. Inevitably this made me keener than ever, until the situation resolved itself thanks to the psychologically adept tactics of our favourite aunt, Dr Muriel O'Brien. She called over one morning ostensibly on a visit to my mother, who after a half an hour or so tactfully withdrew, leaving the field to her. 'I think your Joseph is a stunner,' she said. 'No wonder you are keen. Tell me more about him.' Which I did, at length. After a while she mused, 'It doesn't bother you that he slicks down his hair every now and then with that blue comb he has in his top pocket?' Thereafter, my eye constantly went to the blue comb sticking out of his pocket. In due course Joseph got his marching orders, but, I gathered, immediately found a more satisfactory replacement.

Meanwhile the pressing question had to be faced: how was I to earn a proper living? Desmond Williams provided the answer. Always the source of excellent advice, he had his networks everywhere. He told me to write to a Czech refugee professor in Swansea by the name of Erich Heller and ask for his views. At the time I was quite unaware of the critical standing of this wonderful scholar, who in the altruistic manner of the post-war British Germanists replied by return. The key sentence read: 'Just because you have failed as a secondary schoolteacher doesn't mean you'll fail as a university teacher. None of us university lecturers are actually professionally qualified to teach …'. I thanked him and started applying for university jobs. The first two were for medievalists, at Trinity College Dublin and St Anne's Oxford, and no doubt non-starters (my PhD thesis was in modern literature) and I duly failed to be appointed. I learnt a lot in the process about Anglo-Irish university culture, so profoundly different at that time in its collegiality and courtesy from the rigid hierarchies I had encountered in Germany, Switzerland and Austria. To be offered a glass of sherry in the TCD Common Room after my interview seemed to me a revelation. In Vienna only senior professors were admitted to that holy of holies, the *Professorenzimmer*. The successful candidate at Trinity, Franz Lösel, proved to be an excellent choice and soon became a good friend. Oxford was rather different. The interview in St Anne's was scheduled for a Friday evening, following dinner at 7 pm. At the time adult Catholics were not permitted to eat meat on a Friday. What should I do if fish were not on the menu? I decided I would pass on the meat, and accordingly, having had no lunch because the plane was delayed, was dismayed to find that my Oxford interview dinner consisted of one cold chicken leg plus two lettuce leaves. Having hidden the chicken under one of the leaves, I ate the other and hoped for a solid pudding to hide the rumbles in my empty tummy. No such luck. Moreover, the 'great conversation' my mother assured me I could expect proved to be a protracted argument about the price of umbrellas in Marks & Spencer's between the all-women College staff present.

The formal interviews got going just after 8 pm but I was not called until 9.30 pm by which time my hunger pangs had become all-absorbing. The interview panel, chaired by Professor Enid Starkie,* consisted of the two senior German staff, the elderly professor of German, James Boyd, known for his edition of Goethe poetry, and the Schiller specialist Ernest Stahl, plus seven other College and Faculty members. Apart from my embarrassment at the chairman's inebriated state I enjoyed the interview including the questions on medieval German literature, up to the point when Professor Boyd declared his intention 'to test my spoken German' and proceeded, in an execrable English accent and hopeless command of idiom, to ask me where and how I had learnt the language. I was so embarrassed to be found showing up the professor by my own near-native competence that I began to stutter. 'Thank you, Dr O'Shiel,' Enid Starkie intervened, 'that will be all for now.' As I left the room, I overheard James Boyd whisper loudly to his neighbour: 'Her German isn't the best.' In those days and for some years to come Oxford (and Cambridge) set little store on the spoken language and the tenured staff didn't even bother to teach it.

I was put up in a most comfortable guestroom in College and was treated to the luxury of breakfast in bed. It was served by a tall and

---

* A distinguished French scholar and sister of Walter Starkie, Hispanist and authority on Roma culture.

somewhat untidy cleaning lady, attired rather oddly in a red dressing gown. I spent the next hour or so prior to my departure worrying about how much of a tip I should give her or whether this would be against College rules. I still hadn't decided when the receptionist in the hall told me to wait. 'Lady Ogilvie wishes to see you in her office.' There, at her desk sat my cleaning lady. She thanked me for coming, told me what I had of course guessed, that the internal candidate had been successful, and warmly wished me well. I left for home feeling no sense of disappointment but intrigued to have had such a fascinating insight into the strange ways of Oxford's academic culture.

It was now August and I still had no job and even fewer prospects. On holiday with my father in Achill I got a phone call from Clodagh – to get through successfully by telephone to the West of Ireland was not a task for the feeble-hearted – to tell me to apply for a lectureship advertised for Manchester University. Beggars can't be choosers, she declared when I demurred, having once visited the city as a schoolgirl. And the place was even uglier and dirtier when, besuited and begloved, I arrived a week later for my interview. I was the last to be admitted, having spent forty of the previous eighty minutes in the company of a fellow interviewee, Rhona Solomon, a year or two younger than me but already married, whose posh Oxford accent had first put me off until she assured me she was a scholarship girl from a working-class district 'up the road' in nearby Salford. Unlike my Oxford encounter I don't recall anything of the interview. I heard nothing of the outcome until in early September, just weeks before the start of term, a letter arrived offering me the job, which I gratefully accepted. I was scarcely a month in post when my boss, the renowned Professor Ronald Peacock, observed with less than perfect tact: 'I have to tell you, Eda, you weren't our first choice. The outstanding candidate, Mrs Solomon, refused our offer and was not to be persuaded to change her mind. And she,' he went on, 'as we were informed by her Oxford tutors, had achieved the highest marks in German and French in Oxford ever awarded to a female student in the history of the university.' That evening I rang Rhona and asked her why she had done what she did. 'I had a husband to support me and you needed it more.' I have had so much kindness in life from my many friends, but nothing has ever come near to this extraordinary good deed – and we had barely met. Six months later Rhona was my colleague in our shared office and every day I had the opportunity to experience first-hand her truly formidable intellect. Yet in the strange dispensation of things, she was so lacking in self-confidence that she seemed to need an almost daily pep talk from me. Our friendship after more than sixty years is today as close as ever, as it would become between our husbands.

But that first term in Manchester, where I had joined the more than 100,000-strong Irish contingent in Lancashire,* was utterly bleak. During the week I stayed as late as I could in the office to avoid the dreary four walls of my flat. It was the first time I had ever lived on my own and I hated it. The weekends stretched endlessly. My other colleagues were friendly but distant. I earned the to me impressive salary of £14 a week (£11 after tax) and as often as I could get the necessary £6 19s. together to fly home to Dublin, I did. How does one make contacts in a new city? True, by the time I arrived in England, Manchester, like Liverpool and Glasgow, was no longer the focus of Irish emigration as it had been in earlier times. With the decline of the textile and heavy industries, the Irish, as shortly afterwards Pakistani and Caribbean immigrants, moved to find work in light engineering factories, construction and transport to places such as Coventry and the West Midlands. However, the Catholic church was still an obvious first port of call for the newly arrived Irish, and some at my new parish suggested that there were plenty of my fellow countrymen around to provide possible partners at next Saturday's dance in the local Irish club, due to start at 8 pm. Punctual as ever I was there on the dot and found myself in the company of large numbers of friendly young Irish women, dressed, unlike myself, to the nines. We exchanged our impressions of Manchester as we sipped our lemonade and waited hopefully for the boys to come in from the bar and invite us to take to the floor. And there was no shortage of them, dressed in their blue Sunday suits, quaffing pint after pint. Three hours passed, conversation had long dried up when suddenly the barman announced closing time

* The 1961 Census put the figure at 107,527.

and a horde of blue suits, the majority unsteady on their feet, descended on us wallflowers and hauled us one by one on to the dance floor. After one Guinness-suffused stumble, I had had enough and departed home, sadder but wiser. The Irish club was clearly not for me. There was to my knowledge only one Irish person on the Manchester University staff, a second-generation classics Oxford graduate, Desmond Leahy, who with his wife Jo and family welcomed me to their home. It would take another generation and the 1963 Robbins Report before the children of working-class Irish Catholics began to access third-level education in significant numbers, among them the four Leahy children. All my other encounters with my fellow immigrants took place outside my place of work, offering insights into how the Irish were or were not managing the process of integration into their new home.

Meanwhile back home the results of the 1956 special census had finally forced Irish government authorities and the Catholic church to confront (in some measure) a few of the realities of Irish life. In pre-Famine Ireland, the population of what would become the territory of the Irish Free State ('the twenty-six counties') had been 6.52 million; the 1926 Census recorded some 2.97 million. Yet despite the fact that the natural increase thirty years later was higher than at any time since 1901 and that under the de Valera administrations social spending had risen, that thanks to cheap labour some 130,000 new dwellings had been built and many new primary schools, and that from 1944 children's allowances (from the third child only) had been introduced, the Free State population of 1956 was now a mere 2.81 and still falling. It was in British interests from the late 1940s to facilitate the movement to Britain of Irish workers, notably to the construction industry, domestic service and the newly created National Health Service. Apart from convent-educated Irish girls who were attracted to hospital work as trainee nurses – at home they would have had to pay a premium to train – the education levels of the Irish immigrants were in general low, condemning the majority to semi-permanent status as an underclass in British society while reinforcing English stereotyping of the 'ignorant Irish'. The Irish state did little or nothing to support its emigrants. As late as the 1970s no financial help was forthcoming from official Ireland for the hundreds of thousands of Irish in Britain. Immigrants in need could only seek assistance from voluntary agencies and the local social services. The Catholic Church in Ireland tended to focus on moral rather than socio-economic issues, but finally in 1957 the Irish hierarchy made the decision to fund chaplains for Irish immigrants, urgently needed, particularly in view of the significant number of girls who arrived pregnant in Britain. The contrasting attitude between the treatment afforded these unfortunate women by their church in England as compared to what they might expect back from the same church in Ireland was brought home to me in the summer of 1959 through the strange experience of two university colleagues. Dorothy Hignett from the English department, another colleague and I had registered for a 'literary weekend' in Nottingham organized by the chaplaincy there and agreed to meet at our overnight hostel, St Catherine's Convent. I waited in vain for them and finally went on to the venue, only to be greeted sometime later by a slightly shamefaced but evidently highly amused pair of friends. Arriving at the door of the severe-looking building they had been greeted by a kindly Irish nun who ushered them into the parlour and invited them to sit down. 'Which one of you is it?' she asked. 'Both of us,' they replied in unison. It was only when the elderly nun proceeded to produce forms requiring a mass of personal details that they began to wonder. 'Sister, are we at the right place? St Catherine's?' 'Yes, indeed,' she replied. 'St Catherine's refuge for pregnant girls.' No superior sniffs, no moral obloquy as would have been the case back home, just practical support. The situation now sorted with a smile the nun directed them to the appropriate St Catherine's.

In due course I made many friends through the Manchester chaplaincy. Only later did it become clear what a vital policy decision and innovative departure from received practice had been taken by the Catholic bishops of England and Scotland when they decided to institute Catholic chaplaincies in a systematic manner in the university sector. Traditionally the Catholic hierarchy had broadly tended to regard third-level education as 'a danger for faith and morals' and hence not to be encouraged. Indeed, as my maternal grandfather Smiddy's case exemplified, for most Irish people of limited means the only access to a university degree was via the seminary or for women entering one of the better-known teaching orders. The minority status of the Catholic Church in Britain, as well as the ancient and endemic suspicion of 'popery' in the mass of the populace, acted as a motive force for able Irish immigrants to keep their head down. However, with such large numbers of Irish in Britain working largely in menial jobs or at best in the lower rungs of middle-class society, the Catholic hierarchy in Britain made the decision to promote third-level education as a proper aspiration for those of their flock who could benefit from it. The bishops proceeded to appoint some of the church's most able members, usually drawn from the religious orders, such as the Jesuits in the case of 'our' Fr Bernard Winterborn SJ (later Master of Campion Hall Oxford) or from the Dominicans the later distinguished Cambridge canon lawyer Fr Aidan Nicholls OP as chaplain at Edinburgh University. All of this at a time when the Archbishop of Dublin John Charles McQuaid continued to refuse to appoint a chaplain to the English Catholic students at Trinity College on the grounds that, unlike the constituent colleges of the National University, it was 'a godless college' and 'good Catholics' should not be encouraged to attend. The persons who provided the early Catholic chaplains to British universities might have been first class but the conditions under which many operated were nothing better than slums. A day or so each week I would go up the three flights of stairs to meet Fr Winterborn, the thick dust rising at every step from the filthy torn carpet, the grime of ages evident on the walls and the shabby furniture barely usable, to hear a talk or have a cup of tea with my new friends. Since Manchester was a so-called redbrick and thus ideologically secular university whose authorities refused to record the religious affiliation of their students, it was difficult for Bernard to contact his flock, apart from word of mouth. But, like myself, the few Catholics in any faculty or department wanted to make friends in their new and unfamiliar environment and the obvious place to start was among their own kind. And thus, after my first thoroughly lonely weeks in what would become my home for the next seventeen years, I discovered the chaplaincy.

My life in south Manchester could not have been more different from the one I had left behind in central Vienna. Great Britain had won the war, as the *Daily Express* wrapped round my lettuce invariably reminded me. Yet the spoils of victory were nowhere to be seen in late-1950s Manchester. The high Victorian buildings in the city centre and their squat suburban equivalents were dark and filthy and each winter deadly air pollution claimed the lives of thousands of bronchial patients and young children. The benefits of the 1956 Clean Air Act came slowly to the north of England. In the winter of 1958–9 the smog was so bad that the two-mile bus trip home to my Withington flat could take two hours or more, with the conductor walking backwards out on the road in front of the bus, his flaming lamp guiding the driver forwards inch by inch.

But there were lighter moments, as for example my conversation with the rosy-faced young nun from Co. Clare in the bus queue who asked me if I liked England and on hearing my negative reply said, 'It isn't too bad, it's just the food is so awful.' And she began to expatiate on her mother's wonderful cooking: breakfasts of lovely porridge with a 'sup' of milk, lunches of beautiful baked potatoes from the fire with a big lump of butter – and then her teas! 'A big plate of mashed potato with a great lake of buttermilk in the centre.' Or the young bus conductor from Ringsend who got talking with me one evening and, like the nun, didn't mind life in Manchester 'if it wasn't for the English'. 'I share a house with five other English lads,' he went on, 'but they're all queer! I don't know what's wrong with them. You can't get them to come out to the pub on a Saturday night. Do you know what these fellas are all up to, every single one of them?' He paused for effect. 'Goin' out with girls.' An older Irish bus conductor used to regularly encourage me when he saw me getting on with my books and notes (my salary didn't stretch to a briefcase): 'Stick to your books, Miss, stick to your books,' he would say. He had been some years in England and had, he told me, four small daughters. One day he asked me if I would like to visit his family 'of a Sunday', which of course I was so pleased to do. The small daughters, the eldest about eight, were delightful, his wife most hospitable in their small and sparsely furnished flat. Just when we were finishing our tea the father said, 'I wanted you to see our family bible,' and carefully unwrapped a massive, lavishly illustrated book, which had had pride of place on a side table. It transpired that it had cost £15, well over a conductor's weekly wages, and that they were paying off the cost in monthly instalments. 'We read it together on Sundays – it's an investment in the children's education,' he added proudly. Given the couple's priorities I am sure it proved to be.

The local Catholic primary schools and especially the Manchester Loreto convent for girls gave every encouragement to the children of Irish immigrants to 'better' themselves through education, and though up to these years the Irish in England had a poor record in terms of upward mobility – a consequence of the low educational qualifications and particularly poor literacy skills of the majority – things began to change on a number of fronts in the next decade. While the milestone in this process was the successful implementation of the 1963 Robbins Report, devised to harness the as yet undiscovered abilities in the English working- and lower-middle classes by making university education financially possible, the children of ambitious immigrant Irish, Indian or Pakistani parents were probably among its principal benefiters. For the Irish even more important had been the 1959 Education Act, which now allowed the state to contribute to the maintenance of denominational schools – the Catholic ones like the churches had been built 'with the pennies of the poor'. Participation rates in grammar-school education among the immigrants' children rose steadily over the next decades, exemplified in a highly ironic scene we witnessed some years later in Manchester's Town Hall. Facing the proposed threat under a Labour administration sometime in the late 1960s to abolish the grammar schools as 'elitist', hundreds of women from working-class communities, most of them Irish, some in their curlers and overalls, a few even with rolling pins as intimidating weapons, invaded the solidly Labour seat of municipal government in Albert Square in central Manchester demanding a reversal: our grammar schools are the ladder for our children, was the message: 'And you, Labour, want to pull it from under our feet!'

Meanwhile my relations with my new colleagues had undergone a sudden transformation due to a dreadfully embarrassing incident. In thanks for the hospitality he had received from Professor Peacock and his department, the renowned baroque scholar and charming visiting Heidelberg University academic, Arthur Henkel, threw a lavish party. On arrival each guest had a large glass thrust into their hand containing an unusual but most agreeable drink. I was thirsty and happily accepted a constant refill. At home we had never tasted spirits though we drank the occasional glass of wine with a meal. I have no memory of subsequent events as the lethal effect of gin and French began its work. However, I woke up in my own bed with the worst headache ever experienced before or since and when I tried to get up, the floor shot up and hit me hard. How on earth had I got there? I finally crept out to the nearest telephone box and told my mother I would shortly be coming home, having lost my job on account of alcoholism. 'Don't be silly,' was her response, 'go in and face the music.' Eventually, like a condemned prisoner, I made it into the department. But I hadn't reckoned with the English – I was greeted like a long-lost friend. 'You were such fun, we never knew you had it in you! You sang endless verses of a Dublin ditty before passing out on Peacock's carpet.' 'How did I get home?' 'Denis Dyer. Elizabeth [his wife] and I,' said the diminutive Rosemary Wallbank, 'carried you off and put you to bed.' The drunken Irish. I had conformed to the stereotype and could eventually live down my embarrassment: I belonged.

The Manchester German department under Ronald Peacock's aegis was one of the best in the country and should have led him to one of the more prestigious British chairs – at Oxford, Cambridge, Edinburgh or one of London University's leading colleges. Only years later did we become aware of the network, which at the time and for some years after determined successful candidacies for the top university chairs in German in Britain, namely those scholars with distinguished military service in the war (such as the medievalist and former Wing Commander Frederick Norman of University College London, Rosemary's supervisor as a graduate student) and / or those who had been members of the Secret Service code-breakers at Bletchley Park.* Peacock was neither, and although unfortunately he left us for the University of London two years later, it was to go to Bedford rather than the more prestigious King's or University College.

Our Manchester students were excellent, coming from right across the country, many of the men more mature than the rest with their two years of National Service behind them. The department offered a broad range of courses, with experts in medieval, early modern (the age of Luther and the baroque) and modern (eighteenth- to twentieth-century) literature and linguistics. The BA thesis requirement set a demanding standard and the degree examination was more searching than most other university departments I encountered in my later career: the student had to gain an average first-class mark in nine three-hour papers plus a rigorous viva in German to qualify for a rarely awarded first. We taught to a syllabus, but with wide-ranging choices of texts determined by the senior members of the department; for junior lecturers, it was a tough but valuable training, since you could be asked at barely two months' notice, as I was, to teach one or more new sets of courses. One morning in July 1960 Peacock, who had just been offered a year's sabbatical in Freiburg, called me to his office to tell me that I would be taking over his second-year lecture course on German history, a module on the Weimar Republic, and his main seminar on drama in the autumn.

And so I found my metier, ending up in my last seven years at Manchester as lecturer on German history for students of German literature. One of my first students in the Weimar course was a fifty-year-old Jewish ex-journalist from Silesia. Ilse Samuel had been sent in 1931 by her boss, Theodor Wolff, editor of the prestigious Berlin Jewish liberal daily, the *Berliner Tageblatt*, to London and was fortunate, unlike Wolff, to

---

* Bletchley Park, the top-secret home of the codebreakers in World War II, drew on the expertise of German scholars to interpret the data, cracked by the mathematicians, in terms of their cultural connotation and hence the import of the information.

survive Nazi Germany. Scrupulously polite, but as a 'professional' most anxious to have the record right, she would diffidently come up after class and tactfully suggest that her memory of some event or personality mentioned in my lectures had been a shade different. From then on, she with her former lawyer husband Herbert,* became my special advisers on Weimar Germany, as well as close friends of ourselves and the Solomons. More important for my own personal research and later career, teaching these courses directed me to link my historical interests to the interpretation of late eighteenth-, nineteenth- and early twentieth-century literary texts, to the branch of our discipline known as the social history of literature.

---

* Herbert's father, a successful businessman from Rostock on the Baltic, had been dubbed '*der rote Samuel*' (Samuel the Red) by his fellow industrialists for 'gratuitously' granting all his employees an eight-hour working day in 1908.

# — FIVE —

# *The 1960s: The Ireland we left behind*

*'While any drudgery or inconvenience in man's work will soon be lightened by invention or improvisation, for women little or no effort is made to ease the burden of their monotonous household tasks.'*[*]

In the decade following my departure in 1958 as one of 43,000 Irish women and men to emigrate in the space of five short years (1956–61), some things were in fact starting to change back home. Personally, I was unaware of them.[†] For rural women there was the impact of the work of voluntary organizations, many if not most founded by progressive members of the Church of Ireland, prominent among them the Irish Countrywomen's Association.[‡] Then, in the mid-1960s the

---

[*] James Andrew Deeny, chief medical adviser to the Department of Local Government and Public Health (1944–56), cited in M.E. Daly (1997), 211. On the enlightened Deeny see DIB 3, 135–7 and his posthumous *The End of an Epidemic: essays in Irish public health 1935–1965*, Dublin: A&A Farmar, 1995.

[†] At the time and for at least a decade or more to come, I was pretty self-focused, so concerned with getting a job and making a success of it and had little feminist consciousness.

[‡] Founded in 1910 by Anita Letter and Ellice Pilkington, great-granddaughter of Henry Grattan, as the *United Irishwomen* to promote women's health and education,

pragmatic businessman Seán Lemass replaced the ailing septuagenarian de Valera as Taoiseach (1959–66) and 'the gruff Stakhonite helped to pull de Valera's comely maidens and athletic youths out of the emigrant boats'.* Emigration numbers started to fall, and the population to rise for the first time since the Famine and, partly in response to international trends, the country witnessed for the first time in decades a period of economic growth, albeit from a low basis. And Ireland too experienced its version of the 1968 mass protest movements in Paris, and other European countries and in the United States. Ireland's student movement may have been comparatively low key, but it politicized a generation that would come to play significant roles in public life.

Among these was the remarkable Dominican nun and pioneer of the academic study of women's history in Ireland, Margaret MacCurtain. The name she chose when she entered her convent, Sr Benvenuta ('well came')† was indeed apt. The timing of her work coincided with the increasing topicality of the issue of women's rights, while her combination of academic rigour, common sense and sovereign sense of humour in her public appearances‡ undermined those many critics of the women's liberation movement who liked to present it as an ideologically driven and humourless fad. Her 1978 edited volume of essays: *Women in Irish Society: The Historical Dimension* (with the UCC historian Donnchadh Ó Corráin) is a founding document of the discipline, her lightly carried learning masking a steely determination to challenge and to change.§

---

reconstituted in 1935, the ICA is one of the oldest organizations of its kind in the world. See Ferriter (1995). The Association's importance in enabling women living in rural isolation to get contact with others in a similar situation was immeasurable.

\* Alvin Jackson, 1999, 344.

† Many women (and men) took or were given a new name when they entered a religious order.

‡ I experienced her laidback wit some years later when several 'representative' Irish women were invited to discuss our personal stories in an RTÉ television programme. Each was asked for our immediate response to being told that 'the world will end in one hour'. Most of us offered would-be intellectual scenarios. She just smiled and said: 'I'd try prayer.'

§ The nonagenarian Sr Ben's retrospective essay volume, *Metaphor for Change: Essays on State and Society* appeared in 2019, the year before she died.

Included in her wide circle was my UCD friend Lelia Doolan. In our College days, Lelia had attracted the ire of our Professor Cunningham for her dedication to Dram. Soc., which didn't however affect her capacity to get a good degree and equip herself for her later profession in the performing arts. She went from UCD to Berlin to train with none other than Bertolt Brecht and soon was widely involved in the media, in the national broadcasting company RTE, as first woman artistic director of the Abbey Theatre and subsequently as pioneer of street theatre in deprived areas of Belfast and much else besides. According to the still all-powerful Catholic Archbishop of Dublin at the time, John Charles McQuaid (1940–1972), Lelia was 'mad, bad and dangerous'. As was no doubt in his eyes the then 25-year-old lawyer and Senate member for Trinity College, Mary (*née* Bourke) Robinson. Mary was already campaigning vigorously to reverse the notorious requirement that women must resign from the civil service on marriage, to promote the right of women to sit on all juries and to secure the legal availability of contraception. This last brought her a denunciation from the cathedral pulpit of her hometown of Ballina, Co. Mayo. Later Mary Robinson would give effective support to her fellow Trinity student and friend David Norris when he took his campaign to de-criminalize homosexuality to the European Court of Justice.

The 1960s, then, was the decade which could give Irish women grounds for optimism – but mainly in retrospect.* Other indicators of future change came from the media. Television first came to Ireland in the 1950s and by the early 1960s some 100,000 houses held a TV licence (increasing fourfold by 1970). In 1962 Gay Byrne began his *Late Late Show*, eventually the second-longest-running of such shows in the world. In his deft and provocative style Byrne, known affectionately as Gaybo, aired long taboo issues in front of a live audience, among them contraception, divorce, domestic violence and homosexuality. He is generally credited with having played a key role in re-shaping Irish public discourse and hence societal norms over the next decades. Yet if

---

* Fergal Tobin's *The Best of Decades: Ireland in the nineteen sixties*, despite being published a decade and a half later, makes scant reference to women.

they had time or the consciousness to think about anything apart from coping with the endless drudgery of their lives, rural and urban working-class women might well have felt bitter at the society which vaunted 'Irish values' yet showed scant awareness of the burden they carried or of the unacknowledged contribution they made to their nation. This was made evident in the state's failure to consult them on issues of concern, exemplified in the pusillanimous refusal of the Dáil deputies in 1943 to support giving children's allowances* to the mother. Even more notorious was the 1950–51 Mother and Child Bill when both the medical profession and the Catholic hierarchy for their own reasons effectively blocked the Minister of Health Noel Browne's efforts to provide free medical services to all Irish mothers and their babies, while Browne's fellow ministers abandoned their controversial colleague. Older children and particularly girls in large families were often robbed of their childhood. A mature student of ours in the late 1980s, Mary from Mayo, eldest of eight, told me how her mother would always snatch a book from her whenever she was caught reading between chores: her 'job' was to mind her mentally handicapped brother. Mary's sheer delight at forty years of age in being permitted to study at university, together with her daughter, was infectious. Both graduated together and she went on to a successful career as a secondary-school teacher.

Perhaps the novelist rather than the social historian can best capture the harsh reality and psychological pressures to conform of so many women's lives,[†] as exemplified in John McGahern's novels *The Dark* (1963) and *The Barracks* (1965), which I read avidly as they appeared. The sheer truth to life depicted in these early works cost the young teacher his job – deference to authority, to the agents of the state as the parish priest, the guardians of the peace (the Gardaí), to the respectable citizens, must never be challenged.[‡]

---

* Vigorously opposed by (well-heeled) government ministers.

† 'Why then … go to the novelist rather than the theologian or the moral philosopher for instructions? Not because novelists are wiser or better than others, but because they are most skilled in revealing the obscure windings of the human heart.' (Cockshut, 1978, 208).

‡ To me, even more powerful in their evocation of psychological violence in family life for many Irish women, tolerated and thus condoned by the state, are McGahern's 1991 masterpiece *Amongst Women* and the autobiographical *Memoir* (2005).

But was it so different in rural Germany? The lives of my Freiburg student friends from the patriarchal worlds of rural Catholic Bavaria, Swabian Allgäu, the Black Forest or former German Silesia (now Poland) suggest that materially it may have been, but that culturally the difference was not marked. Family duty came first, especially for girls, regardless of whether the academically gifted ones had qualified for university through their *Abitur* (final school-leaving examination). And even then, parental views rather than student choice generally determined what 'useful' discipline one might study. My Swabian friend Gertrud, finally permitted by her father to go to university at the age of twenty-seven after she had spent six years as the sole carer of her bedridden mother who had just died, wanted above all to study literature. No, as a member of a hard-working Swabian family, she must do something useful, Father ordained, something that would help the family. It was pharmacy or nothing, and after graduation she was sent to work for years in her aunt's pharmacy. It didn't dawn on her, she told me, to demur. That was how it was in their patriarchal culture.

I continued to keep closely in touch with what was going on in Ireland, still hoping and planning to get back and live my life at home – even after a few years in my fulfilling career I regarded England, like many of my compatriots, as a temporary interval. In that interim, however, I had to get on with that career. If I was to get over the three-year hurdle from junior lectureship to permanent staff member, which then tended to be the exception,* I needed to produce some worthwhile research. Manchester may have appeared to my neophyte immigrant self as a rather miserable place, at least by contrast with Dublin, Cork or Galway. But nationally, Britain in the 1960s presented itself as a nation full of creative energy. True, Harold Macmillan's prime ministership ended in 1963 in failure – the lot, according to the sour Tory genius Enoch Powell, of all politicians – but his Labour successor, Harold Wilson (1964–70/ 1974–6) soon brought the energy of a younger generation to power.

* In the then British system few were invited to stay on at the institution of their first appointment but were obliged to seek a further post to gain experience at one or more other universities.

Wilson was not only a Northerner but came with the promise of a formative role for science and technology in the re-making of Britain. Macmillan's government had introduced a key policy document for Britain's future, the Robbins Report on higher education (1963); Wilson oversaw its implementation. With this came seven new universities, among them East Anglia, Exeter, Sussex and Warwick, which rapidly established themselves as serious competitors for the older, redbrick institutions, and with all seven of which I would be involved in one capacity or another later in my career.

One of Manchester's distinguishing features was its vibrant Jewish community, from which the university in general and its German department greatly benefited. Several professors had been or were the sons of refugees from the 1848 revolution. Henry Simon, founder of Manchester's famous Simon steelworks, who gave his name to the Henry Simon chair of German (1896), had been a prominent revolutionary in 1848; his magnificent library provided me with the primary materials for my first book. The Levite grandfather of my friend and colleague Rhona Solomon, *née* Gold, had fled from the pogroms in Lithuania following the defeat in the Russo-Japanese War of 1905, when Tsarist Russia resorted to its well-tried policy of directing public anger away from its disastrous policies towards its Jewish communities. While the more orthodox tended to live in north Manchester, the men standing out in their long black coats, beards and sidelocks, the more secular Jews favoured the southern suburbs where the university was situated and where most younger lecturers lived; I often heard Yiddish spoken in the local bus. As an offshoot of sixteenth-century German, it sounded familiar to me, but the meaning elusive, on account of the different accent, syntax and the many Hebrew expressions. The faithfulness of the first generations of Manchester Jews to their German cultural heritage expressed itself in lively local societies, such as the Goethe Society and, thanks to its namesake's ethical philosophy, the even more popular Schiller Association, both of which had been important cultural fora for the community well into the twentieth century. Even in the 1960s, when the students put on their annual drama, we could be assured of strong support in the audience from older members of the Jewish community. Education had been the ladder for most of the families. Rhona and her husband Gerry, children of small businessmen, were representative of the substantial percentage of Jewish pupils at the two leading schools, Manchester Grammar (25 per cent) for boys and Manchester High School, for girls (between them, Rhona and Gerry scored 19 'A's in their O-level *exams). Anti-Semitism was latent, but more in the form of social envy, such as referring to the Didsbury area where many Jews (and later we) lived as 'Jidsbury' and its main thoroughfare, Palatine Road as 'Palestine Road', or in the incongruous prohibition of Jews as members of the many local golf clubs. By contrast, the Jewish golf club, Dunham Forest, where I occasionally played, was always warmly welcoming to non-Jewish visitors.

A novel teaching experience for me only a couple of years after arriving in Manchester was my involvement in the Workers' Educational Association. From its foundation as Owens College in 1856 Manchester University had had a fine record in adult education. In 1960 I was recruited to make my contribution on behalf of our department. The work consisted of giving evening courses and classes both in the university and in outreach centres across Lancashire. A few years later I started intensive German language residential weekends, which proved popular and drew a diverse audience, among them former refugees from Nazi Germany who had lost touch with their native language. For some twelve to fourteen hours intensive teaching and tutoring over the weekend I received £9, which funded many a household purchase. One of my happiest memories of the WEA was the first cohort who came in the mid-1960s to do the new modular BA degree course and were offered the option of taking beginners' German. I certainly learnt more from them for my future teaching than they learnt German from me.

---

* Our friend Jack Zussman was the first British scientist to be entrusted with examining samples brought back from the first Moon landing. Shortly after, my husband and I brought him to tea in our local golf club, where the Irish stewardess made lovely scones. We were hardly sampling them than a committee member came up and asked us to leave with our guest: we were infringing the 'unwritten rule': 'no Jews here'…

They were a class of only four, two men and two women, all of whom had left school between twelve and fourteen and had never had the chance to learn a foreign language. I taught them basic grammar and vocabulary, using simple poetic texts, as some of the greatest German poets including Goethe have written in very accessible language. In their second term they were required to master the notorious Subjunctive II (today's students are expected to have only a passive understanding of this splendid but demanding linguistic tool). To make it palatable as well as accessible I gave them a hand-out with the Romantic poet Eichendorff's lovely *Mondnacht* (moonlit night, set to music by Schumann). We went through the vocabulary of the eight-line poem, and in its simple syntax they found their command of the past imperfect tense reinforced. I explained how the subjunctive was formed and what its function was, promised them that when they had mastered it that they would be able to do all sorts of wonderful things with it, and asked them to study the poem for next week's class and give their views. They came back full of enthusiasm, and their spokesman, a factory worker, said proudly: 'We have only been learning German for four months and now we can read and understand great German poetry.' They probably spent too much time on their German, only one of several subjects in their degree, but all four passed their end-of-year exams, and they all scored a first-class mark in German.

At Manchester University as elsewhere in 1960s Britain we began to experience the hugely positive effects of the 'academic blood transfusion' of clever students of working- or lower-middle-class origin who in pre-grant days would have been understandably slow to postpone entry to the job market for years of study, only to end up with substantial debt. Soon the cultural scene was being transformed in all sorts of ways by their presence. The beneficiaries of the new scheme found that their grant covered fees and maintenance and left something over for other activities. I was only in my second year of teaching when one of my tutorial students presented himself in my office as a possible candidate for a part in our annual student drama. The student performances, a mixture of inspired and ham acting, attracted all the local schools taking

German for A Levels. A second-year student named John McKenzie, a fishmonger's son from Formby, got the three-word part of the misanthropic coachman Melchior in Johann Nestroy's *Einen Jux will er sich machen* (1842).* Melchior's mantra in heavily accented Viennese dialect: '*des is klossisch*' (classic!), repeated lugubriously at every appearance, brought the house down. It proved to be the start of a notable academic career at Exeter University where John would become a co-editor of the prestigious standard edition of Nestroy's collected works. But in the 1960s he had a much greater claim to fame than his bit-part acting: he had been at school with three of the Beatles. During his O-level year at his Liverpool grammar school the French master had picked on a couple of them: 'You and you,' he allegedly said, singling out John Lennon, Paul McCartney (or was it George Harrison), 'if you don't buck up and learn your French irregular verbs, you'll never earn an honest penny.' I was equally unaware of the launch, across the road in a disused church in the scruffy Manchester suburb of Rusholme where I was then living over a bank, of what would become *Top of the Pops*, the longest-running BBC pop show.

Was it the ever-present undercurrent of the Cold War and the nuclear threat, which latter loomed ever nearer with the erecting of the Berlin Wall on 13 August 1961 and the Cuban Crisis of November 1962, which gave such an edge to British satire, in the cinema, the radio and the innumerable popular magazines such as *Private Eye* (1961)? We all, academics and students and the general public, were, as in Ireland, dedicated cinemagoers. Our absolute favourite was Peter Sellers, especially in his most famous role, a splendid satire on strike-torn Britain, *I'm Alright Jack* (1959).† Two conversations at the time suggested just how close fiction was to real life. My younger cousin Eoin O'Brien, then a Royal College of Surgeons medical student, spent a summer in the

---

* In Thornton Wilder's translation: *The Matchmaker*, later adapted for the film *Hello Dolly*.

† Here he played the arch-villain of 'respectable' employers, the Communist shop steward Fred Kite opposite Terry-Thomas as the hapless personnel manager Major Hitchcock.

early 1960s working in a Manchester factory. His job on his first day was screwing together large sheets of aluminium, which he did with his usual efficiency. On the following morning he presented himself to his line manager expecting at least a pat on the back. Instead, he found himself directed to 'unscrew all those f...ing screws and when you've finished screw them back. How else will we keep our pay rates?' Between 1948 and 1963 the productivity of the average British worker remained lower than that of their opposite number in France and even lower than that of 'defeated' Germany, which might help explain the resentment of the average Joe Soap towards the 'foreign worker' and specifically those of the two major players of the EU.* The other conversation involved myself and the wife of a businessman as we set out to play golf one morning in the early 1960s in my new club in the posh suburb of Wilmslow. 'We do admire you, Eda,' she said, 'you seem to manage your students so well and never complain. My husband [managing director of one of the largest firms in the area] tells me students are just like trade-union workers – troublemakers and impossible to please.'

## LIFE OUTSIDE THE UNIVERSITY

For, while most of my leisure time from 1959, my second year in Britain, was spent in the company of university and especially departmental friends and their expanding social networks, I had already acquired another little world of my own, namely golf. My colleagues regarded the game with mildly amused contempt as a pursuit for dull bank managers but hardly a milieu or activity suitable for academics. My only transport apart from the bus was my bike (with the golf clubs slung over my shoulder), but since the first green field† was at least thirty miles outside the Manchester conurbation, the golf course began to provide an outlet for my physical energy and a welcome contrast with working

* The productivity of Irish workers at that time was only half that of their British counterparts.

† There were no such things as 'green' fields in heavily polluted industrial Lancashire before the clean air acts of the later 1960s: even the sheep were a dirty grey.

life. With my handicap of 27 I was no luminary of the game, but an easily accessible local club needed lady members and offered membership at £1 per annum for me as a 25-year-old, rising in each subsequent year by a further £1. In no time at all I was spending hours in summer evenings and at weekends practising or playing this fascinating sport, whose elusive challenge I first truly understood when I discovered the essay *Das Marionettentheater* (*The Puppet Theatre*) by Heinrich von Kleist (1770–1811). Can we ever, he asks, achieve the balance between the rational mind and intuitive grace? Not that my many and varied golfing partners over the years would have had much truck with a German poet. They, or rather the male golfers, just got up and hit the ball as hard as they could and thought no more. Between matches and later in county, regional and, briefly, even national competitions over the next few years, my handicap dropped to four. I played successively for Lancashire and Cheshire and enjoyed myself no end. Sometimes this involved getting up at 5 am in the summer vacations, travelling 100 miles to North Wales or wherever, playing thirty-six holes and then straight back through Lancashire's industrial rush hour traffic on pre-motorway roads (by this time marriage had brought the additional benefit of use of a car). Thoroughly exercised, it was a pleasure then to get back to my research, which made pretty slow progress in the first decade or so of my career.


EDUCATION BACK HOME

In Ireland, meanwhile, an even slower reform process was about to get off the ground, which would in time change the face of Ireland. In its initial objectives the Education Act of 1967 was thoroughly restrictive, certainly by comparison with the 1944 British Education Act and indeed with the wide-ranging Robbins programme. Yet in the context of Ireland in the 1960s it was a bold decision of Fianna Fáil's minister of education, Donough O'Malley, to respond to the findings of the Commission on Education chaired by the former senior civil servant and then Professor of Applied Economics at UCD, my sister's former final-year tutor Patrick Lynch, and to introduce free secondary schooling for all pupils.

O'Malley's initiative would prove nothing short of revolutionary. Up to the 1970s some two-thirds of Irish children left school at fourteen. When I left Ireland in 1958, of a population of some half a million under-nineteen-years-olds, less than 80, 000 were enrolled in secondary or vocational schools. In 1966 the education system in the Irish Free State and the Republic was characterized by its extreme discrimination against the poorer classes. As far back as 1915 my grandfather, Timothy Smiddy in his capacity as dean of the University College Cork's Faculty of Commerce and Economics, had urged the authorities to place greater focus in primary schools on the practical skills needed by children who would be earning their living from the land. Unfortunately, from the early 1930s the very opposite happened. Manual skills were dropped to make room for the mandatory minimum of five weekly hours for the Irish language. Yet after fourteen years' obligatory Irish instruction most Irish school-leavers could not, and many today outside the *Gaelscoileanna* (Irish-speaking schools) still cannot hold a normal conversation of any length or sophistication in the Irish language. If this was the case for us, a privileged elite in terms of educational background, how was it for those hundreds of thousands of Irish children who up to sixty years ago could never have aspired to the benefit of secondary education? And more particularly for those forced to emigrate with minimal literacy and numeracy skills[*] to join a despised, because 'Irish', labour force in Britain.

## MARRIAGE AND FAMILY

In January 1959 I returned after the Christmas vacation at home to my depressing flat and was 'meithering' about it to a colleague in the French department when she said that there was a vacancy in a staff hostel in Fallowfield, a suburb closer to town and the university. Donner House, named after the original owner and located between the Vice-Chancellor's residence and the local convent, known as the 'Hollies', proved to be

---

[*] Because the teaching of obligatory Irish, a complex language, was frequently enforced by often brutal corporal punishment, the child's capacity to learn, as my later friend Paddy Maugham would tell me, was invariably severely damaged.

quite *sui generis*. It wasn't so much the high-ceilinged, slightly dilapidated rooms that spoke of better days, but the very mixed bunch of inmates. We were an odd lot. All were single members of staff, a few like me in their twenties or thirties, most middle-aged or elderly. There was the professor of medieval history, spare and earnest, who liked to remind us that Yorkshire men ate cheese with their apple pie. There was an elderly former maths instructor at Dartmouth Naval College, a confirmed bachelor, who spent his leisure time knitting baby clothes and his working day trying to realize his ambition to get into the *Guinness Book of Records* as the person who had calculated (on his little self-invented machine) the mathematical term π (pi) to its farthest degree. When the computer was invented his whole world fell apart – almost, that is, as he still had his knitting. As we all had our breakfast and dinner together, we soon got to know each other's idiosyncrasies. There were several clever Jews, two of them former refugees from Nazi-occupied Poland and Czechoslovakia, my colleague in French, Fanny Bogdanov, humourless and self-absorbed almost to an entertaining degree, and the sophisticated psychiatrist Dr Honig (like the fictitious Oxford detective Morse, he never revealed his given name). He was tremendous company on any subject you could think to raise. Then there was the belligerent but diminutive maths-physicist Dr Wolf Mays, across whose high-domed bald head its owner carefully arranged his three or four remaining long strands of hair. His total preoccupation, as he would tell any available audience, was the design of a billiard table with the number of sides so that a ball however struck would always return to the same spot. Unfortunately, when at last he found the answer (π sides), it was quickly pointed out to him that a billiard table never has more than four sides.[*]

I soon became friendly with the Londoner Jack Zussman, a crystallographer only a few years older than myself and for a few months we went out together, briefly each with serious intent until I felt his

---

[*] It never occurred to him to have a conversation about pi with his fellow mathematicians. An academic snob, he regarded intellectual engagement with the instructor at a naval college as 'beneath him'.

evidently very orthodox parents would be distressed with a *shiksa* daughter-in-law.* And I, if I married at all, would hope to find a Catholic life partner. When I told him that I felt we had no real future, I was dismayed to see for the first time a man break down in tears, but we remained staunch friends as long as he remained in Manchester. Most of my social life was now spent in the company of Jack's colleagues in the Department of Geology, virtually all of whom would go on to make a name for themselves in the field of science, but none more so than Jack himself. When samples of the moon rocks were made available for scientific research in 1969, it was he who was chosen to work on them and in due course he became professor of crystallography at Cambridge. Back in 1959, as we discussed our plans for the long vacation, mine to holiday and research in Germany, I felt a pang of envy when Jack and his best pal in Donner House, an organic chemist and petrologist working in the Department of Chemical Engineering, told me of theirs. They would take a trip across France in his friend's recently acquired Austin Sprite sports car to spend their holidays with his brother's family at the Catalan seaside village of Port de la Selva.

Up to then I had only exchanged polite good mornings with this silent and evidently self-contained man, admiring his highly polished shoes and smart leather jacket and waistcoat, while being mildly if absurdly irritated by the fact that he carelessly let drops of milk splash on the latter when pouring it on to his cornflakes. He enjoyed regular arguments on all sorts of subjects with the psychiatrist Honig. On one occasion Honig, who loved to tease, proposed a bet: that his friend wouldn't kiss the hand of the Vice-Chancellor's wife during the annual reception for the academic staff, a stuffy bun-fight with sour wine styled the *Conversazione*. Yes, he was on for it, provided his mate followed suit. Lady Mansfield-Cooper was as down-to-earth as they come, refusing to adapt her working-class accent on the elevation of her husband to the 'new nobility'. We later got to know her quite well and they even came one evening to dinner when we lived in Didsbury. On this occasion however, as Albert, at least a foot taller than our hostess, took her hand

---

* i.e. a Gentile.

and bowed over to kiss it in true Spanish style, she let out an audible yell, persuaded that 'this foreigner' was going to bite her. His companion had lost the bet, but was dispensed from his part of the bargain, and the pair melted happily into the crowd to entertain us with their doings. A few months later ten of us from Donner House went to the theatre together. During the long and lively discussion on our return home over a cup of tea I was surprised to hear how forthright Albert was in his views, especially when provoked by his sparring partner. And what strong and clearly much reflected moral principles the man appears to hold, I thought to myself. A pity he is so old, he seems to be a man of parts.

Back in Manchester in September 1959, as Jack enthused about their holiday in Catalonia, Albert announced the pair of them had plans to visit Dublin, ideally some weekend when I would be home. My mother, when I told her, with her usual flair put on a lively garden drinks party with my grandparents and a couple of aunts, notably Muriel. In the course of that sunny evening Muriel,* who had been having a long chat with both visitors, with her uncanny ability to read another person's mind, remarked: 'Dr Sagarra, I wonder what is going on behind those dark glasses of yours?' The weekend was a great success and an invitation to dinner was issued to my mother when she told Albert she would be coming to visit me early in October. Albert took us to a celebrated old restaurant in the city and during dinner oddly asked me if I wouldn't mind going to get the waitress. Later my mother told me when I was gone that he had very formally asked her permission to ask me out. A man in his early forties asking a modern young woman's mother for permission to invite her out on a date? How extraordinary. It took several thoroughly decorous outings, always preceded with his leaving a white rose outside my door at Donner House, for me to solve the mystery. Catalan culture at that time among established Barcelona

---

* Muriel, a medical doctor and an extremely clever woman, had put up her plate beside that of her husband, the physician G.T. O'Brien, when they got married. No patients came, and after some months she took it down and never practised. She had been the first woman in Ireland to gain a gold medal in both medicine and surgery when she graduated from the Royal College of Surgeons in 1937. See the forthcoming memoirs of her eldest son, the cardiologist and Beckett scholar, Eoin.

families was far more traditional and conservative than in Ireland, not to say northern Europe. Young men and women in their circles, almost all of whom had been fellow students at Barcelona University (unlike in the rest of Spain, where women students were rare) socialized in large groups, skiing, mountaineering, performing music or staging amateur theatricals together, and attending concerts, theatre and cinema. When a man invited a young woman out in their culture it was understood that he was expressing a wish to marry her, having first informed himself about her family and giving her plenty of notice for her parents to do the same. When, the following spring, Albert proposed to me, he explained that the actual engagement must wait until I had met his family – his father, not he, would give me the engagement ring. We would drive in the summer vacation across France to Barcelona to meet his father, a widower, and then after the engagement ceremony to spend the rest of the holiday with his brother and family at the sea. My father, normally most agreeable to his daughters' plans, wouldn't hear of it. If his family wanted to inspect me before agreeing to the engagement, I certainly wasn't to put myself in an ambivalent position: I would travel by plane. Accordingly, we arrived at three o'clock in the morning via chartered night-time plane (the cheapest form of travel then) at the front door of Sr Sagarra's elegant third-floor apartment, there to be embraced by a tall old gentleman in pyjamas. He spoke no English, and I had hardly a word of Catalan despite my efforts to learn the rudiments of the language.* Albert's father's eloquent if brief address was very moving when I learnt what he had said: 'Thank you for agreeing to marry my son: he has always been especially close to my heart.'

The next couple of days in the hot and humid city were packed. I went to early mass each morning with my future father-in-law, whom I learnt I must always address with the formal *Vosté*. Albert's sister, Montserrat, had written to me before I came, telling me that in Catalonia (unlike Castile), the husband provided everything for the house – the

---

* Learned from a small grammar published in Oxford – at the end of the Spanish Civil War Franco had had all Catalan libraries, book shops and publishing houses destroyed, and any copies of Catalan books discovered burnt.

bride just came with herself and her clothes. She took me round the house, showing me stacks and stacks of her mother's beautifully embroidered linen. I feared I would be expected to demonstrate my non-existent skills in that department but had yet to discover that Catalans were not like that: they took you as you were. There were visits after visits to every conceivable relative and connection to meet the new member of the family. I soon had three favourites: Ramon, Albert's genial godfather fifteen years his senior, who had made a fortune in cotton dealing, and two aunts by marriage, Tia Paca and Tia Engracia. The two could hardly have been more different but for both Albert was clearly a firm favourite. Tia Paca Sagarra was a formidable old lady, the widow of Tio Ramon, a former naval attaché in the Spanish diplomatic service. The Cuban Tia Engracia de los Molinos de Zacarini, thoroughly laid back, had married Albert's mother's brother. He, having fathered four boys, had taken his own life in a fit of depression leaving his widow to live with the four sons, augmented in due course with three grandsons of the eldest whose wife had left him, plus a male servant. Even the dog was male. The household was extremely hospitable, though you were never sure at what time the lunch or dinner to which you had been invited would actually appear; on one occasion 9 o'clock dinner made the table at two in the morning. Albert's godfather, a cousin and godson of Sr Sagarra, would always be our first call on arrival for the holidays in Catalonia. His two sisters were equally absorbing company: Carmen, tall and spare, a former air hostess, married in middle age to an elderly husband, the hypochondriac brother of the famous Catalan poet Josep Maria de Sagarra,* whom she happily indulged; Guadalupe, by contrast was a comfortable spinster, short and broad with an evidently slightly murky past – she had apparently eloped and lived unmarried with her life's love in France till in respectable old age and 'widowhood' she could return.

My efforts to learn Catalan rather than the clearly more useful and beautiful Castilian were greatly appreciated by all and sundry. It was after all the language of home and family, banned by Franco from use in public; had I not learnt it, as a Castilian-speaking foreigner I would have

* Ours was the bourgeois branch of the family.

always remained a bit of an outsider. From the various family members' libraries, I was presented with volumes of poetry from the Catalan *Renaixença*, the same period as the Irish literary Renaissance, and a great source for the learner, plus novels by the dozen. Unfortunately, the only available dictionary to escape Franco's fascist bonfires was a Catalan–French dictionary, published decades earlier. I knew French but not Catalan. But eventually I managed, thanks to our twice-yearly visits and the somewhat dubious aid of translating a wonderful new novel. Mercè Rodoreda's *The Pigeon Girl* in my English translation, done largely during some sixty hours of fortunately event-free exam supervision, was published thanks to the late Diana Athill's support in 1965.[*]

After the Barcelona days with temperatures in the high twenties and a humidity factor of c. 95 per cent it was a relief to escape to the seaside. Sr Sagarra, whom I was now since our formal engagement to call 'Papa', would follow in a day or two. I was lodged in a small room in the narrow ex-fisherman's house of Albert's brother Bepe (Josep-Lluis) and his wonderful wife Isabella Trias, plus their nine children aged nineteen to two (ten that December): four sisters in one small bedroom, four brothers next door, the littlest with them. When we sat down to supper, I thought I was in a madhouse. One sister started teasing another, who seized her glasses, the rest took sides, and all hell broke loose. The Spanish voice is in general not just a great deal louder than the Irish and in moments of emotion several pitches higher. The window of my bedroom looked out on a small farmyard whose cock crowed unmercifully from 3.30 am onwards. For two weeks I hardly slept and though sea and sun were glorious and Isabella and her five sisters a delight, I couldn't wait to get back to sticky but peaceful Barcelona.

In Manchester work piled up, leaving little time for wedding plans apart from a vague timetable for 'next summer'. In the event the date was arranged for 4 April 1961, a cold, rainy and otherwise delightful day. We were only twenty-two, close family and Maryanne and Fin, as my mother

---

[*] *La Plaça del Diamant*. London: André Deutsch.

had generously if reluctantly agreed to my wish to have the wedding break-fast in our house. My father-in-law, who had come with Montserrat and his godson Eduard, Ramon's son, and his young wife, whom we lodged in the Marine Hotel in Dún Laoghaire, later wrote a letter to relations back in Spain to the effect that Ireland is a wonderfully green country where everyone is a Catholic and none of the windows close properly. Speeches, seven in all – including two lengthy ones by the two lawyer fathers* – took most of the afternoon. My grandmother had trimmed her hat in the monsignorial purple of her old rotund friend Alfred O'Rahilly, who had just been thus promoted after a mere two years as priest of the cloth. He insisted on putting himself in the front of every possible wedding photo. Eventually we set off on our Connemara honeymoon to Sweeney's Hotel Oughterard, forgetting just how bad Irish roads were after Galway, arriving just before midnight to be shown into a three-bedded room! Albert, as he told me later, thought that I had arranged it on purpose, but he was too tactful and I at that point too diffident to comment.

After two lovely weeks touring Connemara in the Austin Sprite, which was so low on the road that you could touch the tarmac when stationary, we were soon back into teaching, examining and marking. I was no cook and had to learn the hard way. Having decided a newly married husband needed a good breakfast, I had started our first morning back in Manchester with the best of intentions but no skill. When I broke the sixth egg trying to produce a fried egg and ended up in tears, I wasn't really consoled by Albert's capacity to clear up the mess and in no time produce a perfect repast (I had been told in Barcelona that his mother had been a famed cook). For our first casserole, I bought six pounds of beef for the two of us, all of which, boiled instead of gently simmered, ended life in the bin. And then my mother sent me a copy of Maura Laverty's cookery book for Irish housewives, *Full and Plenty* (1960), and I served my apprenticeship.

At last the summer vacation came. In those pre-motorway days, it was a multi-hour journey to Southampton airport where an elderly

---

* I was much moved by my father, who wasn't given to expressions of emotion, describing me as 'a giver', one of the nicest things ever said of me.

ex-RAF aircraft carrier flew us and the Sprite with three other cars to Cherbourg. For the next week we wandered through rural France from Romanesque church to Romanesque church, staying where the Michelin guide advised there was good cooking at a modest cost, arriving finally at Port de la Selva to find the small village of some 600 overrun with some 13,000 mainly British tourists. And a multiplicity of Sagarras and Triases too – almost twenty families, all with children. 'Tia Eda speaks funny,' was the constant refrain from the three- and four-year olds. There is no language laboratory that can compete with that age group when it is a question of reinforcing endlessly repeated basic phrases and vocabulary in a foreign language. Before the holiday was over, they had taught me enough for me to be able to take part in family chat. The Trias family as Republicans had had to flee to France during the Civil War and all spoke French, which was a help. Unlike monolingual England and Ireland, these Mediterranean people, the family and their large circle of friends holidaying at the Port moved easily between Catalan, Castilian, French and Italian, often in the same conversation; none of them at the time knew English. My one problem, one that would recur each summer for the next few years, were the probing questions from the menfolk. During the *tertulias* (chats) sitting round on the beach one would look in my direction making a rocking gesture with their arms and ask pointedly, 'When is it to be?' In vain that first year I would protest that we were only married four months. Catalans are mad about babies, but they are quite uninhibited, not to say earthy, about everything to do with their production. Even my dignified father-in-law, when his first great-grandchildren were born, would report in detail in his regular letters to us on the stages and outcome of his respective grand-daughters' pregnancy and labour.

During the months of our engagement Albert and I had of course talked in a very general way of our hopes and plans for children but never of sex. Women of my generation were extremely reticent about sexual matters; it was a topic I can never recall any of my friends raising, let alone discussing among ourselves. Within the immediate female family circle that was different, where reference to sex was common enough, invariably mediated through humour, though how untypical we were of the prudish society we inhabited, I cannot judge. We (me, my sister and my cousin Berna, Muriel's daughter some eight years younger), our ears flapping, thoroughly enjoyed the witty exchanges, jokes and innuendo on the subject between my mother and her favourite sister, which would add, we felt assured, to our stock of (theoretical!) information on the matter. I certainly wanted a family of at least four and expected that Albert, like all Spaniards, would be equally enthusiastic. I took for granted that we would observe the Church's teaching, namely that the so-called 'safe period' was the only form of contraception available to practising Catholics such as ourselves. I would, for example, not take the pill.* Despite my erstwhile membership of the Newman Society I had never encountered Newman's teaching on the role of 'the informed conscience' for the laity. In the event, for us the situation did not arise. The longed-for children did not materialize. My original concern had been not to get pregnant too quickly so that I could have a bit more time in the career I so enjoyed. (I also had the sneaking ambition to reach the dizzy salary, due with my fourth increment in 1963, of earning £1,000 p.a.) But as the first years went by it became clear to us that something was wrong and that we needed to get ourselves checked out by the medical profession. This we proceeded to do but not without an incident that nowadays might have landed me in court. We had several doctors in my family, so it took a while to reach consensus on the best gynaecologist. Eventually one Raymond Cross was declared the one, and Albert and I duly presented ourselves at his Fitzwilliam Square consulting rooms. Cross had, I was warned, a reputation for gruffness, but I wasn't prepared for his rough handling. At one point I whimpered, 'You're hurting me,' but when he took no notice and became unapologetically rougher, I buried my teeth in his arm and bit it as hard as I could. 'Now you know what it's like!' I shrieked as he looked at me in horror. Various stressful investigations over the next couple of years brought us no nearer to answers. Involuntary childlessness is a hard cross to bear. People can be insensitive – 'Of course, being a careerwoman

---

* See chapter 7.

you won't want to complicate your life with children,' being one such common remark. Whenever my friends had a baby, I felt dreadful pangs of silent envy. But fortunate to have been born an optimist, I didn't get depressed – I began to rationalize it as God's will for me – but I did have bouts of sadness, which I endeavoured to hide from Albert. Eventually, prompted by my wise mother who took the long view, the question of adoption arose. By then it was 1967 and Albert, who would be fifty in the autumn, felt he was too old to take on the responsibility. But on our next visit home she urged me to persuade him to talk to Fr Michael O'Carroll, who, though we didn't know it then, had for years arranged many adoptions. He had even managed, with his enlightened superiors' consent (and these were very unenlightened days in Ireland) to 'place' some eight orphaned children over several years with the unmarried daughter of his and Vincent Kelly's great friend, Mrs Partridge.* He was permitted by his Holy Ghost (now Spiritans) superior to give all his earnings from his journalistic work for the maintenance of that unorthodox family; though brought up in near poverty all eight had happy and useful lives.

Fr Michael invited Albert to come and see him. When I tried to find out what they talked he was non-committal and I didn't press him, because I felt him preoccupied with the thought that his family would find it near impossible to accept a child that was not 'of the blood'. We took our holiday with the Sagarra family a bit later that year and in the evening of our last day in Barcelona, went for a long walk and talk in a large public park at the top end of the massive street known to us all as the Diagonal but in 1967 still officially the Avenida del Generalissimo Francesco Franco. Normally diffident in such matters, even after seven

* Mrs Partridge is one of my heroes. Married to the brother of the Duke of Marlborough (in Sarah Marlborough's wedding dress from the 1700s), after he deserted her, she married or lived with four other men and had five children with five different fathers. She dined with Stalin in her Bolshevist period and went on a pilgrimage to Rome where she converted to Catholicism. When I met her as a fragile old lady, she had been thirty-eight years in the Harold's Cross Hospice, surviving twenty-six cancer operations, but her penetrating mind, wit and humour were undiminished. From her sickbed she would regularly counsel priests with personal problems. She is buried in the Benedictine Glenstal Abbey, Murroe, Co. Limerick.

years of marriage, I said outright that evening that I couldn't contemplate a childless marriage, and could he agree to what was clearly a very tough decision for him, to adopt a child. I should have known by then: Catalans are straight. The indirect approach never works. Suddenly all was agreed, but in the meantime, darkness had fallen, and we realized we were locked in – not a good idea in a police state. If we were found there or if we were caught climbing over the high railings, we risked interrogation as 'plotters' and possible arrest. Luck was on our side. We managed, with an effort, to negotiate our way over the three-metre-high railings without being detected, I full of euphoria at having finally reached the decision to apply for an adoption.

At the time legal adoption in Ireland was problematical. But Fr O'Carroll 'had connections', and evidently had been long involved in helping couples in similar circumstances to our own, given that I had remained an Irish citizen. Having been contacted later that year through his religious order by someone whose unfortunate pregnant daughter had 'been sent to England' where her child was due to be born in spring 1968, Fr Michael had arrangements put in place that, unless she changed her mind, we would duly adopt her baby. In Britain, while the bureaucracy was considerable, the whole process was fair and transparent. We were visited at home several times by a social worker, always without prior notice (we had recently moved from our flat over the bank to a house in the suburb of Didsbury). We had medical check-ups and were advised that, prior to the adoption order going through the courts I must have first given up my job; it was unlikely that the judge would countenance a mother in full-time employment taking on responsibility for a child. My then Swiss boss, Professor Keller, never enamoured at the idea of female colleagues, agreed to consider my request for a part-time contract. A day or two later he came back with a take-it-or-leave-it offer. I would have no more administrative duties: 'You are not very good at it anyway, Eda.' Otherwise, I would keep my full load of teaching, tutorials and examining, and generally 'do my bit' in the department and be expected to get on with my research. And I would receive all of one-eighth of my current salary, some £180 per annum. Would he have even thought of offering such a 'bargain' to a male colleague? I think not. In going part-time, I had to cash in my pension contributions, a mere couple of hundreds of pounds after ten years' service (which I invested on a well-recommended Liverpool stockbroker's advice and duly lost). Scarcely were we back from Ireland in April 1968 with our nine-week-old daughter than my boss sent his wife to visit me, ostensibly to see the baby but in fact to persuade me to think twice about continuing in post. Could I in conscience decide not to be a full-time mother, for the child's sake? Some things do indeed change for the better.*

The actual adoption process was nothing if not anxiety-inducing: it was poignant to walk into the orphanage at Stamullen in Co. Kildare on a cold March morning in 1968 and be led into a great hall, where all the windows were open, and see ninety-six cots, each with a small baby. I was aware that the mothers had either conceived ignorant of the consequences or in some cases by rape or incest. And then, forced by family and social pressures, they had had to give up their child to avoid 'bringing shame' on family and community. Stamullen was not one of the notorious mother-and-baby homes for illegitimate or abandoned babies; it was heart-warming to see how the nuns cared for the infants, overwhelmed as they must have been by the sheer numbers. As we walked by the babies in their cots, 'our' nun told us of the sisters' efforts to get as many as they could adopted by Irish families. One little eighteen-month-old, she told us, would put up his arms when anyone passed to be taken up and cuddled, but nobody seemed to want him. It was not until much later that we learnt of the fate of those who were never adopted. Many ended up in harsh institutions, orphanages, 'reformatories' and industrial schools. These were run by religious orders with the connivance of the Irish state, as ever ready to wash its metaphorical hands of its social responsibilities for the unwanted. As we reached halfway down the long hall and stopped at a cot with a very tiny

---

* One of my friends, a distinguished UCD professor, told me recently that when she got her first contract post there in the early 1970s, she had been required to submit a doctor's certificate each year in September to prove she was not pregnant before her contract could be renewed for the coming academic year.

baby, dressed incongruously in yellow and turquoise garments, Albert put out a finger and immediately the small person grasped it. This was the one arranged for you, said the nun. That was the start of a lifelong bond between the two of them. The only thing remaining to be done was to go back to Manchester and, instructed by our marvellous Mrs O'Connell, up to then my help in the house but from now on my bible in all things baby care, to equip us with everything we would need. Incidentally, we were never given information about our daughter's background, apart from being told by Fr O'Carroll that her parents, a medical student and a trainee nurse, were from Galway. Without exactly saying so, he implied that her father was someone who believed his family's 'respectable' position in the community would have been 'seriously damaged' by the 'shame' of an illegitimate child. Our baby's young mother had evidently been 'exported' to England for the duration of her pregnancy where she gave birth in a London hospital, and only days later handed over her baby to one of the Stamullen nuns to take back to the orphanage for adoption.*

On 27 April, the feast of Our Lady of Montserrat, patroness of Catalonia and of our marriage, we travelled to Dublin to collect our future daughter and brought her back to my parents' home in Rathgar en route for England. The extended family with Fr Michael were all there to welcome her. What was her name? It must, we had decided, be some version of Maria. Albert had wanted the Provençal name of Mirèio after Frédéric Mistral's celebrated epic poem,† but I pleaded problems for her future Lancashire school mistresses. We compromised on Mireia. Later that evening, blissfully happy, we went off to bed, having carefully prepared her night bottle as the nun had shown, including a small amount of egg mixed with the milk. Alas, however I had done it, she kept on vomiting the contents and cried for the rest of the night with hunger. Eventually we got some milk into her and set off for the airport. The

---

* Though we asked her on her eighteenth birthday and occasionally thereafter, if she would like to make contact with her birth mother, she said she didn't wish to.

† Mistral (1830–1914) was the leading poet of the Provencal literary Renaissance. *Mirèio* appeared in 1859.

trip was not without its lighter moments. As we waited for our flight a group of about forty hung-over young Mancunians evidently returning home after a stag night eyed the three of us, whispering among themselves: Albert with his already greying hair in his black Catalan beret and black raincoat with its scarlet lining, me and the tiny whimpering infant. Eventually one reluctant volunteer, pushed forward by his mates, came over and asked Albert in somewhat blurred tones: 'Is that your grandchild?' 'No,' he said without batting an eyelid, 'as you'll appreciate, we are not happy with the English school system and have been in Ireland looking for one suitable for my youngest sister.' 'Thank you, sir, thank you,' mumbled the red-faced youth before stumbling back to the safety of his mates.

The next few weeks were full of anxiety. Mireia, born in February and weighing eight pounds when we collected her, had not gained but at nearly three months had lost weight, her poor little head covered in sores. We did everything the weekly baby clinic advised but to no avail, until at my next visit a new doctor, an elderly Frenchman, examined her and said: 'Has no one told you that the child is allergic to eggs?' From then on, she throve. Only two worries remained, one to get her birth mother's permission for her various vaccinations, which took weeks to come and made us extremely nervous for the last step – the final agreement before we could call Mireia our own. Her mother was (rightly) given up to nine months to change her mind. I wouldn't wish to have to go through that waiting again but in late October her letter of consent arrived and in November the court granted our order of adoption. The judge advised that we must pledge to tell her that she was adopted before her seventh birthday, adding the kindly advice that it was a good idea to use the term 'adopted' as a term of endearment. That Christmas we spent in Barcelona and Mireia, now ten months old and sitting up and taking notice, hadn't a moment to herself. All her ten Sagarra cousins, aged from twenty-four to eight, wanted to have her on their laps, a blonde baby being an utter novelty among the uniformly black-haired family clan. Everyone we met expected to be kissed by the baby in the manner all Spanish children were taught to do from the cradle. My second fear, that the Sagarra family would not accept a 'stranger', could not have been more misplaced. If you are part of the Catalan family, that is it. Surprisingly, though he never said anything to me, it was my father who evidently had problems. After his death in 1970 I found the draft of a letter he had written to his brother explaining that 'Clodagh now has two girls, aged three and two, and Eda also has a child.' It didn't bother me apart from feeling sorry that he thought that way.

Meanwhile there was the question of my research. I had effectively wasted the first six or seven years since my appointment to a lectureship on an ill-advised general history of Germany. German in Britain was a 'minority language', partly in consequence of the two World Wars. Staff numbers were relatively small (Manchester's, with some eight to ten tenured staff, was one of the largest German departments in the country) such that, thanks to our well-attended conferences held each year in the Easter vacation at different universities throughout the country, we got to know most of our colleagues in England and Scotland. (Our Welsh colleagues rarely attended meetings outside Wales.) Moreover, German departments in Britain were often known for their sociability, for we tended to keep in touch between conferences. Given the recent past, the relationship between the senior members of our profession in Britain and post-war Germany was unusual. It was the consequence of several of the leading names[*] having been refugees from the Nazi era and several of whose British colleagues had had a material role in bringing them to Britain. There was, for example, Edna Purdie,[†] Professor of German at Bedford College London, who, as one of her colleagues told me, had

---

[*] For example, the professors of German at Oxford, Cambridge and University College London, Peter Ganz, who had spent two years as a teenager in Buchenwald, Siegbert Prawer and Peter Stern and my kind mentor at Swansea, Erich Heller. Charlotte Jolles for years after the war worked as a nursery nurse and later assistant at a girls' school. When her published work became known she got her first university appointment in her late fifties.

[†] Unusually for a female scholar, Professor Purdie had successfully gained her doctorate in Oxford in the 1920s but on the grounds of her gender had been refused conferral (and title) as this would have given her the right to be a member of Senate, which was barred to women. Miss Purdie thereupon got a post in Germany and gained a second doctorate there.

spent weeks standing in queues in front of the Home Office in boiling London sunshine in 1939, despite suffering from dangerous varicose veins, to get her later colleague, the Schiller expert Ilse Appelbaum, out of Germany. Early in 1949, when Germany was still occupied by the four powers and anti-German feeling in the UK was still rife, a group of British professors of German had managed to persuade a reluctant Home Office to grant visas to six of their German colleagues to share in their planned celebration at the University of Cambridge of the 200th anniversary of the birth of Germany's national poet, Wolfgang von Goethe. None of the six had supported the former regime but as German scholars they shared in the general defamation of their discipline, which had been notorious for most of its exponents' eager support of the Third Reich and promulgation of extreme racist views in their teaching and published work. The six gaunt survivors of the Nazi regime were overwhelmed by the warmth of their colleagues' welcome. Important personal and research networks were formed and for years to come British Germanists played a central role in appointments to chairs at German universities. Many of them had been involved as experts both during the war (as at Bletchley Park) and like my third boss at Manchester, Professor Idris Parry, in the interrogation of German prisoners of war and suspected Nazi criminals thereafter.

My generation benefited in our careers from the readiness of many of those senior colleagues to promote young lecturers, getting us invited to conferences and introducing us to publishers. One such conference invitation to join a group of British historians at a meeting organized by Professor Johann Wolfgang Mommsen* at Düsseldorf was memorable for those we met, among them the widow of Bernhard von Stauffenberg, brother of Klaus, the leader of the 20 July 1944 plot against Hitler, which had led to the gruesome execution of thousands of Resistance members. One evening I listened in open-mouthed horror as one of the Oxford historians present (who himself was Jewish) asked Frau von Stauffenberg

---

* Mommsen, and his twin brother Hans, grandsons of the famous historian, were highly influential younger German scholars challenging received views of the origins and workings of the Third Reich.

where she had spent the last years of the War. 'In Württemberg,' she replied. 'That must have been a nice place to live.' 'It wasn't,' was her laconic reply. She didn't elaborate. Virtually every member of hers and the Stauffenberg families, including small children, had been imprisoned as part of *Sippenhaft* (mass arrest of extended families), Hitler's revenge on the families of the executed. The other memorable meeting was with Alexander von dem Bussche,* who almost uniquely among Hitler's senior generals had been prepared to take matters into his own hand and assassinate the Führer. A tall, extremely handsome officer and imposing figure, he had got as far as a planned meeting with Hitler at Cologne to display the latest uniform in 1943, having successfully secreted his pistol undetected on his person. An hour before the encounter, Hitler, with his allegedly uncanny prescience of personal danger, had cancelled the meeting.

Another chance encounter at one of our annual Germanist conferences led to an introduction to the famed Professor Roy Pascal of Birmingham, one of the most generous of colleagues with his time and connections.† He invited me to contribute the 1830–90 volume to his series, *Literature and History*, published by Weidenfeld and Nicolson. As history was my first love I tried, as was customary in British humanities scholarship but not in its German counterpart, to situate the literary figures of this fascinating period in the context of their time. In other words, not as we saw those seminal years of Germany's industrial revolution and the rise of Prussia from our contemporary perspective, but as Germans living at the time thought and felt. The supreme example of such writing was George Macaulay Young's *Portrait of an Age* (1936). 'Read until you can hear them speak' and 'Always remember what was happening when a young man was twenty,' he advised. And I began to read and read, fat volume after fat volume of novels beloved of mid- and late nineteenth-century German writers. These were accessible in the

* I still have his visiting card which he presented to me.

† We younger colleagues often wondered why Pascal had never moved to one of the most prestigious chairs of German, at Cambridge, Oxford, Edinburgh or University College London. We learnt the reason only years later: he had never been at Bletchley Park, for years an unspoken 'qualification' for such advancement, and 'worse still', the Pascals were Communists, his wife a Russian Jew.

stacks of Manchester's splendid university library, to which staff and students still had access, and the bulk of whose excellent German collection had been brought to Manchester by Henry Simon. The manuscript was duly submitted in 1968 to the publishers, Weidenfeld and Nicolson. I heard nothing for a year and was so absorbed in our new life that I forgot about it. The blow fell when Mireia was five months old. A letter advised me that the manuscript was incoherent and that the whole thing must be rewritten. Having now spent eleven years in post without a single publication, I was aware that if it failed to be published, I had no hope of ever getting my job back, something we planned I would apply for as soon as Mireia started school. The only time in the day that she was invariably asleep were the hours between about 5 and 7 am. And so began a routine I still have today, writing or reading each early morning apart from Christmas Day and birthdays. Eventually, over the course of many early mornings, a completely rewritten manuscript was with the editor a year later.[*]

It was not the last time that a senior colleague felicitously intervened in my career. In 1971 Lilian Furst, though only a few years older than me already head of Comparative Literature in Manchester, shared her worries about her father. Her mother had died recently, and he was feeling bereft. I asked them to tea and Mireia, aged three, decided he was her new grandfather. Lilian and her parents, both dental surgeons, she a German, he from Hungary, had trained in Vienna and established a highly successful practice in the city, before having to flee their home in March 1938 days after the *Anschluss*. Like so many other of his fellow Jewish refugees, Dr Furst had been interned as an enemy alien for most of the war on the Isle of Man but retained his irrepressible Hungarian sense of humour. The afternoon was such a success that Albert and I, and Mireia revelling in all the unexpected attention, were delighted to repeat it. On one such occasion Lilian asked me about future research plans.

---

[*] It finally appeared in 1971 under the title *Tradition and Revolution. German literature and society 1830 to 1890* and in Munich in 1972 as a paperback: *Tradition und Revolution. Deutsche Literatur und Gesellschaft 1830 bis 1890* in List's *Taschenbücher der Literaturwissenschaft* (Literature paperbacks).

If I was interested in writing something more extensive on German society as reflected in its literature, she would secure me a contract. *A Social History of Germany 1648–1914* was completed four years later and published by Methuen in 1977. Lilian went on to have an outstanding scholarly career in the United States, where her father happily re-connected with friends and colleagues of better days from Central Europe.

# SIX

# *The 1970s: Return*

*'I'm just one for equality – equality of opportunity.'*[*]

*'… the vitality of the intellectual and creative energy of the 1970s'.*[†]

The 1970s were an uneasy decade in Europe. In Germany mentalities were beginning to change perceptibly, in some respects radically. The two Germanies had been formed in 1949, in the east from the former Soviet zone of occupation (1945–9) and in the west from the three merged American, British and French zones; both states were now a generation old. By the beginning of the 1970s courageous voices in East Germany critical of the regime had begun to command a following, especially among the educated young. This time, unlike the abortive East Berlin workers' revolt of 1953, the media, particularly song and cabaret, and literature more generally, became the vehicle of protest, ruthlessly crushed by the party, but not before a whole new generation

---

\* Thekla Beere in an interview for RTE's Radio One in 1974 with Tom McGurk (Bryson, 160, n.86).

† Margaret MacCurtain. *History Ireland*. vol. 2, no. 1 (Spring 1994), 54.

had become politically sensitized. While DDR Bürger, citizens of the German Democratic Republic,* were proud of what their Socialist state had achieved against the odds and identified with it, many were increasingly resentful at what they saw as the authorities' failure to reward loyalty, hard work and acceptance of restrictions on the citizen's liberty, particularly the right to travel to the West. In the Federal Republic, meanwhile, the state's spectacular economic growth over the previous decade and a half no longer provided a distraction for the younger citizens from political challenges to the status quo, as it had done for their parents' generation. Courageous political leadership by the Social Democrat chancellor Willy Brandt (1969–74) was epitomized in his dramatic gesture during a state visit to Poland in December 1970, when he knelt and wept before the memorial to the Warsaw ghetto. His deeply symbolic action was angrily condemned by members of the opposition in the Federal Republic, but it forced the issue of confronting Germany's relationship to its past firmly into the public arena, anticipated in bestselling novels of West German writers. In the longer term, American-educated young German historians in research and teaching at school and university level, many of whom were former prisoners of war in the US, would prove to have a formative role in one of the most important tasks of the Federal Republic, facing and dealing with the nation's past as the responsibility of every citizen.†

---

* East Germans, citizens as well as party bosses, regarded the term 'German' as being tainted and avoided using it of their state. Germans in the West referred to themselves as *Bundesbürger* or Federal citizens rather than West Germans. But the Federal Republic claimed to be the legitimate heir to the 'German state', including the Third Reich as well as its predecessors, the Weimar Republic (1919–33), Imperial Germany (1871–1918) and the German Confederation of 1815–67 (1871). It was on this basis that Konrad Adenauer institutionalized the payment of restitution to the state of Israel.

† I admire how the Federal Republic and its citizens have acknowledged their past history in the Third Reich as so many others, notably Russia and Turkey, have failed to do their own. But see *Law in West German Democracy. Seventy Years of History as Seen through German Courts* (Leiden/ Boston: Brill 2019) for a dissenting view by Hugh Ridley, professor of German at UCD 1979–2008.

In Britain meanwhile, the nation's stagnant economy* and troubled labour relations were having an impact on people's pockets and their lives. Following the first oil crisis of 1973, millions of Britons and with them Irish labourers lost their jobs, while prices shot up. Wildcat strikes made life miserable for virtually everyone. For weeks during the winter of 1973, we had neither gas nor electricity, neither light nor central heating. Being the fortunate owners of an ancient Aga, we had an abundant supply of hot water (until the fuel ran out). So at least I was able to keep up with my student corrections lying in the warm bathwater with candles on both sides of the tub and a towel wrapped round my wrist to keep their essays and language exercises dry. The authorities had shown admirable *sang-froid* in the rapid process of dismantling the famed British Empire in these years and Prime Minister Edward Heath finally succeeded where his otherwise more dexterous Tory predecessor Harold Macmillan had failed, namely, to negotiate Britain's entry to membership of the European Economic Community.† The oil crisis however brought down his four-year administration in 1974.

The mood in Ireland offered a welcome contrast to that prevailing in England, as I experienced on my visits home in the early 1970s. Here the euphoria of 'Europe' seized the popular imagination and was endorsed by 83 per cent of our population in the 1973 EEC membership referendum. At last, it seemed, we could 'get out from under England's all-encompassing umbrella'. The extraordinary changes that flowed for Ireland from that membership in terms of opportunity were epitomized for me, but very much later, in the form of two conversations, the first in 1990 with two shy young women sitting beside me on a plane to

---

* Britain suffered economically far more than Germany. As the war had been mainly fought until the ultimate stages beyond her then borders, the German economy survived relatively intact. The addition of some twelve million German refugees from the former East German territories, which were now part of Poland, Czechoslovakia and Russia, infused immense energy into the re-building of Western Germany.

† Yet, despite Britain's entry, together with that of Ireland in 1973, what Chris Patten termed the 'psychodrama' visited on the English nation by President de Gaulle's notorious blocking of her original application in January 1963, continued like some imperfectly diagnosed blood condition to poison relations with Europe for decades to come.

Lithuania, where I was doing some work for the European Commission on university exchange with former Soviet/Eastern European countries. The two nineteen-year-olds were trainee laboratory assistants, working at the kidney unit of an Irish hospital. This was their first time abroad, they said, and they had made friends the previous year at a conference in Dublin with some Estonian fellow trainees, whom they planned to meet at that year's conference and maybe create their own little 'international' network. The enlargement of these young women's horizon and their sense of now being part of a greater whole was palpable, and exciting. From small beginnings... The second occasion was the night of 23 December during the great freeze of 2010. Having just travelled some five hours from my sister's home in North Yorkshire, I was sitting up all night, squashed together with some 800 fellow travellers in Holyhead waiting for the mail train from London's Euston station packed with returning fellow countrymen following the closure of London's airports. My neighbour, a well-dressed man of about forty, told me that he was travelling home for Christmas from Dubai where he now lived. 'Home' was a small holding near Ballina in north Mayo ('where my father, when we were children, only had an old bit of twine to keep his trousers up with. But thanks to the chances he had had', he told me, 'from my secondary school and college education I now have my own construction business in Dubai and employ some 200 men, Jordanians, Lebanese and Pakistanis, all of them great workers').

1970 was a memorable year for Clodagh and me; our father Kevin died in the summer after a long coronary illness, which kept him often confined to bed, but left his energies to record his memories of the struggle for Irish independence undiminished. From the comfort of that bed, with his bookshelves covering the wall beside him, he wrote some eleven hundred pages of memoirs enlivened by anecdotes and vivid pen portraits of those central players he had known and worked with, among them Michael Collins and Arthur Griffith. He would joke that every time he had to write the name of de Valera, whom he bitterly blamed for his absence from the Treaty negotiations and his part in provoking the Civil War, while acknowledging his achievement in having kept

Ireland out of the Second World War, he would suffer another attack of angina.* My father's final year was greatly saddened by the outbreak of the euphemistically named 'Troubles'. Coming from the mainly nationalist area of 'west of the [river] Bann', his native Tyrone had been, relatively speaking, less devastated than Belfast and surrounds. He did not live to witness the horrors of the 15 August 1998 bombing of his native Omagh. But when in 2015, nearly half a century after my father's death, my sister and I went to visit the cemetery in Altmore near Dungannon where many of our ancestors were buried, we would read alongside 'our' much older graves, the names on the neighbouring gravestones of a number of young Tyrone IRA members who had died in the infamous 1980–81 hunger strikes.

My father had gone into hospital for the last time on St Patrick's Day, 17 March, and died on the unionist holiday, 12 July 1970. His sense of humour never left him. During his illness Clodagh and I had been summoned to his deathbed from England all of nine times. When we came for the penultimate time just before Easter 1970, I on crutches after an operation on my leg, he apologized for yet another 'unnecessary' journey, his last words on our departure being: 'Girls, I promise I'll go next time.' Which he did. We were fortunate to have lived well into our thirties with both parents. And yet whatever age one is, to lose a parent gives a sense of having been assigned to the 'older' generation. My mother, who had cared for him for so long, was now free to travel, even going to Hong Kong, where my brother-in-law Bill Forshaw was serving in the British army, and making her first visit to China. When Bill was transferred to Northern Ireland in 1972, she happily looked forward to their spending that Christmas together. 'I think not,' said Clodagh in her down-to-earth way, 'I could come with the children, but not Bill. "They" would only tar and feather me, but they would murder him.'

The 1970s undoubtedly did bring Irish women substantive reforms at legislative level, triggered by external forces and established women's reformist organizations in Ireland. In 1970, under pressure from the

---

* Available online as NAI Witness Statement 1770.

United Nations Social and Economic Council,* Taoiseach Jack Lynch's government set up the Commission on the Status of Women in Ireland and appointed Dr Thekla Beere (1901–1991) to chair it. It was a first-class choice. 'The ultimate civil servant,'† Beere had in 1959 become the first female head of an Irish government department (Transport and Power) since the foundation of the state. With her characteristic efficiency she initiated a programme of intense research. She and her colleagues on the Commission presented their report, which was published by government in 1973 and described by Mary Robinson, as the charter for women in the modern Irish state. Most of its forty-nine recommendations were implemented in the following years. 1974 saw the Anti-Discrimination (Pay) Act become law, further developed in the 1977 Employment Equality Act to include recruitment, conditions, training and promotion; a year earlier the Civil Service (Employment of Married Women) Act had ended the highly discriminatory marriage bar. Attempts by the Irish government to seek derogation on the key measure of equal pay came up against the new reality of Ireland's obligations as member of the EEC. The government was directed to implement equal pay with effect from February 1976. The 1970s saw the setting up of the first Rape Crisis Centre, whose founders faced malicious or ribald criticism; it would take a further generation before the issue of domestic violence was finally addressed by the Oireachtas in 1994. The 1973 and 1974 Social Welfare Acts had dealt with outstanding issues such as the plight of marginalized women: hitherto deserted wives in Ireland had been entitled to no support from the state. Deserted and prisoners' wives, widows and single mothers were Beere's particular concern. In her 1974 interview she expressed horror at the findings of some of the Commission's research. 'A lot of us were absolutely amazed at the things we found … People like me – we hadn't realized – I don't think that anyone there [on the Commission] did know a lot of these things.' This certainly was true of

* The international body set up in 1946, based in New York, to enhance the status of women and promote gender equality.

† President Mary Robinson at Anna Bryson's presentation of her biography: *No Coward Soul. A Biography of Thekla Beere* at Áras an Uachtaráin in March 2009.

myself and of people of my background and education: we were simply out of touch with the reality of so many Irish women's lives.

Legislation could change a certain amount. Culture was quite another matter. Legislation *per se* cannot alter mentalities. What did change in Ireland of the 1970s was Irish women's awareness of their situation, the pre-condition, according to Karl Marx's mentor, the German philosopher Hegel, for change in substance. To arouse and promote consciousness of their unequal condition was the driving force behind the Irish Women's Liberation Movement, founded in 1970, which focused on new methods of 'direct action' in order to highlight women's unequal condition. Direct action included spontaneous demonstrations, some of them stunts to attract media attention. One of these, the 'Belfast contraception train' sought to stress the absurdity of the legislative situation, when several members travelled to Belfast, bought contraceptives and returned with their contraband to Dublin. The radical impact of the Irish Women's Liberation Movement did not last, partly on account of in-fighting among its members. The movement 'may have been chaotic,* short-lived and riddled with class tension, but an irreversible start had been made in making the status of women a political issue'.† It realized one of its key aims, to involve women on a nationwide basis in the cause of greater equality. Contacts with other women's organizations in the following years helped promote vital services for women, such as support for victims of domestic violence and rape. Here too directives from the European Commission proved to be key in translating aspirations into law.

I had meanwhile and very belatedly reached a small milestone in my own career. My first-ever brief article (on Viennese comic theatre) was published in 1970 through the good offices of Gar (W.E.) Yates in our 'house' journal for British and Irish studies in German literature and language, *German Life and Letters*. In 1971 my first book appeared

---

* I and the other members of my seminar on *Frauen schreiben* ([German] women's writing) around that time were intrigued at the demand of a radical Berlin feminist who signed up to give a paper but only on condition that the sole male member of the group leave. Her argument: a 'proper' feminist seminar must exclude men, the 'enemies of the people'. Hard to know how they planned to ensure the future without them.

† Ferriter, 2007, 664.

followed a year later by its German translation. *Tradition und Revolution*, the most successful of my books in terms of sales, was evidently widely read by German graduate students who were attracted to the idea of setting literature, its production and consumption in its contemporary historical setting. When a number of these readers became university lecturers and the Munich group set up the research centre for the social history of German literature, I was invited to contribute and made many valuable contacts and some new friends. Professor Keller showed himself agreeably surprised, but when I made tentative enquiries about getting back as a permanent member of staff – Mireia was now at morning school – he was unenthusiastic. Fortunately, he had been joined by a new professor, the lively and creative Idris Parry from Wales, who took over the headship while Keller was on sabbatical and in 1973 organized my re-instatement. On his return Keller summoned me to his office to tell me that in terms of seniority it was now my turn to take over responsibility as departmental examinations secretary. 'I have decided,' he said, 'to give it to [my younger colleague] David Blamires – you have more charm than efficiency.' I thanked him for the compliment, which slightly fazed him. A year later, with my next book well in train and a contract with Methuen's in hand, I was again summoned to his office to be told: 'Eda you are in line for promotion to senior lectureship, but as you have a husband to support you, I have decided to give it to Ray Furness, as a married man he needs it more.' It speaks volumes for our very different mentalities at that time that I thought it was a perfectly rational decision.

The first half of the 1970s were years of great contentment. Mireia, as blonde as her father was dark, was a constant delight. For some four years six small children of my colleagues filled our house a couple of days a week with laughter and tears, devouring astonishing quantities of pancakes and fish fingers at teatime. On the other weekdays I would read and write while she went off to Mrs O'Connell's or to play in her friends' houses. In their fifth year all the children went together to Beaver Road primary school, just a street away, where extraordinary teachers managed mixed-ability classes of up to forty-five English,

Pakistani, Indian, Irish and continental European pupils to admirable effect. Ritual, so reassuring to small persons, was evidently always the same. At the end of the morning cleaning, Mrs O'Connell would take Mireia home with her on the bus, for me to collect her after tea. As soon as they came in the front door of their house in Levenshulme, Mireia would go to get her apron from its hook at the back of the kitchen cupboard door and wash her hands. After lunch she sat with a picture book or toy, followed by a walk or a visit to one of the neighbours. Just before teatime 'Uncle' Arthur would return from work, with Mireia, who idolized him, rushing to hug him. 'No-aah, child,' he would say in his strong Mancunian accent, (which Mireia then shared), 'first a wash, then a hug.' Arthur O'Connell, as small as his wife was tall and spare, worked as a semi-skilled labourer in a steel factory. They lived frugally, saved all their lives and had managed when property prices were low to buy their two-up-two-down home on a mortgage. Once a year they would take their two weeks' holiday, one week to visit a sister and in the second to take day trips on the bus to the coast, on these occasions always accompanied by Mireia for whom Blackpool was the zenith of human bliss. Later, when they were retired and became ill, they, unlike feckless neighbours, were entitled to nothing from the state; after all, the argument went, they were property-owners.

When the O'Connells' daughter got married in 1972, Albert and I were afforded a unique insight into some of the norms and practices of old Lancashire working-class culture. Mireia, to her utter delight, was to be bridesmaid. I asked what I should buy for her, to be told: 'Mrs Sagarra, our taste might not be your taste, but this is our occasion and we pay for everything.' 'And what shall we wear?' 'The men a suit and the ladies a silk dress and a hat.' I acquired a hat and silk dress, while the four-year-old Mireia duly appeared, delighted with herself, in a St Patrick's Day-green long satin frock with bright yellow socks. When we arrived as bidden at the O'Connell house, Albert was given a white carnation and directed to the small sitting room, now packed with male relations of the bride and Arthur's mates, while I, presented with a pink carnation, joined the ladies in the kitchen. When I fixed the carnation upright on my dress, a headshake from Mrs O'Connell indicated I had got it wrong, I must pin it upside down: that was the way it was done.

After the church service we were all invited to lunch at a long table in the local pub. As the silent meat-and-two-veg. meal progressed, I tried to animate things, until the man opposite leaned over and said: 'Missus, when we eat, we eat, when we talk, we talk.' I haven't often been so effectively silenced. Afterwards we moved across the hall where there was a bar and dance floor. The two 'sides' separated, the bridal party to one side, the groom's to the other (for practical reasons, each side paying for their own drinks). As we sipped our coffee, Arthur and two of his workmates came up to Albert: might they ask him a question? 'We,' said one, 'work with our hands, tiring work. You work with your head. Do you ever get tired that way?' As the friends of the newlyweds arrived and before the dancing could start, all the men queued up to kiss the bride. A moment's panic for me when Albert whispered, 'but I don't want to kiss the bride'. It would have been a dreadful insult so, normally impervious to such promptings from me, he submitted with reasonable grace. At that point Mireia, who had been very silent throughout, turned a pasty green. As soon as we got her home, she came out in spots – with measles.

Just as the monumental neo-Gothic Jesuit church where we often went to mass on Sundays is now a mosque, when Mrs O'Connell's neighbours died and their houses sold, they were one by one bought by the recent immigrants from Pakistan. 'They are pleasant, but the women don't go out and they don't keep their gardens,' she would sigh. She took our departure, or rather the loss of Mireia, very hard. Mireia herself remained inconsolable for a long time, bursting into tears whenever their name was mentioned, but we gave them a gift on two successive years of (most successful) summer holidays with us in Dublin. Arthur was able to fulfil his long-held dream of visiting Bray, in his and his mates' mind the Irish equivalent of Blackpool. When Edith died in 2005 Mireia and I flew over for the day to attend the funeral from her daughter's house, now an elegant small semi in Thornton Grove, two doors down from where Friedrich Engels had lived with his common-law Irish wife Lizzie

Burns. Ritual was just as her mother would have wished: we women sat in the sleek funeral car, and the men, nominally Church of England but hardly church-goers, processed behind us on foot around the local streets to the church. After the ceremony we drove to the Southern Cemetery for burial and back to a local hostelry for lunch, where we met Edith's and Arthur's eldest grandson, now a physics student at one of the major universities.

In the early to mid-1970s life in Manchester University's now fourteen-strong German department could hardly have been more agreeable. Eight of us were roughly of an age and enjoyed the subversive collegiality of us versus them, which Manchester's excessively professorial culture fostered.* Many of our group were now Albert's and my close friends: from the department Rhona Solomon and her husband Gerry, Rosemary Wallbank and her medical doctor brother Bill, Peter and Celia Skrine, both Germanists, whose daughter Juliet was Mireia's special chum, together with Gill and Tony Cockshut, at the time an English master in the renowned Manchester Grammar School and later professor at Oxford, and colleagues from the Italian, French and Classics departments.

A further friend for a couple of years in the 1960s was one of the German assistants, who with his fellow language assistant Dietmar liked to make impromptu evening calls to our flat over the bank in Wilmslow Road in the hope of being asked to stay for supper (they always were). On one occasion we divided our six ounces of cod and four potatoes into four and imagined the rest – all a further occasion for amusing exchange. We knew him as Max, always great fun, who once wrote a light-hearted Viennese comedy for me, which I alas lost in one of our house moves – doubly to be regretted in the light of his later metamorphosis into the celebrated author W.E. Sebald. We had some difficulty when his first novels appeared in recognizing in this deeply serious and haunted voice of Germany's conscience our erstwhile so entertaining friend and

---

* When the senior lecturer Ruedi Keller was promoted to a chair, his wife informed one of our colleagues' wives that 'we must understand that as a professorial wife she would now no longer be able to socialize [as she had done] with lecturers and their wives'.

colleague. A contemporary of ours as assistant in the Manchester French department was Max's close friend, the later creator of the *nouveau roman*, Michel Butor. Most of us in due course succeeded to chairs in Britain, Ireland or Germany (Peter Skrine to Bristol, Ray Furness to St Andrews, Rhys Williams to Swansea, Martin Durrell to London, later Manchester, our former language assistant Wolfgang Kühlwein to Trier and David Blamires to a personal chair at Manchester). As lecturers at that time were not particularly well paid and most of us had young children, our socializing consisted almost entirely in dining turn by turn in each other's houses. Inspired by the cookery books of Elizabeth David[*] and by Gill Cockshut's adventurous menus, we tried our hand at all sorts of recipes, extending our circle to friends in the English, French, Italian and classics departments. The academic side of life seems in retrospect, at least by comparison with today's bureaucratized university, relatively stress-free. All were expected to do research and progress was monitored annually but teaching and the intellectual and critical formation of the next generation of the nation's leaders was regarded as the central purpose of our profession. Thus Jim (T.J.) Reed, lecturer and subsequently professor of German at the University of Oxford, could afford to publish virtually nothing in the fifteen years before his magisterial study of Thomas Mann, *The Uses of Tradition* (1974) appeared. We had some excellent students at Manchester; classes were enlivened by a sprinkling of Jewish refugees from Nazi Germany, a handful of whom were mature students who could now afford to attend university.

The university had an effective tutorial system, which allowed us to anticipate and help resolve psychological problems. When Mireia was small, I found an effective way of getting over-anxious students, usually the high achievers, to deal with pre-exam stress. I would invite them home to spend the afternoon and 'help' me with Mireia; they returned home physically so exhausted that they could generally count on a decent night's sleep.

Besides my own courses on nineteenth-century German literature and teaching the language, I was now in charge of the history courses

---

[*] Author, among other publications, of the landmark *French Provincial Cooking* (1960).

for students of German. I only gave my first conference paper in 1973 to our annual Conference of University Teachers of German in Britain and Ireland (CUTG). The latter occasion was memorable if for the wrong reasons. The lecture hall at the University of East Anglia was packed and I was predictably nervous, especially when I saw Peter Ganz, professor of medieval German at Oxford, eyeing me, as I thought, sardonically (he was actually full of his usual good will to younger colleagues). My topic was the changing image of Frederick II of Prussia (1712–1786) in the century after his death as indicator of nineteenth-century German nationalists' developing political awareness. As I made reference to the Franco-Prussian war of 1793, my nervousness let me add the absurd rider: 'it's an easy date to remember, it's my butcher's telephone number'. The whole hall howled with laughter and the ice was broken.

Passing my fortieth birthday, I would have been quite happy to have spent the rest of my working life with my congenial colleagues. I had no career ambitions apart from briefly nurturing a secret hope to 'make it' in golf, which I played two or three times a week after work on a seven handicap. In 1968, the day before we travelled to Ireland to collect two-month-old baby Mireia, I had been invited to play in the Lancashire trials for a place on one of the county teams. The event, thirty-six holes at Pleasington in north Lancashre, a championship golf course some forty or fifty miles distant, was staged under the eagle eyes of the team selectors. My delight was mixed with horror as at the end of the day I was told I had been selected to play for the second Lancashire county team. In due course, and with Mrs O'Connell's help and some judicious swapping of babies with our golf professional's golfer wife, I managed to fit in memorable matches all over the county and later, when I had got down to a four handicap, to play in the North of England and the British Strokeplay Championships at the wonderful Hoylake (Royal Liverpool) and Birkdale golf links. On the latter occasion I came second last. So what? I had finally played at national level. For the next seven years I juggled work with children's and dinner parties, golf tournaments and leisurely weekend games with Albert, now an expert on the physics of the game, which he found more important than achieving a score – a great life, we both felt. And then, almost like a bolt from the blue, everything changed.

As so often in life the upheaval in our existence was the result of an accidental encounter. Our mature student Ilse Samuel who with her husband Herbert had become close friends, rang to draw my attention to a job advertisement for the chair of German at Trinity College Dublin. I burst out laughing at her suggestion that I apply, but she persisted. Over the few days we thought about it, reflecting that Albert would be retiring in nine years and that we would probably want to end our days in Ireland. I would also need to supplement the family income in some capacity. I reasoned that, if I were lucky enough to get an interview, it would be a trip home and an interview experience, which I hadn't had in seventeen years. Surprisingly, Trinity called me for interview. It was likely that the College authorities were toying with the possibility of diluting the unjustifiable British image of the university by including on their shortlist a candidate from one of the 'other' Irish universities. Whatever persuaded the College to interview me I shall never know.


TRINITY

Trinity College's assessment process was nothing if not thorough. For two days in March 1975 I was questioned, observed and engaged by different groups, deans, academic, library and administrative staff, and of course members of the German department, for coffee, lunch, tea, drinks and dinner. I enjoyed every minute until it came to the serious business, the formal meetings with Board and Council under the chairmanship of Provost Lyons. In retrospect it had its moments: 'Wheeere were you at school, Mrs Sagoora?' asked the formidable Dean of the Arts Faculty, Professor Jocelyn Otway-Ruthven, who had no truck with foreign names. I had a surprise for her: 'You won't know the school, a Church of Ireland primary school – it used to be called Avoca, now Newpark.' The next question: 'Did your faaather go to Trinity?' 'Yes indeed.' I didn't feel it necessary to mention that he left without a degree.

After a sleepless night in a damp bed (my mother didn't believe in central heating), I was both physically exhausted and unaccountably nervous. Apart from an excellent British scholar from a Canadian university, I do not know who else was on the short list. All I learnt from the two externs after the event, Roy Pascal of Birmingham and – to my utter dismay when I saw him across the Board Room, my Manchester boss, Ruedi Keller – was that I made a right mess of one of the formal interviews. However, the distinguished candidate evidently let slip that he was keen to use the Trinity chair, as he so tactfully phrased it, as 'a steppingstone back to the UK'. And as the former Church of Ireland bishop of Clogher and at the time my colleague as professor of theology at Manchester, Rev. Richard (Dick) Hanson, had remarked to me before I went, 'Trinity has a habit of appointing the least likely candidate.' The next morning before we took the plane back to Manchester, I rang the College Secretary, the legendary Gerry Giltrap, to ask him to convey my thanks to the Provost and the College for their hospitality (and to remind him, without actually saying so, that he hadn't so far mentioned expenses). He interrupted me in full flight of the hitherto one-way conversation, 'but Dr Sagarra, if you let me speak for a moment, we are offering you the job'. I gasped and blurted out: 'But why would you do *that*?' And I meant it. It was by no means good news for me, Albert or seven-year-old Mireia.

We left England where I had lived for half my lifetime (seventeen years in Manchester and four and a half at boarding school in Hampshire) with many regrets, above all for our friends and colleagues. England had given me a great deal. I had no sense of having encountered real discrimination in my profession or any racial abuse, though there was always a bit beyond the walls of the university. One day our grocer, who was perfectly aware of my husband's nationality, confided in me with a worried look as I waited for my half-pound of bacon: 'Spaniards have bought next door and are going to open a restaurant. I hope they are clean.' Having wiped his nose with a cloth he proceeded with the same cloth to polish his knife before inserting it into the side of bacon. There is a nice counterexample to this story: I did my shopping for Mediterranean groceries in the Armenian store a few doors away and was just paying the bill when an old Irishman standing by heard my accent and asked: 'Are yiz married?' 'Yes.' 'And are yiz married to an Irish man?' 'No.' 'You're not married to a Brit?' 'No.' 'Then who are yiz married to?' 'A Spaniard.' 'Ah, God helps us, all these nice Irish girls marrying coloureds!' I later took a mean revenge. Just before we left for Ireland in August 1975, I was ordering forty-eight four-and-a-half-litre tins of Spanish olive oil to take with us in the removal van – just in case – when my Irish friend asked what in God's name did I want with 'all that stuff'. 'Oh, my husband likes to bathe in it.'

In Ireland and Irish universities in the 1970s women university lecturers constituted a tiny minority and female professors and heads of departments were as rare as hen's teeth, rarer in 1970s than in the years of the Irish state's foundation. True, Trinity, a pioneer in 'these islands' in affording women access to university education in 1904, had a better record than most with its two distinguished chair-holders of the previous generation, the professors Frances ('Fanny') Moran in law and Constantia Maxwell in history. Maxwell's successor since 1950, Jocelyn Otway-Ruthven, had in 1968 been one of the four first women Fellows of the College. For women, as my wise old Viennese professor of history Heinrich Benedikt liked to reflect, thirty-five to fifty is their golden age. At forty-two I certainly didn't feel that way. In fact I never felt so old before or since than in those first two distressing years back in Dublin. I had virtually no administrative experience but had been told by Mr Giltrap in no uncertain terms that the administration of the depart-ment would be entirely my responsibility.* My new colleagues were friendly but reserved. I knew no one in the College and hated going in for coffee or lunch on my own where everyone except me seemed to know each other. It was heart-warming to be approached and welcomed by a stranger – Corinna Lonergan, the head of Italian as it turned out.†

---

* Professor Keller had told me after the interview that he had been asked by the Board if I was a good administrator. 'No,' he had said, 'but she will try hard.'

† And then there was the incident with Gerard Simms, a member of the history depart-ment and brother of Archbishop Otto Simms. I had gone into the busy Common

It took all of two years for me not to wake up each morning wishing we had never come. I still insisted on trying to run the house as well as the ever more demanding job. Albert as a petrochemist had hoped that the recent discovery of oil in the Celtic Sea might open employment prospects in the research side of petroleum industry. This proved abortive and with Mireia at school all day, he began to find time heavy on his hands and decided to take over the home front. My mother after meeting him with his shopping basket (he had been raised in a home in Barcelona with two maids and a cleaning lady) phoned to instruct me: 'Eda, tell Albert that men in Ireland don't carry shopping baskets.' When I did so he smiled and said: 'I will always treat your mother with all the respect she deserves, but if I want to carry a shopping basket, I will carry a shopping basket.' One afternoon when he went to collect Mireia at school, a classmate pointed out: 'Your daddy is very old.' 'Yes,' she replied, 'he may be old, but he is very distinguished.'

We had been fortunate to find a tall three-storey terraced house at 30 Garville Avenue in Rathgar, a couple of miles from the College, but at more than double the price (£31,000) we had got for our Manchester home, despite the fact that Rathmines and our part of Rathgar in the mid-70s were run-down areas of dilapidated bed-sits. The Northern Troubles were at their height and our next-door-neighbour's, number 32, we afterwards learnt, was for years a safe house for the IRA.* Some years later next door became the distribution centre for the area's drug trade. The charming-looking young lady I encountered in the dock in her cashmere twinset and pearls, who had evidently been arrested using my stolen credit card, was, the Garda informed me subsequently,

---

Room hoping to find a chair where I could sit quietly, when a tall gaunt man came up and asked: 'Were you a Miss O'Shiel?' When I confirmed this to be the case, he continued: 'You probably don't know that my parents-in-law sheltered your father when he was on the run from the Black and Tans. They felt the Tans wouldn't come looking for him in a rectory.'

* Eleven-year-old Mireia woke up one morning in 1979 when we were both out to see a tall member of the Garda Síochána standing over her: might he look under her bed? There had been an IRA kidnap of a public personage. She, thrilled at the excitement, was sorry to learn: 'wrong house'!

the chief drug-runner into the country. The final unorthodox tenant at number 32 proved to be a poor demented woman with a long history of arson. Called from the office one Friday at 4 pm in time to see fire and smoke billowing out a top window next to my study, we watched the fire brigade quickly bring it under control and, as the guards ushered a small hooded figure in black out the front door, the crowd of onlookers starting to turn nasty and attempting to assault the poor woman. A moment later two nuns emerged and took her over. 'They always look after her,' one of the Gardaí said, 'though she always manages to escape again.'

The problems of adjustment to our new life began to challenge us on all sides. Back in 1975–7 interest rates were 18–20 per cent and taxes far higher than in the UK. My professorial salary of £6,000 p.a. barely stretched to meet the mortgage, feed the family and pay the first bills. Where our two Manchester salaries, mine at c. £1,600 and Albert's at £2,300, had given us a warm house, a good social life and a trip to Barcelona and several to Dublin each year, in November 1975 we found that after paying the mortgage and heating bill of our high-ceilinged house we were left with precisely £20 a month. We switched off the oil heating, wore three or four layers of clothes when we were at home and made soup every day. Even so, we shivered through that winter and the next. I recall spending a week in the Christmas vacation working on an article in my study at the top of the house looking out through the bare beech trees to the Dublin hills, tucked in a sleeping bag plus two hot-water bottles and mittens on my fingers, the temperature just above 4 degrees centigrade. The next blow was a solicitor's letter from the neighbour on the other side, alleging that our drains were polluting her water supply. Poorly advised, we engaged a builder to investigate: all our drains were dug up and replaced at a cost of £9,000, precisely the sum Albert had just received when he cashed in his pension payments from his employer of twenty-five years, the Manchester University Institute of Science and Technology. He had retired three years short of pensionable age in order to help Mireia and me settle down in Ireland. Our drains had not been the problem.

Much worse was to come. Eight-year-old Mireia, hitherto the happiest of children, was not her old self. She had been a little cock of the walk in her old mixed primary school, but in her new class of just fifteen little girls and apart from Irish, which she took to like a duck to water, she found she had done the work before and was getting bored. Above all she missed her Manchester friends. We asked the teachers to move her up a class, which they reluctantly did. She appeared to be coping well with schoolwork, often coming out top of the class as her term reports showed, but suddenly started bed-wetting. We tried to make little of it, while gently trying to find out the reason. It took us more than two years to find out why.

One day when Albert went up to collect her, a new dinner lady approached him. 'Did you know that no one in her class will play or speak with your daughter?' It transpired that this boycott had been going on practically since she joined her new class two years earlier, organized by one of the older girls and her pals and triggered by Mireia's English (read Mancunian) accent and her constantly 'correcting' the history teacher when he regularly portrayed England as the villain of the piece. None of the teachers had noticed anything amiss. We should have moved schools then and there and sent her to the local school with our neighbours' children, her friends Anne, Catherine and Sinead Lennon. But we didn't, and though in other ways it marked her for life, as bullying almost invariably does, she developed a quite extraordinary capacity for empathy with the feelings of others, such as I can honestly say I have never encountered in another person.

A disconnected sense of place, of not belonging, such as many Irish immigrants experienced it in post-war Britain* was my own experience of the Ireland of the 1970s, which I had left two decades earlier and romanticized ever since. Ireland was for me a new society. Albert, on the other hand, for whom it was much tougher experience, had no time for regretting past decisions. 'What's the point? We've done it, and for reasons we thought best, so why bother wasting time thinking about it?' Family always took precedence for him over individual preferences.

* Delaney (2000).

One motivating factor for the move had been an increase in racist discrimination in his own department in Manchester by two successive heads of department in the late 1960s and early 70s. One was a Cambridge-educated Lowlands Scot, the other for several years a professor of chemical engineering in Soviet Czechoslovakia; both had fought in the Spanish Civil War as idealistic young men on the Communist side. No one had been a more reluctant combatant than Albert and his brother Josep-Lluis. Franco was, to virtually all Catalans, an abomination. But that in civil wars young men are forced to take sides and that a Catholic could not possibly join the *rojos* (the reds, i.e. the Socialist and Communist Republicans), was something that British Communist veterans of 1936 were simply not prepared to accept. Nor could his two heads of department with their very different experiences, both embittered by the outcome of the crusade they had fought for in their youth, entertain the fact that Albert had been forcibly recruited by Franco's so-called Catholic forces.

From the first day in Trinity's Michaelmas term 1975 I greatly enjoyed teaching but had an increasing sense of not being able to cope. Over that winter and for months to come I developed boils all over my body and was having problems sleeping. The lighter moments were few and far between, one such being opening the bottom drawer of my predecessor Hugh Sacker's large filing cabinet, where he had kindly listed practical hints on things that had to be done and those to be avoided, and where, finding his forgotten snacks, which included half a pound of butter with blue hairs six inches long. Or the evening he called round to our house to see how we were getting on and brought in a dead badger, which he had run over on a Wicklow road and was bringing home as food for his dogs, to show Mireia. Unfortunately, the badger was covered in fleas, which promptly found a new home in our sofa.

And then towards the end of the summer vacation of 1977 I received a brief holiday postcard from my colleague Gilbert Carr, saying that they were glad that I had come. It was just a postcard but for me it proved to be a turning point. The regrets about coming back to Ireland began to fall away. I felt accepted and able to look forward to the future. Albert, meanwhile, took up trout-fishing (all his life he had enjoyed sea-fishing) and began the collection of his beautifully tied tiny trout flies. With the same intellectual passion he brought to all his other hobbies – music, art, sailing, the history of science, sea-faring – he now started a serious study of insects, river plants and the geology of trout streams, building up a substantial library and expertise in each and in river-fishing in Ireland. For Mireia the acclimatization, though it took longer, would in the end be total.

# SEVEN

# The 1980s: Changing Ireland

'*The cracks became more visible from the 1980s, and have been widening and deepening ever since.*'[*]

## THE FEMALE ACADEMY

It was only in retrospect that I have come to realize how radically the College has changed during my lifetime in terms of its female membership. What role had women played in its twentieth-century evolution? How did I feel during my years as a female member of staff in this unique Irish institution, with its centuries of often contested history behind it? By the early 1980s life in Trinity was becoming familiar. I had always sought out my friends in the first instance among women. Who was there in the 'female academy' to whom I might look to for friendship? At first there had simply been no time to consider such matters or even look beyond work and family concerns.

---

[*] Gerry O'Hanlon SJ. 'The Catholic Church in Ireland Today'. *The Future of Irish Catholicism. Studies* 106, no. 421 (Spring 2017), 10.

In April 2021 Trinity College broke with its 429-long history in electing the Professor of Engineering and the Arts, Linda Doyle, to be its first female Provost.[*] And yet, despite its proud record of having been the first university in these islands to permit women to graduate, the institution had remained long into the twentieth century, quite simply, 'a man's university'.[†] And although the general culture of the constituent Colleges of the National University of Ireland, founded in 1909, may have been less liberal than that of Trinity, women students of University Colleges Cork, Dublin and Galway, by contrast with their opposite numbers at Trinity in the same period, had enjoyed from the outset equal rights and in theory if not in practice equal opportunities with their male peers. For over half a century following the graduation of their first cohort in 1907, women students at Trinity had been subject to absurd and, not just from a contemporary perspective, pettifogging regulations.[‡] They were, for example, required to be off the premises by 6 pm each evening. Should any of them, having received explicit permission to read in the 1937 Library Reading Room till 10 pm and signed on at Front Gate as required, need to use a toilet, they had to sign out, leave College and seek relief in a nearby café. They might not eat with their fellow male students but were corralled in their own common room in No. 6 College. Nor were they permitted to join the leading College societies, the Hist or the Phil, the training ground, as was UCD's Literary and Historical Society,[§] for public life 'in the hereafter'. Neither women staff nor outstanding women students might be members of the body corporate of Trinity College before 1968; the former, however distinguished internationally, were not eligible for

---

[*] No male candidate had put himself forward for election on 7 April: all three candidates were women.

[†] A freshman student, Rosalind Mills, writing in 1954: see *Trinity* 6 (1954), 19–21.

[‡] Captured with nice irony by Susan Parkes in the title of her centenary history: *A Danger to the Men? A history of women in Trinity College Dublin 1904–2004.*

[§] It is striking how many women graduates – Marian Finucane as one example – who had honed their public-speaking skills in UCD's Lit and Hist subsequently made a name for themselves in Irish broadcasting, and how it took time for Trinity women to follow them.

fellowship. Nor might female students, sitting the examination with their male colleagues, regardless of their scholarly achievement, be elected as Foundation Scholars, though they could be awarded what was known as non-Foundation scholarship. On the day of their election, new scholars were traditionally invited to dine on Commons at the Scholars' Dinner, where they would be joined by former scholars 'of the decade', some going back forty or even fifty years. With the proviso that they were male. For years Anne Crookshank, later founder of Trinity's History of Art and Architecture department, refused to dine on Commons. Elected to Scholarship in 1947, she had suffered the humiliation of being barred from joining her male peers in the Dining Hall.

Constantia Maxwell (1886–1962) had been the first woman lecturer in the university, appointed in 1909 and raised to the prestigious Lecky Professorship of History in 1945, but she was never elected to College fellowship. The real breakthrough only came in 1968 when, after a long battle, two long-standing female members of staff were elected to fellowship, Frances Moran (1893–1977), a towering presence in the Law School since the 1930s, and Jocelyn Otway-Ruthven (1909–1989), Maxwell's successor to the Lecky chair since 1951. Their striking double portrait by Derek Hill now greets College members and their guests from its prominent position on the stairway leading up to the staff Common Room. But of even greater significance for the future was the election in the same year of three young lecturers to fellowship, Barbara Robinson (French), Ita O'Boyle (German) and Catherine MacNamara (Economics). While the last two left the profession on marriage, Barbara (1935–2020), married to Bill Wright, a professor of engineering, went on to have a long and distinguished career in College, *inter alia* as Dean of the Faculty of Arts in the 1980s.

1968 may indeed have been a historic year in the annals of the College, but as evidenced in staff numbers, more particularly at senior level, progress for women, while rather better than in the rest of the Irish university sector, remained painfully slow. When I joined the academic staff in 1975, Otway-Ruthven and I were the only female full professors, and few women held positions of seniority in their department.

Compare that with today: in 2015, 26 per cent of Trinity's chair-holders were women; in 2021 they count for 32 per cent.[*]

I never really got to know 'the Ot'; after my first encounter across the Board Room, I continued to be too much in awe of her formidable presence. Whereas Maxwell was remembered as a somewhat retiring personality and an uninspiring teacher, her lectures allegedly read from a volume of notes with the date of their compilation, 1927, clearly visible to the more alert of her audience, her younger colleague evidently relished the hurly-burly of College life. The Ot's achievements were remarkable, both as a scholar and as a high-profile member of the College community, not least since as a woman academic she lacked the kind of mentoring her successors enjoy today. I never happened to experience that side of her which so many of her former students recall, her personal kindness in times of crisis, nor was I aware of her strategic approach to the betterment of women's position in College.

But that her mannish voice and Oxbridge indifference to dress and personal appearance masked a surprisingly feminine streak was delightfully captured in an incident involving my predecessor. Before he resigned the chair of German, which he had held from 1971–5, to pursue his self-appointed messianic ambitions for humanity, Hugh Sacker, formerly of the University of London and ever shrewd in his eccentricity, had made preparations for an event to mark the 200th anniversary of the founding of the four chairs of modern languages by Provost Hely-Hutchinson in 1776.[†] The celebration was to include a commemorative volume of essays by staff members in *Hermathena: A Dublin University Review*. Sacker illustrated his piece with a cartoon by the Weimar Republic's Hungarian-born artist, Georg Grosz (1893–1959), featuring a besuited bureaucrat perched in evident discomfort on the edge of a sofa beside a large naked woman of mature years.[‡] 'What possessed you,' Hugh told me she had demanded, 'to include THAT

---

* Information from Vice-Provost Jürgen Barkhoff, March 2021.

† As such, the first ever chairs of modern languages in a university.

‡ 'The vision', from Grosz's collection *Ecce Homo* (1923). Reproduced in *Hermathena*. CXXI. Winter 1976, 212.

in your piece?' 'It reminded me of you,' he retorted. 'Was she furious?' I naively asked. 'Quite the contrary, she was delighted.' (The Ot was a lady of ample proportions.) As befits a College character of the first order, anecdotes about her abounded, which she evidently relished. In her later years she was known to enjoy a glass or two of whiskey; when her Cambridge friend and colleague came as external examiner, the two women, having agreed the final results, would allegedly sit down in her College rooms for some serious drinking. By midnight, the bottle having been emptied, the Ot would, in her own account,* set off home to Rathgar in her Morris Minor with its characteristic little arrow in the centre of the bonnet. 'How did you manage to get there safely?' 'I would go out the Nassau Street gate, fix the arrow on the unbroken white line in the middle of Merrion Street and stick on the line till I got home.'

That this 'pillar of the Protestant conservative establishment' could also be mischievous and radical was made evident when she made a public gesture of joining IFUT, the university staff trade union, as a protest against alleged infringements of academic freedom by the Roman Catholic bishops in the constituent college of the National University of Ireland Maynooth. But her finest hour was surely the evening on which she singlehandedly rescued the College's reputation among our political masters. Provost Lee Lyons had conceived the idea of inviting Taoiseach Charles J. Haughey and his cabinet to dine on Commons to try and counter the suspicion, if not downright hostility of official Ireland towards Trinity as a putative 'last outpost of the British Empire'. Knowing of Haughey's interest in and collection of old Irish silver, the Provost had ordered an impressive display of the College's silver to adorn the tables in Dining Hall. Alas, in the frosty temperature of the meeting, this was evidently seen by the visitors as a 'typical Trinity' attempt at social intimidation. When the parties adjourned upstairs to the Common Room after Commons for dessert and fine wines, which had been planned as offering the opportunity for a relaxed exchange of views, Haughey ostentatiously led the entire government party across to the far end of the spacious room, leaving their embarrassed hosts

---

* Or so a former student of hers informed me.

standing awkwardly around. After a tense minute or two the Ot strode across the room and in her customary stentorian tones and impossibly West Brit accent declared: 'Mr Haughey!' Pregnant pause. 'Mr Haughey! I wish to offer you my thanks for what you did for my family.' Puzzled silence. 'Yes,' she went on, 'it was a magnificent act on the part of the Irish government to bring the remains of my mother's cousin Roger Casement back to Ireland where they belong.'*

The Ot took a lively part in College life, well beyond her department and faculty. When she retired in 1981, having been in so many ways a true pioneer, she had no obvious successor. Apart from myself there were simply no women in senior positions in College to take over her mantle or to act as role model for younger colleagues and students. And I, frankly, was at the time unaware of the issue of gender equality – had I had thought about it at all at that time, it would have seemed to me a mere distraction. I was still fully preoccupied with trying get to grips with Trinity's arcane ways and dealing with the more pressing issues in our department. Among the most urgent were student recruitment, how to facilitate our young staff in their research, given the lack of any financial support and the poor publication record of our predecessors, and, as will be familiar to most working mothers to this day, the problem of juggling the day job with conflicting demands on the home front.

It was not until the new Provost W.E. (Bill) Watts, elected in 1981 following the somewhat premature retirement of Lee Lyons, invited me to become University Registrar and join the 'inner cabinet', the six-person College officer group,† that my comfortable mindset began to be challenged

---

\* Salters Sterling, present in his capacity as Academic Secretary of the College, who re-lived the scene for me much later, has described the incident in Parkes (2004), 265f.

† They were the Provost, Vice-Provost Aidan Clarke, Senior Lecturer and sociologist John Jackson, the Bursar, physicist Dan Bradley, the Registrar, College Secretary Gerry Giltrap and the Treasurer, Franz Winkelmann. Giltrap, reminiscent of the all-powerful civil servant in the British TV series *Yes, Minister*, teasingly observed to me that he wrote Board Minutes before the meeting and just had to tweak them thereafter. The tall and bronzed Winkelmann was the son of an immigrant from the Sudetenland, whose German population had been expelled from the restored Czechoslovak Republic in 1945; he liked to provoke the few women members on Board with his pink tie adorned with the letters *m.p.g.*, which he was always only too

and I was forced to witness the mothballing of my planned epitaph from Manchester days: 'She never sat on a committee.' The academic year 1981–2 had barely begun and the new Provost installed in Number 1 College than I found myself not just a member, but the chairman of more than a dozen committees. (I never could take to being called 'a chairperson';* logically, we women should then be referred to as 'wo-persons'.) Over the next four years the tally reached, I think, twenty-five, for Trinity governance was a mix of benign cabinet government and democracy, in this so unlike the hierarchical character of UCD as I had known it. The Provost is elected by all academic staff members, chosen for his scholarly standing (up to 2021 always *his*), enjoying both moral authority and considerable power. He was supported by some four College Officers,† chosen by him from the academic community, and by the College and the Academic Secretaries, both members of the administrative staff. The day-to-day business was then organized through a proliferation of committees, with the assistance of a relatively small administrative staff. In the election to choose a successor to the historian Provost Lee Lyons, I had campaigned vigorously but ineffectively for our friend Charles Holland, internationally renowned geologist and Lancastrian, whose range of informed interests encompassed most of the arts and many of the big questions of life.‡ I was still somewhat naive in terms of university politics, for when a call came to my office that Provost Watts wished to see me, my first reaction was dismay. What can I or the department have been doing to incur censure? His daughter Sheila was our Senior Freshman student at the time, and accordingly I added two and two and got five.

---

ready to decipher: male chauvinist pig. How nicely ironic that his successor, Grace Dempsey, would become Ireland's first female College Treasurer (1997). Incidentally, Winkelmann rendered Trinity staff incomparable service when he moved the entire pension fund in the 1980s, first into yen and then into D-mark – a risky enterprise, but which resulted in his doubling the fund.

\* As in: 'the chair addressed the floor, which in turn challenged the platform'. I see it not in gender but in Orwellian terms as part of modern de-humanization of language.

† Vice-Provost, Senior Lecturer (head of academic staff), Bursar and Registrar.

‡ When he died at ninety-six in December 2019 Charles, who enjoyed parading his atheism, was engaged in two research projects: 'What is beauty?' and 'Why are we here?'

But Trinity never ceases to surprise, and I emerged from my first visit to a Provost's office as a thoroughly dazed candidate for Registrarship, as the first woman, I subsequently learnt, to hold this office in Ireland or Great Britain. I was to combine this post with the deanship for foreign students, which I had held since 1979 in succession to Dermot McAleese, who after only a year in this newly created post, had been appointed to the Whately Chair of Political Economy. The Chancellor and her or his deputies the Pro-Chancellors are, as is the Registrar or Keeper of Records, University rather than College Officers. As the responsible officer for the University's records and therefore for the conduct of Commencements,* the Registrar chaired the coordinating committees regulating the University's external links, at that time with several institutions whose degrees Trinity validated. Otherwise, the job in 1981 was ill-defined. But this paradoxically conferred a certain freedom, as so often in Trinity, of allowing you to explore the terrain and find your own way. The two most important things I learnt from my five years as a College/University Officer were that things look very different when you carry responsibility for them, and that, for me, Trinity's salient character as I experienced it throughout my career, was trust. Apart from making it very clear at my original interview for the German chair in 1975 that in Trinity, students 'come first', nobody ever told me what any new post of responsibility entailed. But here too, I felt trusted and therefore able to cope. I enjoyed preparations for Commencements particularly, though having to sign up to one thousand degree certificates by hand in ink in a week for the winter and summer Commencements while we were still in teaching term was arduous. But it was an important part of Trinity's tradition of giving personal service.

An illuminating feature of the job as providing novel insights into Irish life I found to be the chairmanship of the coordinating committees with our partner institutions, the Church of Ireland College of Theology and the School of Ecumenics, the three Colleges of Education and member colleges of the Dublin Institute of Technology (now

---

* The Trinity term for graduation conferring, so termed in the sense that the bachelor's degree constitutes, not the end, but the start of the educated person's life.

Technological University of Dublin). The first proved one of the most agreeable. I had scant acquaintance with bishops of my own church. As a member of the laity and as a woman, I felt and probably was regarded as being of lesser account. My first meeting with the representatives of the governing body of the Church of Ireland College of Education, which included the two archbishops (of Armagh and Dublin) and the bishop of Meath, Donald Caird, later archbishop of Dublin, was a revelation. That they were courteous was to be expected, but the tone of the meeting and all subsequent ones, though business-like, was relaxed and constructive throughout, even when problematical situations arose, as they inevitably did. A thorny issue proved to be the complaint by somewhat fundamentalist-minded students for the ministry from Northern Ireland that they were unhappy being taught part of their theology by a Roman Catholic, the internationally distinguished Werner Jeanrond.

It is worth interrupting the narrative at this point to recall, as an example of the parochial attitudes of that time, just how distinguished their lecturer was. Jeanrond, though a native of the German Federal state of the Saarland, had just been recommended for appointment to the chair of theology at Strasbourg University aged only in his mid-thirties, all interview proceedings having been conducted in French. As required by their Concordat, the French authorities had to seek approval from the Vatican for the appointment – which was refused by the then Prefect of the Society for the Propagation of the Faith, Joseph Ratzinger.* Was it perhaps because Jeanrond's Swedish wife was the daughter of a Lutheran pastor? We shall never know, but I recall phoning my friend Wolfgang Frühwald, Professor of German at Munich and adviser on matters aesthetic to the German Catholic Bishops Conference, to share my distress. 'How can one continue to be a member of a church which does such things?' For the Jeanronds were people of deep faith. 'Eda,' Wolfgang replied, 'we remain members not *because* of but *in spite* of.' Werner Jeanrond went on to be the first Catholic professor of theology in Sweden since the Reformation (at the University of Lund), later the first lay head of Oxford's Benet Hall, moving from there to the chair of theology at Aberdeen.

* Later Pope Benedict XVI (2005–13).

To return to our 'problem'. It didn't particularly help to assuage those theology students' suspicions of Trinity that the dean of their faculty was the ex-Muslim former South African free-thinker Kader Asmal. After one meeting on the matter the shrewd and ever practical Academic Secretary Salters Sterling advised – he was the one member of the senior administrative staff who always marked my card for me – 'Eda, you will have to have a party in your house. When people sit around the table eating together, it's amazing how much common ground they find.' And so, with the assistance of my mother and my cousin Geraldine O'Brien who had worked for Aer Lingus for years as an air hostess and was now in charge of training in the organization, we put on a good supper, to some effect. Towards the end of the evening my mother asked the Archbishop of Armagh if she might invite his chauffeur in for supper before their long trip back to Armagh. 'He has had his supper,' was the amused reply. 'How so?' 'I am "his" chauffeur.' My mother couldn't believe her ears and, forgetting her usual tact, blurted out, 'Catch our boys driving themselves!' Salters was invaluable in smoothing out the many and often seemingly unending difficulties in our relationship with the three Colleges of Education whose BEd degrees Trinity validated: The Church of Ireland College of Education, the Christian Brothers College at Marino, and the Dominican Sion Hill. Not on the colleges' count, for they had long years of experience in teacher-training. The problem was on our side with some senior members of staff of our own Department of Education. I'm afraid in common with both my predecessors and successors in the job, I had little success in their resolution. Many years later, two of the three colleges would take the decision to break the link with Trinity, one to move to Dublin City University at their St Patrick's campus, one to Maynooth University.

Unlike my new colleagues, I was unused to power. Furthermore, the Registrar's brief, apart from having charge of record-keeping on behalf of the University and thus responsibility for Commencements, and of College's links with other third-level institutions, was still evolving. As Registrar chairing numerous College committees, it didn't take me long to realize that in virtually all of them I was the sole female member.

My proposal at one of our regular Friday Officers' meetings, to do a systematic trawl of the various committees with a view to identifying women staff qualified and prepared to serve, met with strong support. And yet it proved difficult to effect, given the still insignificant numbers of women staff and the sense shared by most that their departmental and domestic responsibilities and generally relatively junior status made them reluctant to put their names forward. But it was a start, and I got to know many of my female colleagues including in the other male-dominated faculties of College such as medicine and engineering What I wasn't aware of at the time, though I was friendly with her stepmother the French professor Barbara Wright, was the historic 'first' for College in the person of Jane Wright. The first female graduate in the School of Engineering in 1970, she joined the Department of Computer Science in 1980, and would go on to become a powerful role model for women in science in Ireland. Jane Grimson *née* Wright was the first woman to hold, among other leadership roles, the offices of Dean of Engineering, Pro-Dean of Research, and in 2001 to be the first woman in the College's history to hold the office of Vice-Provost, which she did until 2005.

Following my report to officers on the committee initiative, Bill Watts, a sound feminist like many fathers of (a) clever daughter(s), set up a special commission on the status of women in College and appointed one of the Department of Economics' most able young members, Frances Ruane,[*] to chair it. Her report, *The Position of Women Academics in College*, presented to Board in 1989, deserves to be remembered as a milestone in helping create a new mindset in those responsible for promotions within the College and elections to fellowship. The report raised consciousness in a measured way, based on the survey undertaken by the committee and good analysis of data in TCD and elsewhere. As Frances Ruane commented to me in retrospect:

> You may recall that we went beyond our remit in advising on how academic positions should be filled and this was not welcomed by some at the Board.

---

[*] Professor Ruane was the first woman Bursar in Trinity's history and, following a distinguished career, was appointed the first female director of the Economic and Social Research Institute.

We set out what would be 'good practice', such as a gender representation on recruitment committees and that a seminar should form part of the recruitment process.

Her committee members were told subsequently by the senior lecturer that 'this was not our business' and they were asked to remove the section from the final report. 'Yet the suggestions proposed became the norm almost immediately – they were too hard to argue against.'[*] What struck her at the time, she said, were the hidden biases against women in areas where they were under-represented. So even after Trinity got gender balance into appointments boards, there were no standards for less formal appointments – e.g. postdocs – and on average women were much less likely to get these positions than men. This made it harder for them to get on the academic ladders especially in STEM areas (science, technology, engineering, medicine). This did not come about until funding standards in the EU and in the Irish Research bodies[†] at the end of the twentieth century allowed women and men apply with equal chances for postdoctoral awards and PhD scholarships.

As Registrar I was a member of the Senior Promotions Committee, which made recommendations to Council and Board for career advancement to senior lecturer and associate professor across College. My own experience in the 1980s and early 90s was of an operation at pains to be fair and transparent. However, there were problems, principally in its dependence on the attitude of the individual head of the department, who in those still hierarchical days was almost inevitably the professor. Or the problem could be simply lack of familiarity with a candidate's discipline on the part of the head of department, or indeed of the Senior Promotions Committee collectively.[‡] This was made evident on one occasion in the case of Anne Crookshank: I brought her name up

---

[*] In our email exchange of 7 April 2021. See also Frances Ruane and Elma Dobson: Academic Salary Differentials – Some Evidence from an Irish Survey. *ESRI Review*, vol. 21, no. 2 (January 1990), 209–26.

[†] See below, Chapter 9.

[‡] An issue which, as I learnt during my association with the German Research Council, was recognized as particularly problematical by the major German research organizations, and duly dealt with.

for consideration at the Committee, only to be dismissed initially by the argument from science and engineering colleagues: 'But look at her list of publications. She seems to have published very little apart from exhibition catalogues.'* It was not difficult to counter that the preparation of major exhibition catalogues was precisely what art historians did and should be doing. Similarly, when I mentioned the name of Helga Hammerstein-Robinson, it appeared that, as neither the relevant dean and nor the departmental head knew the language,† her earlier research which had appeared in prestigious German publications had not been taken into consideration. Following her promotion to senior lecturer, a necessary qualification for College office, Helga became a truly innovative Dean of Graduate Studies. Her appointment came at a critical moment for College's functioning and public reputation, given the rapidly increasing numbers of graduate students from Ireland and further afield, and of the then relatively novel propensity for students disappointed with the outcome of their studies to seek litigation in the public courts. In her period of office Dr Hammerstein brought about the standardization of graduate study at Trinity, from application to admission, the selection, training and monitoring of supervisors, appointment of external examiners and oversight of the examination process across College.

But 'promotion stakes' were not necessarily always a gender issue. I remember trawling through the College Calendars looking for possible candidates for promotion who might have been bypassed and noting that Terence Browne, whose publications in Anglo-Irish studies had won him an international reputation, was still just a lecturer. The English department in the early 1980s, while it may have had some high-profile and popular lecturers such as the poet Brendan Kennelly and the later Senator David Norris, whose perorations on James Joyce's *Ulysses* attracted record numbers, had for some time been in the doldrums and

---

* Her major book publications came later.

† Which may have been a further problem, since at the time virtually all external examiners and referees for candidates for promotion to senior positions at Trinity came from Britain, who may not always have been proficient in the relevant foreign language.

lacked any kind of serious leadership.* The bottom line was that in the paternalist culture still obtaining in universities at the time, including Trinity, women were more likely to be overlooked than men.

Prominent in Trinity's female academy were my contemporaries in the modern language departments. Barbara Wright, who held undergraduate degrees in music and law as well as French and Irish from Trinity, was described by my colleague in German, the then undergraduate Tim Jackson, as 'a breath of fresh air' in the somewhat staid French department when she joined the Trinity staff in 1966.† She had come from Manchester University following her Cambridge PhD and remained active well after her retirement in 2000. Barbara had an impressive family pedigree: her suffragette grandmother had served time before the First World War in Portlaoise prison with three of her colleagues for their public activities. Exceptionally, she was promoted to a personal chair in French at a very early stage of her career in 1978. Some academically distinguished women only won appropriate College recognition at a relatively late stage in their careers, if at all. Common to many of them was the fact that they were members of small departments for which they had assumed responsibility (or had it thrust on them) shortly after their recruitment as young scholars. The international Dante expert, Corinna Lonergan, current Fellow Emerita, is was one of College's icons, her elegant figure instantly recognizable in the interplay of lilacs, purples and mauves of her dress and jewellery,‡ as she makes her way several times a day between Front Square between the Common Room and her office, where so much of her life has been spent. Corinna's

---

* I remember getting into conversation one Monday in the 1980s with the middle-aged man standing next to me who told me he had been a student under the recently retired chairholder in English. The professor had ticked him off publicly as a Junior Freshman for not taking notes at his lecture. 'But I told him, very politely, that I didn't need to: I had my father's lecture notes.'

† A decade later, a graduate and staff member for some years, the Huguenot scholar Ruth Whelan reluctantly resigned from the College to move to the chair of French at Maynooth, a motive force, according to her own account in Parkes (2004, 286) being that 'the French department had changed little since I was a student'.

‡ Her wonderful sense of colour is finely captured in her portrait by Carey Clarke in the Common Room.

friendship with the former Professor of Modern History, Gordon Davies – not to be confused with the equally high-profile College personality of that time, the geographer Gordon Herries Davies – seemed somewhat surprising to their circle of friends, given Gordon's penchant for provoking Corinna's devout Catholicism by his eighteenth-century style atheism. Both Gordon's appearance and splendid irony belonged to the Age of Enlightenment, which provided the context of his massive scholarly contribution to the history of the American Revolution. Tall and lean, his long white hair emphasizing rather than concealing a high-domed bald pate, his long nose seemed to lead the way as he stalked across Front Square. He certainly made his students sit up: 'The semi-colon,' he liked to remind them, 'is not, despite what you think, a last residue of British imperial oppression of the Irish. Use it!' When in the 1970s American ambassador Bill (William V.) Shannon invited him to a reception in his honour in the lovely American embassy in the former Vice-Regal Lodge in the Phoenix Park to mark the 200th anniversary of the Revolution and the publication of the twenty-first and last volume of his edition of the *Documents of the American Revolution*, Gordon ensured that his departmental colleagues, plus all his other TCD friends, were included in the invitation. I had never set foot inside the embassy and was standing admiring the house's splendid restoration, which is still a monument to Elizabeth Shannon's tenure in Ireland. Beside me, Gordon was deep in conversation with the ambassadress and his colleague and Trinity character R.B. McDowell, who was leaning against a gleaming pale-yellow pilaster. Then, to our huge embarrassment, McDowell, never a man to lay too much store on his personal appearance, moved to talk to another group, leaving the black imprint of his hand on the once-pristine surface. Like all his friends in College, I greatly enjoyed Gordon Davies's company and wit – who wouldn't? – despite his pointedly disparaging remarks to me about Germany, German history, and culture and Germans generally. It transpired, as he later told me, that on his 1945 release from a particularly unpleasant and lengthy sojourn in a German prisoner-of-war camp, he weighed just over four and a half stone (c. 27 kilos). No doubt Corinna enjoyed Gordon's teasing as much as he did.

*Kevin O'Shiel and Cecil Smiddy on their wedding day with Cecil's father, Professor Smiddy, on the left, 1929.*

*Eda (left) and Clodagh at Loreto Convent Foxrock, 1942.*

*The first pupils of Loreto Convent Foxrock, 1941. Clodagh (second row, first from left), Eda (second row, third from left) and Eda's friend Maryanne MacDonald (second row, fifth from left).*

*Farnborough Hill first hockey team, 1951. Eda is back row, third from right.*

*Eda in Manchester, 1959.*

*Albert and Eda on their wedding day,*
*4 April 1961.*

*'Monsignor' Alfred O'Rahilly:*
*always in the centre of things.*

*The writer W.E. (Max) Sebald, on the right,
at a soirée at Manchester University with
Eda and Albert, 1967.*

*Max Sebald's postcard to Eda,
sent from Vienna in August 1967.*

*Provost Lyons, on Eda's left, receives German Embassy book donations, 1977.
The German cultural attaché inspects the stock.*

*Chancellor Helmut Kohl visits Trinity, 1996.*

*The UCD German class of 1951–4 at home in Rathgar, 1980: (left to right) Mella Carroll; Madeleine Margey, Lelia Doolan, Eda, Katie Kahn-Karl and, partly hidden, Maryanne MacDonald.*

*Golf practice, 1966.*

*We reach our destination: Santiago de Compostela, 2016. On Eda's left is Aidan Redmond, his wife May (†January 2020) and their brother-in-law Kieran O'Mahony OSA.*

*Trinity runs the Women's Mini Marathon, Dublin, 2017*
*(Eda comes 11,993rd out of 12,000).*

*Mireia, 2019.*

*Trinity's first female College officer in 1981 becomes a pro-chancellor in 2000.*

She must equally have enjoyed her revenge in 1986 on the occasion of the filling of the Erasmus Smith Chair of History – Gordon had retired somewhat prematurely in 1985, allegedly, as he assured me, because of Trinity's proven inability to provide him with a competent secretary. There was consensus around College and in the wider community of Irish historians that far and away the outstanding candidate to succeed him was Aidan Clarke. We assumed the appointment would be something of a foregone conclusion.[*] I was a member of the selection committee, which had been unanimous in their recommendation of Aidan Clarke. Alas, on the day of the interviews, things did not go according to plan. The first and only female candidate to be called was a former pupil of the UCD medieval historian F.X. Martin and now a lecturer at the university of Innsbruck, where her husband was professor. Picking her way along the narrow space behind the serried ranks of the Senior Fellows to her seat in the Board Room beside the externs, she was clearly enjoying the impression made on her audience by her statuesque figure, Titian-red mane of hair, expensively dark blue tailored suit and ostentatious (but genuine) jewellery. Even I, seated at the other side of the table, was not immune to the waves of her pungent scent. The next candidate, a lecturer in Bulgarian history, left no impression, at least on me. When the final and much-looked-forward-to candidate appeared, he looked wretched – he was apparently suffering from the excruciating pain of a severe middle-ear infection.[†] The first part went as well as could be expected in the circumstances – but when Keith Thomas, the Oxford extern, began probing questions on European history, a field of research then poorly represented among Irish university historians, Aidan Clarke, evidently struggling with pain, asked to pass: he was clearly completely exhausted. That evening we were horrified to learn that the Chair of Modern History had been offered to the Bulgarian historian and that he had accepted. 'I rang Corinna,' Gordon Davies told me, 'and asked her to

---

[*] Never underestimate the eccentricity of the Trinity Council and Board in the matter of appointments, as Richard Hanson had once advised me.

[†] I had suffered from it once as a graduate student: no pain I have ever endured in my life could equal it.

spend the night in prayer.' Which she allegedly did. At precisely 10.30 am next morning, the College Secretary received a phone call from the successful candidate: for a variety of reasons, he had decided to turn the offer down. Aidan Clarke had been recommended for appointment and duly accepted. 'The ways of the Almighty ...' Whatever way one wanted to look at it, we, not least Gordon Davies, agreed that we certainly owed something to Corinna's intercession.

And yet despite her being such a popular figure round College, it took too many years before Corinna Lonergan achieved the official recognition in the form of promotion to Associate Professorship (1997), which her erudition, ranging across medieval and early modern Italian literature, philosophy, art, theology and cosmology, so clearly merited. The problem, in hindsight, was systemic, typical of small departments common in the modern languages area as then constituted, which were headed by young and inexperienced scholars. Corinna Salvadori had joined the Trinity staff in 1961, aged only twenty-one, following her acclaimed MA (NUI): *Yeats and Castiglione, Poet and Courtier*. In her mid-twenties she found herself head of department, in those days virtually a permanent post, remaining there for some forty years. Such a system is no longer possible, and it was indeed unfair to young scholars to give them the burden of administrative responsibility before they had the chance to develop their scholarly profile, especially in a department whose size made sabbatical leave effectively impossible. It takes time to produce the body of published work necessary to attain the level of seniority which allows one to compete with colleagues in larger units, who have enjoyed the advantage of mentoring by their seniors, minimal administrative duties and regular sabbatical research leave, a situation naturally compounded for married women with children.

The situation was at least in one specific sense not dissimilar for Winifred McBride (Mrs Greenwood) in the Russian department (now Russian and Slavonic Studies). She had joined the staff (of the smallest department in the faculty) in the mid-1960s not long after her graduation, to find herself shortly after in sole charge of the only Russian department in Ireland, where she remained as head until her retirement some four decades later. A former scholarship pupil from Glasgow, proud of the strong work ethic and stoicism of her working-class noncon-formist background, and who had earned high honours at university, her academic career must have seemed at the time most promising. A careful and overly self-critical scholar and teacher, who had had none of the kind of mentoring colleagues in larger units might hope to enjoy, Winifred, now Mrs Greenwood, never succeeded in completing a research degree. This had the effect of making her possessive of her area,* but also to becoming defensive towards her more ambitious and better-qualified male colleagues, both in the department and faculty. She made some excellent appointments, notably the historian Patrick O'Meara and later Senior Lecturer, who returned to Britain in 2004, and Sarah Smyth, from 2004 Associate Professor and head of her department, who has been one of our outstanding faculty colleagues. Sarah Smyth's command of her discipline includes internationally acclaimed expertise in several discrete areas: narratology in Russian literature, Dostoevsky studies, Russian sacred icons, linguistics and language-teaching methodology and prac-tice. She holds an honorary doctorate from the Gorky Literary Institute, University of Moscow and is, to the best of my knowledge, the only Irish recipient to have been awarded the prestigious Pushkin prize (2010) by the Russian government. She has combined College and Faculty offices with extensive outreach activities in the Russian-speaking community in Ireland, and as part of her advisory work with government departments.

During our time as faculty colleagues, the relationship between Winifred Greenwood and myself could only be described as one of mutual irritation. An early source, not of conflict – we were too polite for that – but of tension was our shared secretary. I, being a Germanic 'lark' and at my desk by 7.30 am, was impatient to get as many of the main administrative jobs as I could out of the way early in the day, but our secretary, officially due in at 9.10 am (till 5 pm), regularly pleaded that Mrs Greenwood (an 'owl') had kept her long after six the

---

* The Public Orator and professor of Latin, John Luce, whom I once consulted about her chances of promotion, accurately observed: 'Winifred's trouble is her complete focus on her department; she doesn't get involved in College life.'

previous evening. I found myself disagreeing with Winifred over almost everything at faculty meetings. But in the strange way things can happen in life, she ended up, after her retirement, not just a good friend, but somebody I learnt greatly to admire and appreciate. Not long after she retired, Winifred, who was living on the eleventh floor of the high-rise apartment block in Pembroke Park, lost both her husband, whom she had met and married late in life, and her health. I only heard of her situation by accident from Vanessa Wyse-Jackson, Methodist minister and the daughter of a former lecturer in Irish, May Risk, who had known Winifred through their church. When I suggested going to see her, I was told that Winifred had indicated that she wished to be left in peace and would probably not wish for a visit. How right she was! I knew it could not be good for a retired colleague living on their own to be alone all day, so eventually I persuaded Winifred to let me drop in with a bunch of sweet peas from my garden. The visit was repeated, until eventually I would spend an hour with her each Saturday afternoon right up until just days before she died in 2006. The situation had been complicated by her memory of my earlier lack of collegiality and by her extreme sensitivity to any appearance of pity for her current isolated state. And something else took me by surprise, although it was some months before she referred to it. 'How pitiable I am,' she burst out one week, 'how pathetic, that the only person who comes to see me now is … a Roman Catholic.' I didn't see myself as having anything much in common with the whore of Babylon, but the particular brand of sectarianism she had been nurtured in from her youth, had clearly left its mark: the Roman Catholic Church for her was the enemy of human freedom and progress, even though her own religious affiliation had long been tempered by enlightened Marxism. On another Saturday she greeted me with a long face: she hadn't slept a wink all night, having watched a BBC documentary on the Spanish Inquisition, which profoundly challenged, she declared, the whole raison d'être of her lifelong crusade against 'popery'. She was clearly distressed, but I managed to persuade her that, while I saw her antipathy to Romanism in terms of what the political scientist and philosophy Isaiah Berlin so aptly liked to call 'a point of view',* we were quite at one in our abhorrence at the role played over the centuries by the Inquisition – epitomized for me in Heinrich Heine's terrible verse about 'their Spanish Majesties', Isabella of Castile and Ferdinand of Aragon, 'savouring from their balconies the scent of old Jews roasting' in the auto-da-fé below.†

Winifred Greenwood deserves to be remembered in Trinity for her role in developing Russian Studies in Ireland, but more especially as a woman who showed extraordinary fortitude when life robbed her of virtually everything she valued. She coped alone and uncomplainingly with a debilitating illness for many years, but towards the end, told me she would no longer mind if I let colleagues know of her situation. I mentioned it to a few people, and in the very last weeks of her life, she was literally inundated by visits from the Trinity colleagues who had wished to visit but feared to intrude. The last time I saw her, the week before she died, her mind as clear as ever, she said to me: 'I haven't been so happy for years.'

Trinity College's celebrated library was perhaps the one area of College‡ where female staff were numerous, librarianship still being seen in Ireland as in Britain at that time as 'a suitable career for women', especially those 'of a retiring personality'. Hardly any in 1981 were represented in middle management, the most prominent being Margot Chubb, whose husband Basil was Professor of Political Science and a man of high profile in Irish public life. Margot and I had been in a position, as we subsequently agreed among ourselves, to give signal service to College, when, as members of the five-person appointments committee for the post of Deputy Librarian in 1979 we managed, after a long argument, to overrule the majority and recommend for appointment the candidate we both felt to be far and away the most able, despite their (and our) concerns at his youth (he was only twenty-nine), relative lack of

---

* That is, a philosophy of life or an opinion, with which he did not agree.

† *'Wo sie auf Balkonen sitzend / Sich erquickten am Geruche / Von gebrat'nen alten Juden'* (*Hebrew Melodies*, 1851). I had formed my image of the Inquisition very largely from Schiller's portrait of the crusading Archbishop Torquemada of Toledo in his drama *Don Carlos*.

‡ Apart from the support staff.

experience and what seemed to be an unsettling youthful brashness of manner in interview. Peter Fox went on to become an outstanding Trinity Librarian and College Archivist, and in due course Librarian of the University of Cambridge and Curator of the Bodleian Libraries at Oxford. Following his appointment as Trinity's Librarian, his deputy post was advertised and attracted an excellent field. I was by then well ensconced in my twelve-year stint as chairman of the Library Committee (it can sometimes be more difficult in Trinity to get off a committee than on). Every candidate was asked the same questions but only one candidate from the north of Ireland, whom none of us knew, impressed us not just by her excellent professional qualifications but by the sheer realism of her response to: 'What would be the very first thing you would do, if you were given five minutes' notice that the students were going to occupy the Lecky Library?'* Lisa Duffin didn't hesitate: 'Secure the loos.'

The Deputy Librarian's brief at the time was very much about keeping the library functioning smoothly. This involved liaising with staff across a wide variety of areas in College. Some of these were not particularly impressed by academics, probably the more so if they were female, as I had soon found out when I vainly tried to persuade the Buildings Office over many months to supply my office with urgently needed bookshelves. It was only when I joined the Dublin University Staff Golf Society and played regularly with Buildings staff that any difficulty I might have had would be solved overnight. The morning after my very first game with one of their members and the sociable meal which followed,† a carpenter appeared in my office. 'And where are the new shelves to go?' I advised Lisa to join, and with her incomparable tact, sense of humour and firm style she soon had everyone she needed literally eating out of her hand. As we were the only female members of the Society, and among the very few academics, one of us invariably won the ladies' prize until we both decided we were well able to compete with

---

* Occupation of key College buildings by members of the Students Union was much in vogue in the late 1970s and 80s.

† Everyone was on first-name terms on these occasions, and although we academics would have been quite happy to continue that way, our new partners considered that to be 'most inappropriate'.

the men and the ladies' section of the DUSGS was accordingly abolished.

In other areas of College, gender equality may have been slower in coming, yet as Trinity's administrative structures were modernized and became more complex, many of the key administrators facilitating the process were female. Some of these had originally been recruited as secretarial staff and went on to develop unrivalled competence in their various fields of responsibility. This was strikingly evident by the end of the century. Then with the large-scale 'restructuring' of the university between 2005 and 2010, new senior management positions were created and those appointed were fairly evenly divided between women and men, some of them recruited from the corporate sector outside the university, some home grown. Meanwhile, not to forget the College 'character' who represented another 'first' for Trinity women: in the 1990s Trinity appointed its first female security guard or 'porter' to use the old term, Maureen Coote.[*] Maureen was quite fearless. One night before the Trinity Ball she told me she had heard suspicious sounds up on the fourth floor: 'I got hold of a chair and burst into the room, chair legs first. I can tell you we both got a bit of a shock when I found I had impaled the intruder: a student trying to break into the cupboard to steal a couple of tickets for the Ball. Better be safe than sorry. He was sorry!'

Looking back across the last forty years, I have the sense that, while there was a good deal of talk in parts of the Irish university system in the early 1980s of the inequitable situation of women academic staff, scantily represented at any level of seniority and barely any of them chair-holders – particularly evident in the statistics of the constituent Colleges of the National University of Ireland – this did not translate itself into action. Political appointments over the following decade will have played some role in promoting a gradual change in cultural awareness, notably that of the first two female Ministers of Education in the history of the Irish state – Gemma Hussey (1982–6) and Mary O'Rourke (1987–91) – and more particularly the election of Dublin University's later Chancellor Mary Robinson to Head of State in 1990. Increasing participation by Irish women in higher education and the professions was a further factor

---

* Parkes (2004) includes Maureen's photo (number 49 of her collection).

but it was not really until the new century that cultural change was reflected in appointments statistics. In 2006 an equality unit was set up at Trinity, headed by a designated Equality Officer; in 2020 the Equality, Diversity and Inclusion Unit was established with a much wider remit, currently led by Claire Marshall.*

A further opportunity to become familiar with a key part of Ireland's higher education system came with my appointment towards the end of the 1980s to what was then known as the National Council for Educational Awards (NCEA).† I had hardly been a week or so in my new job as Registrar when Salters informed me that we were going to Athlone for the annual delegates conference of the Institutes of Technology. We went but I found the endless sessions and the rubber-stamping of item after item unbelievably dreary and the whole thing seemingly useless. Salters, however, reminded me: 'It's a public relations exercise, but an important one.' And how right he was. It is perhaps difficult to appreciate how deeply rooted public prejudice still was in the 1980s against Trinity as 'this elitist, Protestant outpost of the British Empire'. I recall one of our then students, son of an army officer, telling us of how on a summer job in Germany he had been quizzed by his fellow workers from the other Irish universities and colleges to the effect that 'with your [Irish] accent, you can't possibly be a Trinity student. They wouldn't have you.' I had already had a foretaste of such received notions when I came to attend my first meeting as TCD representative on the NCEA Board,

---

* In the last two decades progress in the College has not needed to have recourse to the kind of 'positive discrimination' that able women generally abhor. In open competition across College for positions of seniority in 2006, 33 per cent of internal promotions to professorship went to women academics; in 2018 the figure was an impressive 38 per cent. Even more significant is the percentage of women who have been appointed to chairs following international competition and a rigorous process of externally monitored interview. In 2006 it was 12 per cent: in 2018 the figure was 28 per cent, and includes disciplines in traditional 'male' preserves, such as engineering and the medical sciences.

† The NCEA oversaw and validated courses in the dozen or more regional technical colleges (since the 1979 Education Act re-designated Institutes of Technology) in Athlone, Carlow, Cork, Dundalk, Galway-Mayo, Dún Laoghaire (Institute of Art, Design and Technology) Letterkenny, Limerick, Sligo, Tallaght, Tralee, Waterford and later Blanchardstown.

which was to be held in the Bolton Street College. I arrived, as always, too early to find two gentlemen, the College's director, and a director of one of the other institutes, deep in conversation. As I approached them to introduce myself, they immediately switched into Irish, as though a Trinity person couldn't possibly know the first national language.

The governance of the NCEA with its headquarters in one of the beautiful Georgian houses of the now dilapidated Mountjoy Square was a thoroughly macho affair, notably under the lengthy term of office of its director, Padraig (Paddy) MacDiarmada. It took many years, in fact well into the new century before one of the institutes got its first female director. I found the contrast in style uncomfortably different from Trinity practice, as in the somewhat condescending way the very efficient in-house administrative staff were treated, among them Attracta Halpin, who now serves with distinction as Registrar of the National University of Ireland. On one occasion Paddy insisted on moving the meeting to finish discussion over lunch to a local pub on Upper Gardiner Street. Here he departed off with all the male members of the Board into the gentlemen-only snug, leaving Attracta, another woman member of the staff and myself to eat our sandwiches in purdah. It was only when the doughty and sure-footed Mary Upton, later Irish Labour Party TD for Dublin South-Central (1999–2011), joined the Board that things began to change and the macho culture to be undermined from within.

The Institutes of Technology were highly politicized and, while the influence of certain powerful personalities could and did affect the culture of the organization, at times adversely, their socio-economic impact on Ireland of the regions is hard to overrate. I must have worked with and for each one of the then twelve, later thirteen colleges for over a quarter of a century. I sat on boards of studies, sometimes as chairman, we conducted institutional reviews, considered applications for the delegation to an individual institute of degree-awarding powers across the disciplinary spectrum, from science and engineering, economics and business to archaeology, modern languages, hospitality and tourism and even on one occasion complementary medicine. Eventually, as the institutes developed and new demands made on them, we were asked to make recommendations on the delegation of degree-awarding powers up to masters and doctoral level. While some were referred for further development, almost all were ultimately successful. At one stage I had the pleasure of being part of a Department of Education advisory group under the chairmanship of Professor Dervilla Donnelly, professor of chemistry at UCD, to consider broader policy issues. During our visit to the second of two leading institutions, the Waterford and Cork Institutes of Technology, I had the opportunity, not for the first time, to witness at first-hand just how knowledgeable some of the Department of Education's Chief Inspectors were. The Cork staff had finished their presentations and withdrawn, and its director was making his few final remarks before we began to consider our report. He concluded with a quotation from Shakespeare's *The Tempest*, which expressed optimism on the outcome. No sooner had he left the room than our team member, the recently retired Chief Inspector for the primary sector, smiled and proceeded to finish the quotation, all twenty-two lines, by heart, offering a delicately nuanced reading of what we had just heard.

What I took from my many years of involvement in the work of the Irish Institutes of Technology was threefold. Firstly, as with the Irish education system more generally, for all their problems there was and is a dynamic informing the institutes and their staff despite the often very restrictive conditions under which they operate. Their social impact across Ireland has been considerable, making third-level education accessible to whole sectors of society. And finally, they have made and continue to make an immense contribution to the development of a modern industrial base in the regions of Ireland. With the assistance of the Industrial Development Authority (IDA) new industries are attracted to the locality, which then work in partnership with the local institute, recruiting staff from its graduates and benefitting from the College's readiness to provide specially tailored short courses to meet the requirements of modern industry and commerce. What strikes me after my years across the water and what seems to me to distinguish the Ireland of today together with Scotland from England is this deeply held and dynamic belief in the value of education.

# — EIGHT —

# *German studies at Trinity and beyond*

From my first term teaching in October 1975, I had been impressed by the Trinity German department's Oxbridge-type tutorial system with each student in the department being assigned to a staff member for weekly essays. This had been a principal feature of the thoroughly radical shake-up of the old-fashioned curriculum, which my predecessor Hugh Sacker had introduced in 1971, together with modern teaching methodology at which my new colleagues in 1975, David Little, Gilbert Carr, Tim Jackson and Amanda McVittie excelled, and the students so evidently enjoyed. But the financial and educational constrictions within which we had to operate were onerous* and inhibited innovation: Irish inflation at 20.4 per cent in 1981, crippling for individuals and particularly for younger workers, meant that our small department budget effectively shrank every year. There had been no research funding in Ireland for the humanities other than the Irish language and Irish archaeology since the founding of the state in 1922. Conference travel

---

* Albert's former department of chemical engineering at the Manchester Institute of Science and Technology had in 1975 an annual budget four times that of Trinity's entire Faculty of Science budget.

had somehow to be found from running costs. Sabbaticals did not exist. German was taught at relatively few schools in the Republic, and the impact of the Troubles in Northern Ireland had led students (and their parents and teachers) of those many schools who traditionally favoured Trinity for their modern languages pupils to look instead to English and more particularly Scottish universities. Our recruitment pool was thus not only restricted but in order to fill our prescribed annual quota, we found ourselves with 'a tail' of poorly prepared and ill-motivated students, some of whom had signed up for our course merely because 'it was easy to get into German'.

Since the Federal Republic of Germany, unlike Ireland, was increasingly prosperous, despite the oil crises of 1973 and 1979, and was now experiencing labour shortages, I approached the Department of Education to see if we could increase the numbers learning German at secondary level. They were not interested, those I spoke to giving the impression, rightly or wrongly, of being resentful of the university in general and especially of Trinity as 'elitist'. The tradition of some Irish civil service departments, notably Education, in contrast with Finance or External Affairs, of recruiting their administrative intake at ages seventeen or eighteen, who then worked their way up the hierarchical ladder meant that not many of their officials at the time had had personal experience of university life. The 1980s depression in Ireland was particularly severe for graduates: in 1987 unemployment rose to 17 per cent. Even today, historians, economists and sociologists speak of 'the lost decade of the 1980s'. For the universities it meant an almost ten-year ban on recruitment of young staff, the lifeblood of a university, while emigration brought the loss of half a generation.

We had been fortunate just before the embargo to have been able to replace our dynamic young colleague Amanda McVittie when she left for family reasons. We were thus still five permanent staff with two language assistants from a long-established exchange programme with the universities of Kiel and Tübingen. And we were doubly fortunate in that her replacement, Jonathan West, a former student of mine from Manchester with a doctorate from the University of Bonn, had four weeks previously just missed out in the interviews for a post in University College Galway. I had been on the Galway interview panel, the entire process being conducted (in flawless German throughout) by the Faculty Dean and UCG Professor of Irish, Géaróid MacEoin. He and I were most impressed with the candidate's performance – since we had last met in Manchester Jonathan had acquired fluency in both Irish and Welsh – and were keen to recommend him for appointment. The democratic process determined that we were outvoted by the three departmental colleagues who preferred the American candidate – to Trinity's subsequent benefit. Scarcely had our new staff member and his Celtic scholar wife Dr Máire Uí Bhreathnach (a pupil of MacEoin) settled in Dublin than he started doing what clever young colleagues should do: bother their heads of department by their plans for a brave new world. He had been out drinking with computer science colleagues in the engineering faculty and he came with a proposal: 'Engineers can't write English because they don't understand language and that's why so much software is simply not user-friendly. We understand natural language, so why don't we collaborate with them and the theoretical linguists?' At our next monthly staff meeting he elaborated his idea: we should create a combined honours degree in computer science, linguistics and German to study the interaction between the 'hardware', artificial and natural language and their practical applications. Timing is all. It so happened that about this time our new Provost, Bill Watts, a quaternary scientist but also a former graduate of the TCD German department, had said to me: 'If you can't innovate when times are bad, you are in the wrong job.' As we digested Jon's proposals, I began to think along the lines of our devising a suite of new combined courses in the department, which would (a) attract better-qualified students, (b) respond to the pressing and highly topical need to make our graduates employable at home and abroad and (c) provide for the specialist interests of each of our colleagues. Together with David Little, who had just moved to be director of the new Language and Communications Centre in the faculty, and his friends in Trinity's Computer Science department, Jonathan developed the Computer Science, Linguistics and German degree programme, which took in its first small cohort of students in 1985. Among them was a former male nurse, Fred Cummins, later professor of neurolinguistics in the USA and currently at UCD, and an inventive young genius from Monaghan, who within two years of graduation was earning thirty times the Trinity German department's tiny annual budget.

The next stage of my five-year plan began with the introduction of an optional extra language to the existing two-subject arts course. Our students were offered Dutch in their German degree programme. Initially the project was funded by an Irish-Dutch businessman and supported by a Dutch language assistant, the funding of which was then taken over by the Dutch and Belgian embassies through their Dutch/Flemish language organization, *Taal-Unie* (united language). Of the group who first took up the option, Siobhán Donovan and Anita Bunyan now lecture in UCD and the University of Cambridge respectively; Caroline Nash became the education officer of the Confederation of Irish Industry; Aisling O'Kane a senior executive in the American Chamber of Commerce in Brussels; while Maria Sherwood-Smith, having taken her doctorate in medieval Dutch literature at Oxford, is currently a senior member of the Netherlands police force. A key element of our plan was that each staff member would be involved in degree course in his or her area of special interest. Accordingly, Tim Jackson developed a BA programme in Germanic Languages (German, Dutch / Flemish and Swedish), necessitating for obvious reasons a change in our 206-year-old-title of 'German Department' to 'Department of Germanic Studies', duly approved, albeit with some eyebrow-raising, by Council and Board. Each of our planned four-year degrees would entail an integral year abroad in the target country. This was also very much in line with the European Commission's emerging Europeanization project, represented by the so-called Joint Study Programmes (JSP) in which I had been involved as a representative of Ireland since 1979, and later developed into the Erasmus Programme. Over the 1980s we negotiated a series of exchanges with over a dozen of Germany's leading universities to place our students on their year abroad. By the end of the decade we found ourselves with immensely increased workloads, made the more easy by the presence of so many able and highly motivated students, for whom entry to the new degree programmes was now, by contrast with a few years previously, not a little competitive.

One proposed new BA combined programme had required a tough apprenticeship. Partly for family reasons – my grandfather had been UCC's first professor of economics, and my sister had taken her BA in the subject at UCD – I had long wanted a combined degree in Economics and German. But it had taken all of nine years to persuade the Department of Economics to accept the idea, even though the cross-faculty combination of mathematics and languages had been functioning well for years. Finally, thanks to the support of John O'Hagan, Dermot McAleese, Frances Ruane and Alan Matthews in Economics, we finally got agreement, though only under the absurd condition that the students would be dispensed from any medieval literature. To celebrate, Alan Matthews and I organized a conference on 'Austria and Ireland: Two Small Open Economies' in 1988, inviting among other speakers the director of Vienna's prestigious *Wirtschaftsuniversität* (Vienna University of Business and Economics), Dr Helmut Kramer.[*]

Thanks to the help of two able colleagues, Richard Cox, a distinguished Cambridge graduate of French and German and a lecturer in the French department, and Professor William Duncan in the Law School, we were able to realize two most successful degree programmes: European Studies and Law and German. European Studies was the initiative of our colleague in French, Richard Cox. Under the first director of the new Centre for European Studies, John Horne (History), together with Gilbert Carr and James Jackson (French), the programme was re-designed to include intellectual and European history, politics and sociology. In the thirty years of its existence, European Studies – which now properly includes Italian, Polish, Russian and Spanish – has proved one of the most sought-after humanities degree courses in Ireland.

---

[*] Published in-house as *Austria and Ireland: economic performance in two small open economies* (1988). Incidentally, Kramer's use of the term *Sozialpartnerschaft* (social partnership) and his attribution to it as being a key element in Austria's successful post-war economic performance, was reported in the Irish media and straight away subsumed, unacknowledged, into official vocabulary by Taoiseach Haughey.

Our proposed degree with law was intended mainly for students who would be employed in business and commerce. They could combine a professional qualification in law with linguistic fluency and, for Germany of particular relevance, acquire an understanding of the cultural references that a high-level German business executive would expect to find in an Irish partner who wished to sell Ireland into the lucrative German market.

Our law students spent their year abroad in some of the best schools in Germany, among them Göttingen, where the poet Heinrich Heine and the then idle Bismarck had qualified as lawyer, and Würzburg. Their German counterparts revelled in membership of the Hist and in Trinity student life in general, while ours groaned at having to ingest the massive bible of German law, the *Bundesgesetzbuch*, but found plenty to compensate them in and outside the university walls. The new degree benefited immensely from the appointment by the German Academic Exchange Service (DAAD) of a legal graduate to act as *Fachlektor* (assistant). We were all much amused, given that French departments in these islands have tended to patronize their much smaller German counterparts, that as soon as our law degree began to be discussed at faculty, senior members of Trinity French department immediately demanded to be taken on board. As soon as we had developed our proposed degree in German and business studies under Gillian Martin's direction, they would do the same – which of course in the European context made good sense. Gillian set up exchange programmes with some nine leading German and Austrian business schools; their staff and ours now teach and examine regularly in each other's departments, a further contribution to the Europeanization of Trinity. Our membership as a university department of the very active Irish-German Chamber of Commerce – the first university department in Ireland so to engage – proved important in several ways. Elmar Conrad-Hassel from the Cologne Chamber of Commerce, married to the DAAD language assistant at UCD, helped to place our students in internships in German law firms, a service which he has generously continued to this day. Thanks to the then President of the Chamber and Director General of the CII (Confederation of

Irish Industry), Liam Connellan, we got good media coverage for our new programmes. Liam, who was also a member of the Executive of the Confederation of European Industry, lost no public opportunity to promote the study of German as a gateway to future employment; his speeches on the subject were always well publicized in the press.

Over the next years we put a great deal of effort into selling German to the Irish public, greatly helped by the German authorities: they sponsored new language assistants in Irish schools* and the Goethe Institute provided professional language training for the teachers in partnership with the *Gesellschaft Deutschlehrer Irlands* (GDI), putting on regular weekend conferences and helping to arrange exchanges with German teachers of English. In 1982 when we started our campaign, 4 per cent of the Leaving Certificate cohort took German; by the end of the decade, it was 22 per cent. Over the next decade virtually every Irish schoolteacher of German had spent at least three months teaching in a German school. As part of our efforts to raise the profile of German studies in Ireland and to promote German as a popular option for the Leaving Certificate, I worked with my new UCD colleague, Professor Hugh Ridley, who in 1983 hosted what could be termed a monster meeting in the largest lecture theatre at UCD's Belfield campus.† In the depressed context of the 1980s Irish economy and the return of mass emigration we argued to an audience of some 700 that Germany with its now booming economy and labour shortage offered real employment opportunities to those with a knowledge of the language. And, moreover, their parents would not be losing their daughters and sons to America or other distant continents: by plane Europe was only a couple of hours away.

Back in the department with our five degree programmes set up and functioning well, though apart from Gillian Martin with the same number of staff, our workload was increased by the number of cross-faculty

---

* Such measures were part of the considered and successful cultural policy of the Federal Republic as integral elements of its European 'Project'.

† Parents had been invited with their school-going children – in the Ireland of the 1980s parents still had a powerful influence on students' choice of discipline both at school and university.

committees we now had to attend. But there was still one experiment left to try. Jonathan West's successor Sheila Watts had studied German and Russian at Trinity during her father's time as Provost (1981–91). She was a most able theoretical and applied linguist, becoming proficient in almost a dozen languages and now lectures in Germanic languages at Cambridge. Sheila proposed introducing a German *ab initio* stream for students with no prior knowledge of the language. It would be necessary to devise a language aptitude test (in a language not known to the applicant), which would be administered to interested schools and which, should the proposal prove attractive, would provide the basis for our selection. Sheila would develop and teach the first-year intensive language course and act as tutor to the cohort throughout their time in College. We would accept students without any knowledge of German into all our degree courses but one,* despite the obvious difficulties in terms of student workload. Over two summer vacations in the late 1980s Albert drove me the length and breadth of the country for me to administer the language aptitude test to interested schools. On a single day we drove from the Quaker Newtown School in Waterford to the local school in Achill Sound, Co. Mayo. Here on one side of the classroom where the test was being taken, pupils' religious education lesson consisted of saying the rosary, while on the other the science teacher, as she afterwards explained, was giving a chemistry 'practical', the school's sole science equipment being her own pressure cooker, which she had brought from home. In a school where there were no indoor toilets, every one of these Leaving Certificate pupils knew exactly how many points they would need for every university degree programme they aspired to, whether law in UCC, marine engineering in UCG, history in Maynooth, European Studies or bio-chemistry in Trinity, business studies in UL or medicine in UCD or the College of Surgeons. The *ab initio* project proved to be a resounding success. The students were required to reach a pass standard in the same Junior Freshman German exams as their classmates who had had five years of the language at school. They struggled, but being intellectually

---

* The exception was the Germanic Studies degree programme, whose students had to learn two new languages.

able, highly motivated and systematically taught, all managed to get through their first year; their linguistic competence improved rapidly in their second year and following their year abroad, everyone who took the course then and over the next decade, achieved on average at least a II/I in their degree, and many a first-class mark.

## THE EUROPEAN PROJECT

The students' achievement was vividly exemplified for me on an occasion four or five years after the first European Studies cohort had graduated. I was attending a meeting in Turin on behalf of the European Commission to discuss elements of the new *Tempus* (European University Exchange Programme) designed post-1989 for the former Soviet satellite states. I was directed to the meeting room to await the arrival of the chairman, who entered shortly, a young man in a smart pin-striped suit. I looked at him again, barely recognizing the former wearer of increasingly ragged dungarees. He was now, he informed us in a brisk business-like manner, in charge of the Polish desk in the programme and was soon joined by our facilitator for the day: another member of the first German *ab initio* class! I couldn't help feeling a certain academic maternal pride in their polished performance, but the surprises were not yet over. I was seated in my economy seat on the plane home that evening when the hostess announced there would be a slight delay – one of the business-class passengers had been held up and would be with us in five minutes. A small figure panted up the steps to her seat in the front row, with bulging briefcase and familiar uncombed hair, and, as I noticed when we met on arrival in Dublin, well-scuffed, high-heeled shoes. It was yet another member of that cohort, who however unlike the rest of her classmates had never been in time with her essays, but always managed to negotiate an extension and was now an obviously successful executive in a European-wide organization.

The Erasmus and parallel programmes had emerged from tentative steps under the leadership of the Welsh-born Director for Education, Training and Youth Policy of the European Commission, Hywel Ceri

Jones, starting with the Joint Study Programmes (JSP). As I had been involved with these almost from their beginnings, our own department's very positive experience with our European university exchange partners made me become something of a self-styled ambassador for an extension of the project in the College. As Dean of International Students (1979–85) and thanks to the good will of the Professor of Greek, John Dillon, and a colleague in the Spanish department who taught Portuguese, I negotiated annual student exchanges with the universities of Thessalonika (Saloniki), Lisbon and, for our own department, Aarhus in Denmark. The next step was to 'animate' colleagues in other departments, among them Economics, to spend sabbatical leave either in our partner universities or in one of Germany's prestigious universities, among them Heidelberg, Göttingen, Bonn and the Kiel University World Economics Centre. The first few who went came back full of enthusiasm for the experience; word of mouth did the rest.

Two significant obstacles to a European-wide extension of the university exchange programme were cost to the student and equivalence, that is, the need for recognition of the period of study abroad as an integral part of the undergraduate degree. In developing what became known as the European Erasmus Programme, Ireland and Europe owe a great and largely unacknowledged debt to my UCD colleague, Hugh Ridley. He had come to Ireland as an indirect (and to the great benefit of German studies in Ireland) result of a chance conversation I had had with the then UCD President Tom Murphy. Tom would regularly ask me to play golf once a year in Milltown Golf club's Saturday mixed foursomes, and on our way round in 1977 I complained about the way he and the College authorities were permitting the then incumbent of the chair of German at my old department to absent himself on a third sabbatical year. The staff and the students, I said, were being neglected and it was simply wrong. Some months later he asked me to use my contacts among British German departments to persuade young, highly qualified lecturers to apply for the now-vacant chair of German in my old department. At our next annual conference of the Association of British and Irish University Teachers of German (CUTG), I approached some younger colleagues, recommended to me by professorial colleagues at Bristol, Cambridge, London and Oxford. A couple showed interest and applied, with Hugh as the successful candidate. He came to Ireland in 1979 together with his wife, the applied linguist Jenny Ridley, from Canterbury. The Ridleys very soon became some of our closest friends, Albert on occasion treating Hugh as a younger brother who needed 'keeping an eye on'. I stood guarantor for him when he took up Irish citizenship, soon becoming more Irish than the Irish. Working closely with the European Commission and the Irish Department of Education he negotiated over several years with the other EC member states on vital but bureaucratically complex issues, notably finance and academic equivalence so that students' work at their partner universities could be accepted by the home university as part of their degree. Monnet famously declared in retrospect that had he and his fellow architects of the EEC/EC to start again from the beginning, he would start with culture and education rather than economics and politics. The Erasmus Programme was officially launched in 1987, with an annual budget as part of the EU budget, open to all disciplines and, unlike many EU institutions, de-centralized in being administered by the universities themselves. For small member states such as Ireland Erasmus has been a godsend in terms of strategy. Moreover, there have been relatively few instances where Europe's young people have been given the opportunity to help build pan-European institutions. Not least thanks to them, the European university and college exchange project has been one of the EU's most successful.

After the fall of the Iron Curtain in 1989, a similar but more limited university exchange programme formed part of the integration process of the former Soviet satellite states into the EEC/EU and was warmly welcomed by the central and eastern European universities. I was involved in the initial years as an assessor: academics were asked by Brussels to prioritize and recommend the most promising proposals. One occasion remains memorable on two counts: firstly, and more importantly, for offering a group of 'western' women a brief insight into conditions of life and study in the Baltic states, which for over two generations had been the victims of foreign occupation, secondly, to gain insight into lives so very different from my own through the personal stories of members of my group. Our meeting was held in Lithuania, in a dreary, former Soviet-style hotel building in the middle of nowhere, in the flat empty country-side ten miles from Vilnius, the nearest town. I arrived for our four-day visit to meet my colleagues only to find there was only enough work for a day and a half. We were all busy professional women, two lawyers from Belfast and Belgium respectively, and a third, a French government minister responsible for equivalences. We were all equally miffed by this poor use of our time. How to fill in the other two and a half days?

We found a local bus, which crawled us in a couple of hours to Vilnius, a formerly magnificent town with a celebrated Jewish quarter with only a few buildings, among them the different Orthodox churches, surviving from the Holocaust, the war and Soviet neglect. There were, however, already a few hopeful signs of EU cultural investment policy. We got to know each other on the initiative of our Belgian colleague by telling each other our stories. Mine was by far the dullest, one career and still the same husband after thirty years. Our Belfast colleague, the youngest and a most attractive woman enjoying a successful legal career, related in a down-to-earth manner the story of her recent and evidently very nasty divorce. Although we all spoke French, our French ministe-rial colleague insisted on English throughout. She was fluent but spoke with such an excruciating accent that we heartily wished she would get back into her own language. Like me, she was still married to her 'orig-inal' husband, but the story of her courtship entertained us for a good part of the afternoon. She had been, as she told us nonchalantly the *premier élève* (top graduate) of her humanities year of the prestigious *École normale supérieure* in the humanities. As such she was required to 'attend' the President of France, clad in long silver evening gown, when-ever he entertained a visiting dignitary at the Paris Opera. On President Pompidou's other side was her opposite number from the *École normale supérieure* in the sciences in his uniform, sword and three-cornered hat. She took no notice of him. 'We were on duty, *n'est-ce pas?*' Repetition makes for boredom and one evening, the umpteenth on duty, she heard a low murmur in the style of Peter Sellers' Inspector Clouseau: 'I am boooored. I vish I cood read a bewk.' 'I vish alsooo,' she had replied. And that apparently was the start of a leisurely courtship and an obviously satisfactory marriage. Our Belgian colleague trumped the others with her dramatically told tale of love for a rising but impecunious young politician, father's insistence on a pre-marriage agreement (*covenant de mariage*), marriage to a serially unfaithful husband whose career she financed, discretion to avoid scandal, until, finally, now Belgium's Foreign Minister, he took his new young secretary on a state visit to South Africa. Madame learnt the news the same day and delivered her ultimatum in person to the Prime Minister: 'Either you sack my husband today or tomorrow the newspapers will reveal ALL.' Which he did. The husband returned begging forgiveness, but instead was presented with a bill for: '1,300,063 Belgian francs, the cost of my total investment in your career.' The *covenant* ensured that he paid up rather than face a jail sentence. Hell hath no fury …

Maybe our days in Lithuania weren't a waste of time after all. Life is a journey of constant learning about human nature.


## BUILDING EUROPEAN NETWORKS

I had been conscious of how difficult it was for scholars of German in Ireland to publish, for we had no specialized journals of our own and, as I knew from England, access to publication in the two major British outlets, the *Modern Languages Review**\** and *German Life and Letters*, tended to operate by personal contact. Given the general absence of sabbatical leave in Irish universities at the time, and budget restrictions on conference travel, this was particularly problematical for Irish researchers.† Thinking on how we might improve our meagre

---

\* House journal of the Modern Humanities Research Association.Languages

† It was somewhat easier for those who had done their graduate work in Britain, as Gilbert Carr had in Durham under W.E. Yates, later professor in Exeter and shortly after German editor of the *Modern Language Review*, or Tim Jackson in Oxford, where Professor Peter Ganz had been his mentor and had invited him to join the lively Anglo-German Medieval Research Colloquium, which he attends to the present day.

200-year-old department's publication record,* we began slowly. Tim Casey, Professor of German in Galway and a Trinity graduate, who had been most welcoming from my first arrival in Trinity, shared research interests in *fin-de-siècle* Austria with Gilbert. It so happened that Eoin Bourke, jobless but with a doctorate from Munich University supervised by the renowned Walter Müller-Seidel, had dropped in to my office in the hope of employment. I referred him to Tim Casey, who had a post coming up to which Eoin was duly appointed.† Together with our Galway colleagues, Gilbert and I put on a series of 'local' conferences taking our students with us, in our case focusing on Austrian literature, while Eoin organized their more politically engaged 'Neglected Progressives'. These meetings offered younger colleagues and graduate students an opportunity to 'place' their first publications and reach a wider audience. Under Gilbert's and my co-editorship we published the proceedings of our conferences in-house (almost bankrupting the department for a couple of years in the process),‡ and every year we each brought our annual student drama to perform to enthusiastic audiences in each other's department, to the great satisfaction and entertainment of all concerned.

But in terms of the department's future and our own careers, it was essential to establish our credentials at a more sophisticated level. We hit on a strategy that seemed to work. If we could persuade the appropriate German/Austrian authorities (embassies and the Goethe Institute) to fund the travel expenses of speakers from the Federal Republic and Austria, we would put them up in our homes and give them a good time and memories of a lively and industrious department to take back

---

* It is difficult for a modern academic to visualize the habitus of Irish university modern languages departments in the early days: for decades they consisted of a professor or lecturer with maybe one assistant and were simply teaching departments where one's colleagues might (or might not) do research. Up to the 1950s, when Lionel Thomas came as head of department, the TCD German department's entire publication record had been one book (a pedestrian history of German literature by the incumbent, A.M. Seiss) plus a handful of articles by his successors.

† Eoin would succeed Tim Casey to the Galway chair of German in 1993.

‡ *Irish Studies in Modern Austrian Literature I* (1982) and *Fin de Siècle Vienna: Irish Studies in Austrian Literature II* (1985).

with them. Some of us had contacts of our own age with lecturers in German university departments who were delighted to be invited abroad, such matters in the hierarchical world of German academia being usually the exclusive provenance of the chair-holders. It was the beginning of a network which with time expanded exponentially. When these colleagues themselves succeeded to chairs, we sent our graduate students to them, some of theirs coming to us to gain experience in another system, adding to our students' exposure to the language and encouraging the building of student networks.

More particularly in the 1990s, when the European project began to take educational and cultural links more seriously and monies became available for research networks, our German and Austrian partners invited us to participate in some of their research networks, and we them. Thanks to an initiative by Tim Jackson in 1980, we made a quantum leap in our contacts with some of Germany's leading *Germanistik* professors. He invited the Anglo-German Research Colloquium to hold its annual meeting in Dublin, which attracted some forty members from Germany, Austria and Britain. How would we entertain them appropriately with our limited budget? If, I asked Tim, they could be persuaded to add another £4 each to their registration fee, I would put on a supper party. Plenty of home-cooked food and decent wine could be provided for £200 in 1980. Should it prove to be a squash in our two large reception rooms, being late summer, the guests could spill over into the garden. They certainly could be persuaded, the ever-constructive Tim assured us. With myself as cook and all our department members displaying their skills as butlers, parlour and kitchen people, it proved a great success, allegedly much talked about in later years.

Following the conference, I was invited by the one of our guests, then chairman of a *Germanistik* sub-committee of the DFG (German Research Council), to join their group of some dozen scholars and heads of their institutions. Our task was to examine and recommend research grant applications for critical editions of the major German writers. German universities were in the process of internationalizing their research. One year earlier the sub-committee had invited their first non-German member, Peter Stern of University College London.[*] Now they were being even more adventurous in including their first female member. For nine years (the three-year term of office was twice renewed) from 1980 to 1989 I travelled to the twice-yearly meetings, starting on the stroke of three o'clock on a Thursday in a medieval castle, the Reisensburg, on the Danube. How the Germans worked! We spent the next seven hours on the job with only a brief *Kaffeepause* (coffee break) and a snack until we retired to bed at 10 pm, re-assembling from 9 to 3 on the Friday. (Interestingly enough, when we were working on the Berthold Brecht edition and were joined by scholars from the GDR, the 'Easterners' at first flatly refused to work beyond 4 pm, arguing that when you are working for the state you work the hours set, and no more.) After the first day's meeting eight or ten of us would go for a night walk along the Danube to clear our heads and get to know each other.

I made many friends with whom I collaborated over the next decades, foremost among them Wolfgang Frühwald, Wolfgang Martens, Jörg Schönert, Louis Gontard of Strasbourg, who joined a year later, Wolfgang Harms, Klaus-Detlef Müller and Richard Brinkmann. Brinkmann would drive us at high speed on the Friday to our trains, a terrifying experience as he had lost an arm and two fingers of his remaining hand in the war and would frequently turn around to those in the backseat to emphasize a point. One thing always leads to another – you recommend someone whom you know personally. Accordingly, from that group I was 'passed on' over the years to a variety of commissions whose chairmen felt that it looked better to include a woman member.

Assessing our first woman applicant for a research grant was something of an eye-opener. My new colleagues were without exception friendly and personable. The applicant's project was worthwhile. Yet when the extremely nervous feminist scholar from Hamburg was introduced by the always helpful DFG official who acted as secretary to the committee and after the usual preliminaries was invited by the chairman to make her pitch, I was struck by my male companions'

---

[*] No doubt from their perspective foreign women colleagues were 'easier'.

reaction. I expect I was the only person who noticed that the applicant was dressed in an extraordinarily unbecoming outfit, making a very un-feminine 'statement'.* When she presented her project addressing her remarks to each of us round the table and sought eye contact, one by one they lowered their eyes to avoid it. I'm sure their action was anything but deliberate: they were probably embarrassed at the lack of sophistication we were used to with these applications. Afterwards I reprimanded them for so systematically avoiding looking at the applicant. All twelve† protested. 'No we didn't!' 'Yes,' I said in my best elderly sister fashion (I was almost a decade older than most), 'you did.' To their credit the applicant received very detailed briefing of how to improve her proposal and she was eventually successful. When a few years later we began to receive many more female applicants who were now better prepared and we had more women members on our committee, I noticed that my colleagues made conscious efforts to put them at their ease. So much was part of a received academic culture, designed by males for males.

During a meeting a decade later with (male and female) senior officials of the DFG during our work as members of the grandiloquently styled Federal and State Commission to assess the German research system (*Bundes- und Länderkommission zur Evaluierung des deutschen Forschungssystems*) in 1997–9, we all sat at a long table. Our chairman, an Englishman, who held the chair of materials science at Oxford and was at the time chairman of the British Science Research Council, sat at the narrow end flanked on either side by us seven or eight assessors for an open discussion. I observed that all the DFG males present had managed to get themselves seated alongside us, and that during the discussion they leaned forward towards the chairman, obscuring their female colleagues and making it harder for them to make an intervention – the women were smaller and their voices less penetrating. These things matter and

---

* It was very un-academic on my part even to notice such matters, but they can have an influence.

† Peter Stern was unfortunately not able to attend on that occasion: he would have been, as always, the soul of encouragement.

women tend to be conscious of them, simply because they have had to deal with an inherited system, which privileged their male colleagues. On that occasion as on many others, I found my German colleagues very open, and appreciative rather than resentful of criticism.[*]


## FONTANE STUDIES AND EAST GERMANY

The 1980s were the decade in which I first visited East Germany, or the GDR as it still was.[†] The occasion was the first conference on Theodor Fontane open to West Berliners, held in the summer of 1986 at Potsdam, the former garrison town of the Prussian monarchy. It had been organized by Peter Wruck from the (East Berlin) Humboldt University with Horst Denkler from the Free University as his West Berlin partner, after endless behind-the-scenes negotiations with the GDR authorities. It had the capacity, as we Westerners were forewarned by Denkler, to do irreparable damage to the East German scholars concerned and make difficulties for future West German Fontane researchers should any untowardly political observations on our side upset the authorities. Thanks to the tact and firm chairmanship of Wruck and Denkler the event went as well as it possibly could, paving the way for extensive future scholarly collaboration.

Fontane had by now become part of my life thanks to an offer from Jochen Vogt of Essen, an Erasmus exchange partner and close friend of Hugh Ridley, to write a book on the novel *Der Stechlin* for a series he was editing.[‡] Even as a graduate student I had never actually heard of the novelist whom Sigmund Freud had admired and Samuel Beckett praised.[§] It is difficult to understand why, given the sophistication of his writing, his humour and the subtlety of his portrait of German society in

---

[*] Admirers of the nineteenth-century novelist Theodor Fontane may recall from his last novel *Der Stechlin* (1898) the figure of the Polish painter Professor Wroschwitz with his mantra: '*der Deutsche liebt die Kritikkk*' (Germans *love* criticism).

[†] The Republic of Ireland had no diplomatic relations with the GDR until 1980 – Irish citizens travelling there were represented by the British authorities.

[‡] *Theodor Fontane: Der Stechlin*. Munich: Fink, 1986.

[§] In *Krapp's Last Tape*.

the key years from the 1848 revolution to the age of Bismarck and Kaiser William II. He had never known in his lifetime the success afforded to the potboiler authors of his time. Perhaps unsurprisingly it was Anglo-German critics who rediscovered him for western scholars and readers, or rather Germans who had found refuge in Britain. Principal among them were Mary-Enole Gilbert, sister of the American-German historian Felix Gilbert, and the doyenne of Fontane studies, Charlotte Jolles, whom I had first met in 1973. With my friend and colleague Peter Skrine I had travelled down to our annual conference in East Anglia. We were making tea after our journey when we met a small figure on the corridor: would she like to join us? This was the legendary Frau Jolles in whose company we both now spent privileged hours.

Towards the end of summer 1979 I had received out of the blue one of Charlotte's characteristic missives: brief and to the point. One of her graduate students at Birkbeck, Jörg Thunecke, was proposing to edit a Festschrift in honour of her seventieth birthday: so kind, what an honour – but oh his lack of tact! 'I will lose all my friends,' she moaned. In other words, would I join him as sub-editor. Jörg had assembled an astonishing panoply of scholars from round the world to pay tribute to his revered professor and mentor. He was a most generous colleague, quite ready to accept my role. I was to be the person responsible for apologizing with the right degree of empathy to contributors who felt bruised by the editor's less than tactful comments on their work; if need be, I must be ready to massage famous egos.

One particularly angry missive came from Katherine Mommsen, a distinguished German-American scholar at Harvard, outlining her objections to Thunecke's comments and request for revisions on her article. It was clad in a thick packet of paper, held together with a massive paperclip. 'Professor Mommsen's hairpin,' Thunecke declared dismissively as he sent it on to me, 'we needn't bother too much.' A response to my soothing letter to Katherine Mommsen came by return of post: as the author of 'a dozen books and seventy-two peer-reviewed articles' she had NEVER been treated so badly by any 'would-be' editor. Further correspondence on my part stressing Charlotte Jolles' concern at my co-editor's manner brought out collegial feelings in Frau Mommsen and ensured that the massive, nearly 700-page Festschrift would indeed contain within its covers, contributions from virtually all the great and the good of West- and East-German and international Fontane studies. It was indeed an amazing achievement by a grateful student, a fitting and moving tribute to the dedicatee's personal as well as scholarly qualities.

The 'Fontane-Renaissance', as it is now called, had started in East Germany before the war and continued under the new Socialist regime for whom Fontane, similarly to Heine, could be presented as a critic of bourgeois Germany. East German scholars had access to many of the original manuscripts located in Berlin und unavailable to most scholars in the West. Charlotte, with her Prussian integrity and determination and British tact, was *persona grata* in East Germany, to which she travelled each summer to work in the archives. She was extremely sensitive to any untoward statement by us editors, which might affect the fragile relationship with the GDR authorities. Among her collaborators from the Potsdam Fontane archive was Gotthard Erler, who with his colleagues from the state Aufbau publishing house had begun the neglected work of editing an up-to-date critical edition of the novels, published in eight volumes in 1969. After the appearance of the Festschrift, he kindly sent me the edition, and we began a pen friendship, which led to his first visit to our department in the summer of 1982. Although he was required to report each morning by telephone to the GDR embassy in London, he was allowed to stay with us. When he came down for breakfast in the kitchen on the first morning to sit in Mireia's chair (she had gone to school) opposite the picture of Pope John Paul II who had visited Ireland three years previously, I offered to run up to my study and substitute a picture of Karl Marx. 'I am not like you, Frau Sagarra,' our guest said mischievously. 'I don't need to have my hero on the wall, I carry him in my heart.'

Although Gotthard did not speak English particularly well at the time, and Albert didn't speak German, they spent many an evening over his new discovery (Guinness) 'correcting' each other's memories of the Spanish Civil War, Gotthard taking Albert's teasing of him for his 'political naivety' in good part. On Gotthard's second visit a few years later – the first had been a resounding success with the students – we all had a taste of his command of Marxist dialectics. I had asked him in his lecture to give our students a sense of what it was like to live and be a citizen of the Democratic Republic since (regardless of any prejudices I might entertain on the matter) it was important for them to have as objective a view as possible of the two Germanies. The students came in large numbers. Although it was an internal affair, the Goethe Institute director and the cultural attaché from the embassy of the Federal Republic arrived, evidently sent by the ambassador. In the discussion after the lecture both attempted to wrong-foot Dr Erler but, politely yet devastatingly, his brilliance in argument reduced them to an embarrassing silence.

A few years later I drew down on myself once more the disapproval of the embassy with which we have always had and have the best of relations. Just after the fall of the Berlin Wall we were able to invite Günter Grass, at the time known to be a forthright opponent of German unification, to speak to the students. Our largest theatre in Trinity, the Edmund Burke, was filled to capacity and Grass, whether you agreed with his political opinions or not, gave a sparkling performance. Early next morning I had a phone call in my office from His Excellency reprimanding me for having given such publicity to 'an opponent of the Federal Republic'. I tried as courteously and tactfully as I could to convey that we were an educational establishment, exposing those we taught to all possible viewpoints. Incidentally, it intrigued (and amused) us in the department that the otherwise so very politically aware Grass showed absolutely no interest in meeting or talking to the students.

The 1980s ended on an unexpectedly high note with one of the most memorable moments of our lives, namely the fall of the Berlin Wall on 9 November 1989. German history is full of (usually tragic) ironies, none more so than the date on which the twenty-eight-year-old Iron Curtain came down. The same date, 9 November, had seen the abdication of Kaiser William II in 1918; on that day in 1922 Hitler attempted the Munich Putsch; sixteen years to the day he launched the curtain-raiser to the Holocaust, the so-called 1938 Crystal Night (*Kristallnacht*) when Jewish synagogues throughout the country were ransacked, set on fire and tens of thousands of German Jews rounded up and imprisoned. The fall of the Wall was a date when we would always recall where we had been at the time. On 9 November 1989 I was sitting at 9.30 pm with two other colleagues, Hans-Jürgen Schings and Wolfgang Harms, at the end of our DFG meeting in the Bavarian Reisensburg, finishing a discussion on some item of business. Would we join the others for a beer? Good idea! Our colleague Schings, however, felt he needed to watch the news: we had been so busy over the previous twenty-four hours we had lost touch with the rapidly changing events. He thus witnessed the historic moment virtually while the rest of us thirsty philistines missed it.

# NINE

# On the threshold of modernity:
# Ireland from the 1980s to the 1990s

The 1980s was a key decade in Ireland's long journey to modernity. The temper of that decade was markedly different from that of its predecessor – or so I found. For if the 1970s had prepared the soil and planted the seeds of change, there was at first scant evidence of green shoots. Yet below the surface of seemingly stagnant Irish society, a change in consciousness had been gaining momentum. In the new decade things really began to move. Materially, middle-class urban and much of rural Ireland began to notice the benefit of Ireland's membership of the EEC, specifically from the structural funds and the agricultural subsidies via the Community's Common Agricultural Policy.* As elsewhere in Europe 1980s Ireland witnessed the rapid rise in the number of women working outside the home, partly because of better education but also because the cost of housing and the mortgage burden made two incomes necessary to support one family. In notable contrast for Ireland with the previous

---

* The Republic, with some 60 per cent of the EEC average income in the 1980s, benefited more than almost any member state from EC membership.

decades the number of marriages rose, together with a lowering of the marriage age and a fall in the number of pregnancies. Where the fertility rate had been 3.87 per union in 1970, it was 3.2 in 1980 and 2.1 in 1990.

## THE CATHOLIC CHURCH IN IRELAND AS ARBITER OF PUBLIC MORALITY? THE BEGINNING OF THE END

The Irish Catholic Church's patriarchal regime of attempted control of women's sexual life continued, directed by it and endorsed by the state through legislation, which from 1935 to 1980 had made the sale or import of contraceptives illegal. In 1979 Charles Haughey's government had introduced the Health (Family Planning) Bill, which became law the following year, with the absurd restriction on the purchase of contraceptives 'to *bona fide* family planning or for adequate medical reasons' – and then only through registered pharmacists with a doctor's prescription. That such legislation had applied to Protestants and non-believers as well as Catholics belied the Irish state's claim to its name of Republic. For Catholic marital practice the decision by Pope Paul VI in 1969, against the advice of many senior members of the hierarchy, to release his encyclical *Humanae Vitae* banning the use of artificial contraception was evidently proving far more significant than any state legislation, but hardly in the intended sense. Prior to *Humanae Vitae* the prominent and devout Irish-American Catholic obstetrician and gynaecologist John Rock, already famed for his treatment of infertility, had turned his attention to developing an oral contraceptive to address what he and others saw as the unnecessary suffering endured by women through excessive pregnancies. Following the publication of his ground-breaking book* and having won Vatican approval for the use of the contraceptive pill in treating menstrual disorders, Rock and other leading Catholic medical scientists had been confident of gaining Church approval for its use as a contraceptive. *Humanae Vitae* may have put paid to those hopes, but discussion on the issue was now internationalized, at least in the West.

---

* *The Time Has Come: A Catholic doctor's proposals to end the battle over birth control* (London and New York: Longman's, 1963).

Practising Catholics in Ireland began in ever larger numbers to ignore the papal mandate against 'unnatural' methods of limiting their family and follow their own judgement as to whether to take the pill.

But by the 1980s the impact of *Humanae Vitae* was going far beyond couples' sexual practice. Hitherto Catholic women had tended to be the most loyal supporters of their Church and key agents in handing on the faith to their children. Over the next years significant numbers of them became alienated from the once-familiar church of their childhood. The Second Vatican Council, convened by the shrewd and eminently pastoral Pope John XXIII in 1962, had given an immense boost to thoughtful parish clergy and those in religious orders who were close to the people, as well as to many lay Catholics. Catholic Ireland – which partly on account of its history as a colonized society, partly from the fact that its clergy were largely recruited from small farming communities of poor educational opportunities – had always lacked a tradition of critical enquiry. 'Catholic Ireland,' as one of its most acute observers, Gerry O'Hanlon SJ, has observed, had long 'provided comfort and fuelled the spiritual and ethical imaginations of its adherents, and had a deeply committed, global missionary outreach.' But by the early 1980s 'its un- and even anti-intellectual nature meant that it was ill-prepared for the challenges presented by a late-emerging modernity in Ireland'.* More and more members of the laity now started to take an informed interest in learning about and understanding their faith.

When we came back to Ireland in the mid-1970s I had seen how many of my own friends from UCD college days were taking an active part in the emergence of parish study groups, supported by former fellow students who were now members of the religious orders, notably Jesuits and Dominicans. These groups, it was hoped, would lay the foundations for a vibrant network across the country and breathe new life into the long-dormant ecumenical movement for church unity. The Second Vatican Council had promised a thorough modernization of the Catholic Church, one which would no longer be about power, but would revive the ancient concept of the church as the people of God, of a

---

* O'Hanlon (2017), 10.

genuine partnership between priest and people. The abundant evidence on the part of the Roman Curia and hence of the bishops rowing back on that promise at the highest level of church governance acted as a kind of counterintuitive leaven among the faithful, both the laity and the more reflective clergy. The centralizing control of church governance put paid to their hopes for real reform and change. We now began to hear of individual priests who sought to challenge what they saw as the betrayal of the spirit of the Council being disciplined or 'exiled' from their parishes, of theologians, even senior members of the church, being silenced without recourse to natural justice. There had been no consultation with the laity prior to *Humanae Vitae* in an area so central to ordinary people's lives. Anecdotal evidence supports this. Women friends in my circle drew the conclusion that since their financial circumstances required them to limit their families, they would take the pill and so could not in conscience return to the sacraments until past the childbearing age. With the result that when that time came, practice in many cases had inevitably become lukewarm.

Two other milestones stand out as marking the temper of 1980s Ireland and precipitating the radical evolution of Irish society in the 1990s and beyond: rumours of the clerical sexual abuse scandals and the 1983 abortion referendum, to which should be added the growing influence of the media, including increasing numbers of opinion-forming women journalists and of the women's movement generally. Abortion will always be a highly controversial and emotive subject and Ireland was no different. To me and my fellow Catholics abortion was morally wrong: for us, as in the less emotionally charged euthanasia issue, it involved the unjustified taking of human life. But we knew that while we might be in the majority at that time, our views did not represent Irish society. Moreover, I felt angered at the hypocrisy of the political establishment – who knew only too well what an electoral disaster any legislative change would bring the government who dared to implement it – and who were content with the so-called 'safety valve'. Namely, that women seeking an abortion could simply take the boat to 'godless Britain' and arrange for it there. That women seeking abortion were 'free to travel', but only those who had the means to do so, did not seem to concern the authorities. High-profile cases, such as the sensational Kerry Babies case of 1984 or that of the thirteen-year-old raped child whose parents were refused permission to travel to the UK with her, which came known as the 'X case' some years later (1992), underlined the injustice of the 'Irish solution to an Irish problem'. Yet given the public temper in the Ireland of the early 1980s the decision to introduce a referendum on the issue of abortion proved premature. It was triggered by politicians' fear that the Irish courts might follow the example of the US Supreme Court in 1982 allowing for a less restrictive regime.

In 1983 Charles Haughey's administration introduced a bill to amend the Irish Constitution, and after his electoral defeat his successor Garret FitzGerald introduced the new government's bill that autumn. Following the most divisive public campaign seen for decades in Ireland, the referendum proposing what became known as the Eighth Amendment to the Irish Constitution guaranteeing the equal right to life of the mother and her unborn child was passed overwhelmingly by 66.3 per cent to 32.7 per cent. It became law in October 1983 but without resolving issues of immediate concern, most notably to the medical profession. Despite pressures, among others from Europe, it was thirty-five years before a radical reversal of the earlier decision would take place. Nothing illustrates more vividly the degree of change in the public temper of Ireland within less than two generations than the 2018 campaign to remove the Eighth Amendment from the Constitution,* promoted above all by those born around or after the time of the 1983 referendum and spearheaded by younger women. It was not until the following decade, notably after the 1994 TV documentary of the predatory cleric Brendan Smyth, that the public was made fully aware of the extent of sexual abuse by clerics. But already in the 1980s rumours had begun to circulate so that when victims were finally emboldened to tell their story, the revelations had a profound and lasting impact at several levels. For a century or more Irish Catholics, especially women, had given their church undivided loyalty,

---

* The Thirty-Sixth Amendment to the Constitution legalizing abortion in certain cases became law in December 2018.

many setting their priests on a pedestal. In the years that followed, the impact of what was a devastating breach of that trust would undermine the moral authority of the Catholic Church, and eventually its political influence in Irish society, regardless of the dedicated lives and work of the vast majority of priests and religious.

To mothers like myself and my Catholic friends the clergy were our allies in our children's faith education, and we were quite unprepared for what we learnt. I remember some neighbours of mine and myself in the early 1980s being annoyed with our own parish priest in Rathgar, the elderly and slightly pompous Monsignor Moloney, for refusing to entertain our repeated requests to set up a youth club in the church for our teenage children. One of his curates, a connection by marriage on my mother's side, used to take some of the children's choir and altar boys for outings to the sea during the long sixteen-week summer holidays. At thirteen Mireia and her friend Martha, both regular choir girls, on one occasion tried to get out of the excursion, but Martha's mother and I insisted they go. If questioned the girls would just say, 'We don't like Fr X.' One day Mireia said there had been a great fracas in the sacristy because he had allegedly violently beaten an altar boy. The allegation was soon forgotten until a couple of years later the boy's name appeared in the press as having received a substantial court award from an abusive priest – our Father X.

Over the following years many of the principles on which Irish society had hitherto operated had been effectively challenged, more particularly the cosy relationship between government and the Catholic Church. Irish women under forty were deserting the church in their thousands. By the time of the publication of the *Commission of Investigation: Report into the Archdiocese of Dublin* in 2009, apart from funerals and weddings they and their children no longer attended church services. But in the media furore that followed hardly anyone seemed to heed the devastating impact of the Murphy and other reports on those innumerable priests, innocent of such accusations, who had given their lives in the service of others, and who now felt a deep sense of betrayal leading in individual cases to serious depression.* Instances occurred when Catholic priests, easily identified by their Roman collar† and black clothes, were physically attacked in Dublin's city centre. One priest told us that he had taken to wearing the grey suits plus Roman collar preferred by ministers of the Protestant churches.

The revelations of the abuse of children and young people by paedophile clergy in parishes, hospitals and industrial schools did not affect my own faith, nor even, when the actual scale was gradually revealed, my belief in the church. This was mainly because I had long been persuaded that many men had entered the religious life far too young, frequently as the result of social and family pressures or lack of career options – or as gay men to put an end to pressure from their families to 'find a nice girl and marry'. In most cases seminarians as future celibates had received no training in how to relate to women‡ other than as 'daughters of Eve', who by their 'fallen nature' constituted a 'danger to men'. I remember my then nineteen-year-old sister roundly scolding the French-educated Fr Michael O'Carroll of Blackrock College, when my godfather Vincent Kelly first brought him to dinner in our house after he had paid her a nicely-phrased compliment: 'That's all very well, Father, but you priests are all brought up to look on us as vessels of sin. You should be ashamed of yourselves.' And being blessed with an above-average sense of humour, he promised repentance, at least in his own name.

Even more shattering to Catholics like myself was the revelation of the official Church's response over the next decades. The preferred

---

* See, for example, Alan Hilliard's analysis of his sample of Dublin diocesan priests' response to the abuse crisis by the Church in *Revisiting the Murphy Report. Studies* 102 (Winter 2013), no. 408, 447–55.

† An article of clerical dress worn only by ordained ministers; originally introduced by a mid-nineteenth-century Presbyterian minister, it was rapidly adopted by other Christian denominations, though generally if erroneously associated only with Catholic priests.

‡ See *Underground Cathedrals* (Dublin: Columba Press, 2010) by Abbot Mark Patrick Hederman OSB of Glenstal, especially his chapter on the Murphy Report.

official church response was the instinct 'to protect the institution', the quite appalling moving on of predatory priests to other parishes, where, given the trust of the faithful in 'the anointed of God', such priests were welcomed into homes and left free to destroy the lives of countless more children. True, paedophilia was nothing new in Irish society as elsewhere. Children were simply not believed if they conveyed unhappiness at what they had experienced. Where could they turn for help, or indeed what resort did mothers of families have who were aware of their husbands' abuse of their own children? The mantra prevailing in Irish society here, as in cases of violent domestic abuse known to the Garda Síochána, was to never interfere between man and wife.

One of the most fascinating phenomena of late-twentieth-century Ireland has been the speed with which a once-authoritarian society collapsed.* From being an extremely conformist, homogeneous, 90 per cent-plus Roman Catholic society, with the highest mass-going population in Europe,† within a generation, church congregations appeared by the start of the new century (and in urban areas even earlier) to be composed of the over-sixties and the very young. The deficiencies of Irish religious education over decades had a material influence on the process, although it only became apparent in the last years of the century. As the hierarchy sedulously refused to agree to have religious education as an examination subject for the Intermediate or Leaving Cert examinations, religious exams didn't count for anything and so were never taken seriously by pupils or parents. In a telling critique of Catholic religious education in Ireland far back as 1966, the publisher Michael Adams acutely observed:

> Students leave secondary school with a good smattering of apologetics and capsules of social doctrine … Their religion is not well integrated with their secular studies (consider the teaching of history and English literature). Their vocational guidance has been nil or casual or confined only to the vocations of the priesthood or the religious life.‡

---

* See the excellent analysis by Derek Scally (2021).

† Some 91 per cent, according to the 1971 Census.

‡ Quoted in Patrick Maume. 'Michael Adams, Censorship and Catholic Activism'. *Studies* 106 (Spring 2017), 49–69.

This lack of connectedness was very evident to us as teachers of literature, the more so since the interpretation of many classical German literary texts is predicated on an awareness of the biblical and general Christian iconography on which the author draws. Obvious examples are Heinrich Heine, Friedrich Nietzsche or Berthold Brecht. As a Jew part-educated by monks, Heine (1797–1856) was long regarded as a dangerous blasphemer by 'right-thinking' contemporary Christian readers. Yet his wit and satire rely to a great degree on an understanding of the range of theological references supplying the subtext of his poetry and prose. This is also true for Theodor Fontane, who was no crusader attacking the crumbling walls of Christian Europe. But to read his best-known novel *Effi Briest* (1895) without an awareness of the structural role of Mariological iconography is to miss much of the work's aesthetic sophistication. In the many years we read it together, I encountered few Catholic students who could make the connection. Yet most came from schools run by religious orders and as children had attended mass regularly on feasts of the Virgin Mary, which play a key role in the work's imagery. It was as if religion and life belonged by their nature in separate boxes, neither with relevance for the other.

## 'IRISHMEN AND IRISHWOMEN'*

The 1990s were packed for me with new activities, while in the public arena both at home and abroad great events were taking place which touched all our lives. Among our personal milestones there was Mireia's graduation from Trinity, only to discover the harsh realities of the Irish job market, which would face most of her age cohort for years to come. Although Albert and I felt she would greatly profit from some time living abroad, she chose not to go and suffered for a time, like many others, from a sense of uselessness and even depression. Then in 1994 my mother died, to whom she had been very close, and less than four years later, I joined the ranks of pensioners.†

---

\* Opening words of the 1916 Proclamation of the Irish Republic.

† We got some odd but excellent advice on our mandatory pre-retirement course: look after your toes and spend your pension.

In August 1993 I had reached my sixtieth birthday and should by rights have been starting to plan for retirement. But our student numbers were still rising, there were numerous conferences to attend and Festschrift articles for retiring British and German colleagues to produce. Up to the age of eighty-seven in 1991 my mother had still been playing golf a couple of times a week, on occasion even caddying for a member of her team fifty years her junior, thereafter, to walk the two miles to shop in Rathmines and back or do some gardening before her evening meal. However, in the summer of that year she had the first of her falls and required increasing care and attention. About the same time, I had a conversation with Paddy McDonagh, a member of the Dublin Vocational Education Committee and now in his seventies, whom I had learnt to admire for his wisdom and common sense, which gave me pause for thought. 'I must start thinking of retirement in a few years,' I said to him. 'Much too late,' came the sage reply, 'you should have been preparing for it years ago.' What would I do with all that time on my hands? I had a privileged life; now was time to give something back. At first, I thought of adult literacy but the linguist Eibhlín Ní Mhurchú, married to our former Faculty Dean and Professor of Irish, Máirtín Ó Murchú, advised against it: 'An admirable project, but disorganized. It would drive you mad.' In the event my mother's frequent and more serious falls, involving long nights in the local Meath hospital postponed any further thoughts on the matter. She came to stay with us for a couple of months but was not happy. She would invariably interrupt the normally taciturn Albert whenever he opened his month to speak, with the result that he lapsed into habitual silence, which made her nervous. She was persuaded that I was putting work first and felt neglected. She sought solace in long telephone calls to my sister in Yorkshire, who came to the rescue and brought her over to stay for two months with her and her family. Back in Dublin it became clear that she wanted to come and live with us. Quite apart from pressures of work, I was naturally torn between loyalty to her and to Albert, whom she unconsciously seemed to want to push aside so that she could enjoy my full attention: easy to understand but fraught with difficulties. It was at that moment that

I realized what it was to have a sibling of Clodagh's empathic but logical character. She rang our great family friend, Fr Michael O'Carroll, for advice. He, who was very fond of my mother but experienced in the ways of the world, was firm: 'Clodagh, on no account allow Cecil to go and live with Eda and Albert. It would put an impossible strain on their marriage.' The next time my poor mother rang to complain about me, my sister was sympathetic but tongue-in-cheek astute: 'Yes, Mammy. We all know that Eda can be difficult, and I am the one you need. But the problem for you is that Eda is the one on the spot. If I were you, I would make a fuss of her and make her think she is marvellous. That way you will find her easier to deal with.'

And then, as so often happens in such cases, my mother had a stroke and had to go into nursing care. Clodagh came over and we made the melancholy round of nursing homes, finally finding a lovely house just off our road, where she had a large sunny room and wonderful care, including beautifully prepared meals. What we didn't appreciate was the effect of lack of stimulus on an older person's mental health. Eventually the nursing home closed and, full of guilt, we moved her up the road to a far less pleasant, commercially run large institution, Orwell House, where to our surprise her gregarious nature flourished in company. She now spent her day in a small sitting room reserved for the four or five 'normal' patients, who were soon friends, until a year later new owners decided they could make more money by giving it over to short-term convalescents. Albert and I took turns to visit her every day and Mireia dropped in regularly.

But it was pathetic and utterly guilt-inducing for me to see her and her friends now seated in front of the television all day alongside dozens of the demented. Inevitably her own mental state deteriorated sharply, but as she was suffering minor strokes, she seemed unexpectedly content now that she had plenty of people around her. A few weeks after her ninetieth birthday in September 1994, celebrated at our home with her extended family, she suffered a further stroke and died on 7 November. That Sunday I called up four times, sat on her bed delighted at her lucidity. Once more her old kind and thoughtful self, she insisted on sending me home on each occasion. Thankfully I came back a fifth time to be with her as she died peacefully that evening. Clodagh, whom we had rung in the morning, arrived alas just minutes after she had closed her eyes.

She was indeed in so many ways a remarkable woman. In her youth she had always been overshadowed by her ebullient and extremely attractive, not to say self-absorbed elder sister Pearl: their parents had felt it necessary to send them in their teens to separate boarding schools. In adult life they shared a great deal, not least the years in Washington in the 1920s, and they had to us a tantalizing relationship. They wrote each other regular letters full of affection and stated longing to meet, Pearl from England where she had married an indulgent husband who had died some years earlier in 1965. An enthusiastic invitation to visit the other came equally regularly but two days after arrival of the guest tensions would arise, and the visitor could not get home quickly enough. One Christmas when they were both in their early eighties, my mother invited Pearl to spend ten days with her. Trouble ahead, my sister and I agreed over the phone. The only question: when would it get serious? On the third day I got a tearful phone call from my mother: 'Eda, could you ever take Pearl off my hands for a day or two? I can't stand it any longer.' Pearl, who had no notion of time, would arrive late for all meals, prepared with great care by my mother for whom punctuality came very close to godliness. Of course, we would. In no time Pearl was settled in happily with us for the duration. We enjoyed her time with us, for she was great company. She was by way of being a staunch Marxist, her intellectual surgeon husband Francis Lewis having been the genuine article.* She had taken up the study of Russian language in her seventies and continued attending Russian weekend residential language courses in the University of London into her nineties. She did Trojan work in our large garden, oblivious of the weather, only coming indoors when

---

* My mother had no time for her political views. When Pearl and her husband joined the exclusive Belfry golf club near Birmingham and Pearl started to complain to her sister of the 'invasion' of the course at weekends by the local 'plebs', Cecil observed with not a little *Schadenfreude*: 'Why don't you go and play in Moscow? You can be sure the proletariat won't be allowed to bother you on any of their elitist courses.'

she heard Albert arriving home. A male audience was all she needed, and she focused her charm on him. Christmas dinner that year went down in our family history as one of the most entertaining on record. Mireia and I sat opposite him, my mother to his right, Pearl to his left. We watched delightedly as Albert divided his attention between the two sisters. As he praised her beautifully cooked turkey Pearl would collapse like a faded flower over her plate, immediately sparking on all cylinders when he turned in her direction. The three of us managed to keep straight faces throughout.

My mother had met my father in 1929, after having been strongly advised in a letter by her rigidly Catholic father against marrying her Church of Ireland boyfriend of many years 'as he was at heart an atheist and you would never be happy in such a marriage'. In those days it was difficult for dependent daughters not to follow forceful parental direction. Perhaps she married Kevin on the rebound; she was an affectionate wife, but their interests were very different. She had trained as an accountant but married before qualifying and never earned her living either before or after marriage. Later in life she developed what proved to be her considerable financial flair. My father had foolishly taken advice from well-meaning friends in the heady days before the Wall Street crash of September 1929, borrowing a multiple of his annual salary to invest on the stock exchange, in Courtauld shares. In the months of their engagement my mother allegedly told him she would not go through with the marriage unless he disposed of the shares. He delayed and sixteen days before their wedding had lost his entire investment. As he would tell us daughters, he never wanted to have to have any dealings with money again, even to the extent of getting her to give him 'his pocket money' on receipt of his monthly pay cheque. We never went on holidays; we lived in the country, so we didn't need to. If we asked why not, the stock answer was always 'Courtaulds'. After twenty-five years, my father being on a solid civil service salary, the debt was duly paid off. Systematically my mother began to study the daily stock exchange reports, taking expert advice from the stockbroker husbands of some of her Milltown golfing friends. For nearly twenty-five years she invested and re-invested and in 1979, with some help from her daughters, she was able to become the owner, for the first time in her seventy-five years, of a small house opposite Milltown Golf Club, bought before the astronomical price rises of Dublin residential property. Unlike my father or me (or Albert), she was quite unsentimental. She lived in the moment, absorbed in the world around her and getting maximum enjoyment from whatever she happened to be doing: looking after the family, at early morning mass, gardening, dressmaking, playing bridge and golf and adding up golf scores – she seemed to be able to add up a column of figures error-free by just looking at them –, or, when we lived in the country, having Saturday evening telephone cocktail parties with her younger and favourite sister Muriel.

After her death I found myself getting involved in the novel area of international institutional assessment. Just about that time pressure from governments via research funding agencies for accountability in the dispersal of public monies was creating a European-wide demand for assessment by panels of external assessors of institutes of learning, including the universities. The system in its early stages, as far as I could gather, operated simply through personal networks: those already serving on one assessment committee would tend to recommend colleagues they knew for appointment to another. Thus Barry (H.B.) Nisbet, professor of modern languages at the University of Cambridge, for many years chaired virtually every appointments committee to chairs in German in England.* British colleagues for whom I had acted as extern examiner would recommend me from time to time for membership of such boards or as external assessor of research institutions in the humanities. But what followed from the time of my appointment as Secretary to the

---

* His experience of how individual universities treated their expert assessors was something of an eye-opener, as I discovered when I was a member of his team in 1996 to advise on filling the chair of German at my former university of Manchester. Having experienced Trinity practice in this regard and the lavish hospitality of Cambridge a year or two previously, I was not a little miffed to have an unexciting sandwich and a cup of indifferent coffee as the only hospitality provided for us by the university during our very long day. 'You are lucky,' Barry said, 'I did the same job three years ago and they made me pay for my own lunch.'

Royal Irish Academy in 1993 was on a different scale, in the sense that it was concerned with the assessment of existing large research institutions and making recommendations for the establishment women of new ones. Coincidentally, public opinion around this time had begun to agitate for representation of women on such bodies. Partly on account of the traditionally male character of university governance, perpetuated in appointments policy over the years, there were relatively few women in senior positions in Ireland available and willing to act.* Here too, personal contacts operated in appointments, though at times, given the strength of traditional patterns of thinking even a female government minister might fail to include members of her own gender.†

'THE WOMEN WHO WERE SINGING IN THE WEST / ...
REJOICING IN / FINDING A VOICE WHERE THEY HAVE
FOUND A VISION'‡

I will ever remember 1990 for two extraordinary events: the first one in Europe – German unification, which took place on 3 October – and the second in Ireland five weeks later, on 7 November, the election of Ireland's seventh president and the first woman to hold that office. Eavan Boland's lines capture the palpable sense among the women of Ireland of, as it were, the tectonic plates of the old Ireland shifting, with a new landscape of equal citizenry about to emerge.

Following a shrewd grassroots election campaign, which saw her canvas local communities throughout Ireland, accompanied by her husband Nick and her youngest child William, Mary Robinson *née* Bourke of Ballina, Co. Mayo, was declared elected as the first woman to be President of Ireland and head of state. She opened her inauguration speech in Dublin Castle on 3 December 1990 by addressing the 'Citizens of Ireland, *mná na hÉireann agus fir na hÉireann*' (women of Ireland,

---

* While the task would usually prove rewarding, it always involved long hours of very intensive work and was not remunerated.

† Minister Harney, see below, 190.

‡ Eavan Boland: 'The Singers' from: *A Time of Violence* (New York, 1994).

men of Ireland) in that order, as she set out her vision for her presidency. True, the change was more symbolic than institutional, since the political powers of the Irish President under *Bunracht na hÉireann*, the Irish Constitution of 1937, are limited, comparable in this to the constitutional position of the German President under the 1949 German Federal Republic's *Grundgesetz* or Basic Law. But as Mary Robinson would later remind us, similar in this to President Richard von Weizsäcker (1984–94) from whose vision of the presidential role as one primarily of moral authority she drew much of her inspiration: symbols are what both unite and divide people. They mark our identity. One such powerful symbol was her placing of a lighted candle at Christmas in the window of Áras an Uachtaráin to honour the Irish diaspora, those hundreds of thousands of Irish women and men who over the years had been forced to leave their country in order to earn a decent living.

## DEUTSCHLAND, WO IST ES? (GERMANY, WHERE IS IT?)*

For those of us who had spent our careers studying and teaching Germany's language, literature, culture and history, the unification of Germany in October 1990 was the greatest historical event we had lived to witness. The 1980s had culminated on 9 November 1989 in the fall of the Berlin Wall. Over the next days and weeks, the world watched the Iron Curtain disintegrate, and the new decade bring radical changes to the map of central and eastern Europe. One of the fascinating features of German history over a millennium, from the time of the first emperor Charlemagne to October 1990, is how much and how frequently the territory of Germany has changed, shifting backwards and forwards or, rather, eastwards and westwards over many centuries. Who among today's students of the language knows that once for centuries Germany's eastern border lay at the far end of the Baltic Sea in present-day Russia

---

* The rhetorical question posed in the tones of high pathos favoured by early German nationalists by the poet Ernst Moritz Arndt in *The German Fatherland* (1813). His answer over half a century before Germany's territorial unification as the Second German Empire in 1871: 'Wherever German is spoken.'

and her western frontier in modern Belgium?[*] In the hectic weeks between early October and December 1989 we had not fully realized that we were living through an extraordinary time in European politics. The Soviet Union's Party Secretary Mikhail Gorbachev had arrived on 7 October 1989 to visit East Germany for the elaborately staged fortieth anniversary celebration of the German Democratic Republic. Instead of the hoped-for military aid from the Soviet Union to repress growing at one time domestic discontent, GDR Party Secretary Erich Honecker and the East German leaders were forced to listen to the shattering phrase in Gorbachev's address that 'Life punishes those who arrive too late.'[†] It meant that the Soviet Union was no longer prepared to shore up a moribund German Socialist satellite state.

The international news had not been as exciting for years, as in the following weeks one after the other the Soviet satellite state leaders and their regimes toppled. What would happen to Germany, the world asked? British Prime Minister Margaret Thatcher might mutter audibly about a 'Fourth German Reich', a little-Englander mantra taken up here in Ireland surprisingly by a man as intelligent as Conor Cruise O'Brien. In the aftermath of the fall of the Wall and the collapse of the former Soviet satellite states the international media clamoured for a 'solution' to 'the problem of Germany', incidentally bringing my students some amusement and me a degree of deserved embarrassment: All our first-year students were required to attend a lecture course given largely by myself on the politics, society and economy of the three German-speaking nations, the Federal and Democratic Republics and Austria, plus Switzerland with its majority Germanic-language[‡] population. Each student had to write a Christmas vacation essay for the course, which I would return individually during the following term.

---

[*] During the so-called Holy Roman Empire, a ramshackle association of territories, which lasted for over a thousand years (800–1806), destroyed by Napoleon.

[†] *Wer zu spät kommt, den bestraft das Leben* (attributed to Gorbachev, the phrase was in fact that of his press spokesman Gennadi Gerasimov).

[‡] Swiss-Germans speak their widely varying Germanic dialects as their native language; many don't feel particularly comfortable speaking High (standard) German.

With our increasing numbers this meant some hundred tutorials, but it was a good way of getting to know the students at the beginning of their degree course and help identify their interests. As I read the papers and listened to every available media report, I became convinced that the Federal chancellor Helmut Kohl with his notorious 'Fifty Points' programme for the unification of Germany, announced in December 1989, was on the wrong and politically dangerous track. My essay question on the subject gave a considerable hostage to fortune: 'Write a robust critique of Chancellor Kohl's timetable for German unity as expressed in his Fifty Points.' By January 1990, when the essay tutorials started, it was clear that not only had he not been on the wrong track, but that he had indeed 'seized the moment'. Not for the last time in my teaching career, I had to put my hands up and tell the students I had got it spectacularly wrong.

A year or so later, together with the University Chancellor Dr Frank O'Reilly and the College Librarian, I was asked to accompany Helmut Kohl on the occasion of his state visit to Ireland to see the Book of Kells. As the only German-speaker I was assigned to walk close by him. Given my height of 1.76cm I am hardly small, but on account of Kohl's enormous height and girth and the fact that his great stomach seemed to bulge at least as far out to his left and right as it did in front, this was not easy. He showed informed interest in the Book of Kells, asking pertinent questions and lingering so long over it that his minders grew restive. Another incident connected with high-level German visitors to Ireland in these years is perhaps worth recalling. In anticipation of the state visit of German President Richard von Weizsäcker, I was invited to Áras an Uachtaráin to offer some pointers for President Robinson's speech at the forthcoming celebratory dinner at Dublin Castle. In honour of the occasion, I felt I should abandon my bicycle and arrive by car. Unfortunately, I had forgotten Dublin's appalling traffic. A twenty-minute bike ride up to Phoenix Park turned out to be a 45-minute drive and I came panting in the front door of the Áras, to be ticked off sternly by the adjutant for being late. Ushered into the drawing room I sank on to the sofa to get my breath back, only to hear, in the sharp Dublin accent of the waitress, 'Get off that sofa, missus, the sofa is for the president. Chairs are for youse.' I obeyed with alacrity.

Back in our department we were fortunate to be offered a DAAD *Lektor* by the German government. Jürgen Barkhoff had been an alumnus of the prestigious Konrad-Adenauer-Foundation; he was a graduate in German literature and language, and in history and education and came with his Basel-born wife, Doris. He had spent a year with us as a visiting student in 1986 and was passionate about Trinity College.* When in 1995 our student numbers allowed us to recruit an additional permanent staff member, he proved to be the outstanding choice.

## THEODOR FONTANE AND EAST GERMANY

In the weeks following the fall of the Wall almost half our students had sensibly begged and borrowed their fare to Berlin to witness the historic events at first-hand. It was almost a year before I had the chance to follow them. The Prussian-born novelist Fontane had long offered his readers a bridge between East and West, and in December 1990 several of us Fontane scholars travelled from western Germany, England, Scotland and Ireland to Potsdam to found the Theodor Fontane Gesellschaft, a literary society along the lines of those dedicated to the classical figures of German literature such as Goethe, Schiller, Kleist, Heine, Mann, Brecht and Gottfried Benn. All but one of us present were unanimous who the new society's founding president should be: unlike Konrad Adenauer in the cliff-hanger first Federal-German 1949 elections, Charlotte Jolles did not vote for herself. We welcomed her with acclaim. 'Who shall our society's patron be?' she asked us. Dismissing the more attractive characters as unsuitable to the times, she nominated the hard-headed businesswoman, Frau Jenny Treibel in Fontane's eponymous novel of 1892. 'Why? Because what our society and unified Germany are going to

---

\* He became Trinity's first non-Irish or non-British College Officer in the history of the College and at the time of writing (August 2021) has just completed his term of office as Vice-Provost of the College.

need in the next years is money, more money and much more money."* It was fascinating over the next years at last to be able to talk freely to ordinary Fontane readers from East Germany. They had formed the bulk of those I had met and whose company I had enjoyed on my first visits to the GDR in the 1980s for conferences, to work in the Fontane Archive and on excursions to the Brandenburg landscape the author wrote about. One such occasion included some smart detective work by Gotthard Erler to locate two missing students in East Berlin. We had a series of former addresses for them and when eventually we found the two unhappy and obviously undernourished young women, who had run out of money and moved to cheap (and awful) lodgings in an East Berlin warren, they gazed at me first in horror and then sobbed with relief, before agreeing to contact their families and return to Dublin to finish their degree.†

In the 'new' post-Wall East Germany our former GDR friends no longer had to look over their shoulders. They offered illuminating insights, positive as well as negative, into life as it was lived under the former Socialist regime. On the positive side: my friend Gotthard Erler and his wife Thérèse lived with their only daughter in a block of twelve one-and-a half-room flats alongside bus driver, factory worker and municipal employee neighbours. Learning that their daughter's wedding was due but guest accommodation non-existent – the few state-run hotels being beyond the means of ordinary citizens of that republic – a delegation of neighbours came to the Erlers, offering to take their annual two-week holidays to coincide with the wedding so that they could have all the family and friends they wished to invite and who could then stay

---

* The life and career of Charlotte Jolles, pioneering editor of nineteenth-century Germany's greatest novelist Fontane, exemplified much of Germany's recent history: born in 1909 as the daughter of a well-to-do Jewish businessman, she had just completed her doctorate at the University of Berlin in 1937 when she was advised by her supervisor to leave for England. Her doctorate unrecognized in Britain, she worked in menial jobs until in the 1950s, her London MA and published work won her a post as lecturer, and later a personal chair at Birkbeck College London University, from where she operated as a skilful mediator between scholars in East and West Germany.

† Would such maternalistic interference in students' rights be permitted today?

in their flats. But the darker side could never be ignored. In a population of sixteen million, one and a half million 'unofficial co-workers'
(IMA: *inoffizielle Mitarbeiter*) were secretly employed by the police
state, everywhere watching everyone else's move and contacts. When
the IMA dossiers were made available to the citizens, the poet Reiner
Kunze (among thousands of others) was devastated to learn that the only
member of his entire family and circle of friends and acquaintances who
had not spied and reported on him to the authorities was his wife. In 1991
I came to give the opening address to the first meeting of the Fontane
Society in his hometown of Neuruppin in Brandenburg and over the
next twenty-five years to the numerous now flourishing local branches
of the Society, giving talks on my research to gregarious audiences in
Schleswig-Holstein, Bavaria, the Rhineland, Berlin-Brandenburg and
attending conferences across the 'new' Germany. And we all saw how
right Charlotte Jolles had been: German unification cost money.

Fortunately, the new sixteen-state Federal Republic was established
on 3 October 1990* at a time of considerable prosperity in Germany,
although that would change within a few short years. The enormous
cost to the exchequer, partly funded by the *Soli* (solidarity tax) of
5.5 per cent additional tax on incomes above a certain level, and that it
was readily paid by West Germans, are eloquent facts often overlooked
nowadays.† There is no doubt that the former Federal Republic, government and people, were extraordinarily generous in response to the needs
of their eastern fellow countrymen. However, too little attention was
paid by either to the need to respect the dignity of former GDR citizens. This was perhaps inevitable, given the enormity of the task being
faced. Physical and monetary union was more easily achieved than
cultural, with growing dismay emerging in the relevant West German

---

* I never accepted the commonly used term 'reunification', since the new Federal
Republic was *not* a restoration of what had gone before.

† Although introduced (as so many taxes are) as 'temporary', it has continued for
decades, raising some €19 billion in 2019. Up to 2012 revenue from the *Soli* tax
exceeded government expenditure on eastern Germany; since then, much to the ire
of taxpayers, the ratio has declined sharply in favour of government revenue; in 2019
eastern expenditure accounted for only €3.6 billion.

officials responsible, as they began to discover just how disastrous the Socialist economy really was. Resentment began to express itself in the West at the lack of 'gratitude' on the part of the 'Ossis' (the flippant term for the Easterners). The latter felt understandably bitter after the euphoria of November 1989 at what they saw as the patronizing attitude of their new fellow citizens, their treatment as 'poor relations'. After all, it had been they and not the fortunate 'Wessis' who had paid the price of Hitler's war in the form of forty further years of dictatorship. There was also a degree of envy among Easterners at the far higher standard of living West Germans had so long enjoyed. Many young Ossis voted with their feet and moved to the West. They still do, which helps explain the current (2021) ascendancy in former East Germany of the populist neo-nationalist *Alternative für Deutschland*, with its mainly older age profile, and of other far-right political groupings, such as *Pegida*, which won a strong following in Saxony's capital Dresden and beyond.

In 1992–3 the German economy suffered a brief setback. Political tensions began to manifest themselves in street protests and attacks on immigrant workers, unleashing dormant anti-Semitic slogans. Towards the end of 1993 I found myself linked to these tragic events by the suicide of our former student and long-time close friend, Ilse Samuel. Her husband Herbert had died a few years before, but thanks to the support of her neighbours and many friends, she coped well at her home in Darwen near Blackburn. Then on the first Monday of December I received a letter from her, enclosing a copy of the letter which her former boss, the editor of the liberal Jewish-owned *Berliner Tageblatt*, had sent from his French exile and which was published in the London *Times*, on the day he took his own life in 1939. Why had Ilse done this? I rang immediately, but there was no reply. A neighbour called and found her. She had taken an overdose on the Sunday night, evidently in despair at the racist outbreaks in Herbert's old home of Rostock on the Baltic; for her this betokened a re-emergence of the Nazi nightmare. Three of us, her former classmate and now my Exeter colleague, John McKenzie, and a teacher friend travelled to Darwen; the Samuels had left us their library in their will. It was a bitter occasion for all of us. The familiar house, which we had so often visited, the photo on the wall of the raving beauty the young Ilse had been, were hard, but worst of all for me were the fine grey hairs on her hairbrush – she had died alone but evidently, as always, her beautifully groomed self. A year later I made a 'pious'* pilgrimage to Herbert's family home in Rostock. It had been confiscated by the Nazis, restored to Herbert in 1990, who gave it to the city on condition of one or two rooms being dedicated to a small museum on Jewish local history. Now known as the Max-Samuel-Haus after Herbert's progressive industrialist father,† the neo-classical villa was located on the Schillerplatz, the square named after Germany's great classical dramatist and poet, Friedrich Schiller, ‡ a poignant example of one of the many ironies of German-Jewish history. Reviled by pan-German nationalists over generations as 'un-German', the secularized Jews of nineteenth- and early twentieth-century Germany had exchanged their religious orthodoxy for the ethical values of German classicism. No sector of the population had adhered to them more faithfully than they have. When I arrived the doorkeeper at first refused to let me in. Vainly I showed him the letter I had written to the director announcing my coming: clearly anti-Semitic incidents had dictated extreme caution. Eventually, after I had told him at some length of our friendship, he grudgingly admitted me, and I wandered round the few sad remnants of a once-vibrant Rostock Jewish community.

Once back in Dublin it was time to put pressure on our publishers, Blackwell of Oxford, to produce Peter Skrine's history of German literature, which we had been discussing and writing for years. We had got to the stage of being able to write in the same style, so much so that even we found it at times difficult to recognize which of us

---

* In the sense Virgil uses '*pius Aeneas*' as describing Aeneas' affectionate and loyal memory to his dead father.

† He was the first employer in the region to grant his workers an eight-hour day in 1904, which earned him the disparaging nickname of 'Red Samuel'.

‡ Author of the *Ode to Joy* in Beethoven's Ninth Symphony, today the national anthem of the European Union.

had written a particular paragraph. The manuscript had been with the publishers since 1991, well in advance of their deadline. Unfortunately for us, we had reckoned without the extraordinary nonchalance, not to say crass inefficiency of Blackwell's then ever-changing editorial staff. When the book finally appeared in 1997 all of six years later and despite our vigorous protests under the extremely old-fashioned title, *A Companion to German Studies*, the character of the student reader had changed. Partly on account of the new commercialist philosophy regarding university education and the reduction of student grants, few British students could afford to buy books other than their set texts. Although a paperback edition followed in 1999, what should have been called: *A History of German Literature 1494–1994* with subtitle *From the invention of printing to the internet* did not have the hoped-for impact.

## IRELAND AND EUROPE

The Republic of Ireland was now slowly but steadily orientating itself towards Europe and the European norm in a variety of ways. It was expressed culturally in the increasing urban/ rural divide made evident in the outcome of the 1995 referendum on the Fifteenth Amendment to the Constitution to remove the prohibition on divorce. The referendum was won by the narrowest majority (50.28 per cent to 49.72 per cent on a 62.15 per cent turnout). Significantly, the only constituencies apart from Cork South-Central to vote in favour were the densely populated Dublin ones and the adjoining counties of Kildare, Louth and Wicklow. Business as well as government were now increasingly looking to continental Europe to offset our traditionally high dependence on Britain. We in Trinity welcomed this warmly, not least as increasing our graduates' employment opportunities. When the IDA opened offices in Germany, one of our graduates was appointed to manage the Frankfurt office. School and university exchanges grew in popularity, creating in time influential cross-European networks of their own. Irish people in search of greater opportunities had traditionally looked to the United States rather than continental Europe, Boston rather than Berlin.* Gradually, however, word of mouth began to favour Berlin. In the USA you could only get a job if it could be demonstrated that no American needed it; in Germany, as an EU-member state, you could just turn up, register with the authorities and fairly easily find a job, much more so if you had a good command of German. And if you made a decent hand of it, your prospects were excellent.

This was exemplified by the experience of two of our recent graduates. One got herself a job as a typist in the office of the Rector (President) of Munich University. After a couple of months, she, a non-native speaker, drew her line manager's attention to the fact that she was frequently having to correct the grammar and spelling of the texts she received, written by native Germans. The boss mentioned it to the Rector, who asked her to come and see him. He congratulated her on her excellent command of the German language and promoted her to an assistantship in his office. In another case, a young graduate got a junior office job with Siemens in Berlin who at the time were involved in building the new rail-less connection between the airport and city of Shanghai. She was moved to a similar position in Shanghai and after some time found herself typing out a fat manual on safety procedures. (During the whole of her university career this eminently practical young woman from Co. Cavan had continued to help run the family farm. Even up to the time of her final BA exams she went home at weekends to help milk the family's cows.) One evening in Shanghai she asked to see her German boss: she had concerns with the text she was typing. 'Why?' he asked, a shade patronizingly, she subsequently told me. 'Because this is written by experts. I know how ordinary people react in a crisis. I don't think the authors of this text do.' Instead of dismissing her, his characteristically German response was, 'OK, if you think you can do better, re-write it yourself.' She did, and after due revision Siemens promoted her to an executive position, which she held successfully for many years.

---

* The phrase in a speech by Tánaiste Mary Harney during the Fianna Fáil–Progressive Democrat administration, which gained wide currency.

For Ireland, as for our graduates, a major development of the 1990s was the expansion of the Financial Services Centre (IFSC) on Dublin's North Wall, the brainchild of the prominent businessman Dermot Desmond and the Labour TD, later Minister for Finance, Ruairi Quinn, and implemented subsequently by the Fianna Fáil administration under Albert Reynolds. I recall a conversation with the then Irish head of Deutsche Bank, Erich Matthiesen, at a meeting of the Irish-German Chamber of Commerce. He spoke of the very favourable reception given him as spokesman of his bank* by the Taoiseach when he inquired what the tax arrangements might be if they were to transfer their pension fund from the US back to Europe, specifically to Ireland. The significance of the IFSC for high-level graduate employment and more importantly for Ireland's international reputation (despite ups and downs) has been immense, with the 2015 Irish Government's 2020 Strategic Plan noting that some 400 plus companies were located there and 35,000 employed.

AN IRISH RESEARCH COUNCIL

One area in early-1990s Ireland which continued to lag significantly behind Europe was the low regard paid by the Irish government to research, particularly in the humanities and social sciences (apart from the Irish language and archaeology). Cultural institutions (which in other European countries had a high profile), such as the National Library, the National Archives or the Royal Irish Academy were traditionally a low government priority. When I was asked in 1993 to take over as Secretary of the Academy, of which I had been a member since 1986, Ireland still had no research council. The Royal Irish Academy is recruited from the leading scholars in their field across all academic disciplines apart from medicine (which has its own organization, the Royal College of Physicians). It is one of Ireland's oldest cultural institutions,

---

* The substantial fee I got for an evening's lecture to some of his visiting German banker colleagues financed a modest but year-long scholarship for one of our graduate students to a German university.

founded in 1786 under royal charter (of George III), as a sister institution of the British Academy and the Royal Society of Scotland, and is frequently called on to advise government. After independence it was thought to change the 'Royal' to 'National'. However, this would have meant forfeiting the many reciprocal rights and privileges as an ancient foundation recognized by national academies throughout the world, though relatively unknown to most Irish people. One of my main tasks, I learnt, would be to make progress on the matter of an Irish research council. For several years I had been part of an RIA lobby group, led by Máirtín Ó Murchú of Trinity and Nicholas Canny who held the chair of history at University College Galway. We had lobbied ministers and civil servants and were advised to wait on Nicholas' former colleague at Galway and then Minister for the Arts, Culture and the Gaeltacht, Michael D. Higgins. He addressed us eloquently for forty-five minutes on his belief in the importance of research and dismissed us graciously, adding as we left the room that his was the wrong ministry, and we should look elsewhere. The CEO of the Academy, Paddy Buckley, who had served in the Taoiseach's department under Charles Haughey, then suggested that we might seek the latter's advice. Though he was now no longer in power, Haughey was well known for his creative interest in the arts and matters cultural. We promptly received an invitation to lunch at his Kinsealy residence, Paddy advising me that we must be punctual not just to the minute, but to the second. As we drove up to the house on the appointed day on the dot of 12.59 pm, the hall door slowly opened and at precisely one o'clock Charlie stepped out to greet us.

Rarely have I spent a more stimulating two hours. His conversational powers were brilliant, his range fascinating. As he finally rose from the table to dismiss us (he had a certain air of royalty), he observed: 'If I were Taoiseach you would be going home with your research council, but I am not.' We sent a summary of the meeting, as requested, but never heard back. The next effort was to invite in 1995 Wolfgang Frühwald, now in his second term as President of the German Research Council to address the Academy on the topic of how a small European country like

Ireland might structure and fund research into the future. He agreed to do so and chose as his title '*Vorsprung durch Forschung*' [progress through research]: '*the management of scientific research in Ireland: a European perspective*'. With the help of the ever-efficient RIA office I convened a one-day meeting, which was attended by the relevant minister of the so-called Rainbow Coalition, Pat Rabbitte, and, among others, senior civil servants from a number of government departments, represent-atives from the European Commission's Directorate for Research and Development and the chairman of the Conference of Irish Universities. Minister Rabbitte opened the meeting and then left without waiting for the keynote address by Professor Frühwald, scheduled to follow imme-diately after the minister's official opening. * Mortified at the minister's discourtesy, I apologized to our visitor, who as a Bavarian from the great and ancient city of Augsburg was politically thoroughly streetwise. 'Don't give it a thought, Eda,' he said, 'politicians are all the same – they just need their *Auftritt* [moment in the limelight].' A handful of civil serv-ants, I noticed, took copious notes during his address, which managed to be intellectually of the highest order, thoroughly practical and on occasion downright witty. Nothing concrete emerged at the time, but perhaps an important seed had been sown. Sometime later I wrote a memorandum on the subject, which I was told was mentioned at a cabinet meeting after the Rainbow administration had been succeeded in 1997 by the Fianna Fáil and the Progressive Democrats coalition under Taoiseach Bertie Ahern. The memo's first sentence read: 'Ireland and Albania have one thing in common: we are the only states in Europe without a research council.'

In 1998 the new Minister for Education, Micheál Martin, briefed by his adviser on education, the UCD historian Maurice Bric, announced the founding of a provisional Irish research council, initially for the humanities and social sciences. This was to be followed in due course by

---

* In 1994 the DFG had had an annual budget of two billion Deutschmark or €850,000, which Frühwald had just successfully persuaded Federal Chancellor Kohl to increase by 50 per cent to three billion.

a separate council for the sciences.* Maurice would hold the key position of secretary, his fellow UCC graduate and then Dean of Research and Professor of Business Studies at Dublin City University, Tom McCarthy, would be finance officer; I was to chair it. Our Council would include leading scholars across the relevant disciplines from all the Irish universities. We reported to the Higher Education Authority and were given a small office in their Clanwilliam/ Mount Street premises but no secretarial staff. †

Being in at the beginning of an institution is arduous – one weekend that year I found myself having to type, in my customary two-fingered manner, 166 letters to members of the various sub-committees we had set up to make preliminary recommendations for the main assessment boards. But we had considerable freedom to devise the structures and conditions, a task at which Maurice Bric proved to be particularly adept.‡ Probably the most politically significant decision we took was that membership of the final assessment boards for all categories (PhD, Post-Doc., Fellowships etc) would be entirely external. No Irish academic would be part of the final selection process for recommendation to the council. This decision, initially vigorously criticized, was a key to the establishment of the Research Council's reputation at home and abroad. In a small country such as Ireland this policy decision protected us against charges of partiality. Within the year the structures were in place, the conditions for each award application agreed and the forms to be filled out by applicants printed and ready. When the Provisional Research Council for the Sciences was established in 1998, it was able to take over its complete documentation from us. To be sure, there were plenty of teething problems, but we

---

* The two Councils were later amalgamated as the Irish Research Council.

† A year or two later, space being at a premium in the offices of the HEA, we had to sacrifice half our own small offices to create a prayer space for an HEA secretary who had converted to Islam. This meant at busy times of the year piling the dozens of boxes of applications on top of one another, involving much heavy lifting and much energetic climbing up on chairs to retrieve and return them.

‡ See his report for the Minister: *The Humanities and Social Sciences. A Case for a Research Council* (1999).

got invaluable help from our experienced British colleagues, under the guidance of the professor of British and Irish history at Cambridge, John Morrill, member of the British Academy. They helped identify suitable international scholars for our selection boards, all of whom would give generously of their time and expertise. Over the years we properly extended our external experts to include leaders in their field from all over the world.

The new administration was indeed proving to be serious about investment in research. In 1998 Mary Harney set up an eight-man 'technology foresight' group to consider the case for what in 2003 became Science Foundation Ireland to fund blue skies* and applied research in the STEM areas. From our very first of many meetings a political agenda became apparent. This was the evident determination of the civil servants of Minister Harney's department to locate the new institution, which would attract a very considerable state investment, on a greenfield site and form part of their remit. Most, though not all, of us academics involved were concerned that unless the proposed SFI Fellows had a university base with their own doctoral and postdoctoral students, it would simply be uncompetitive with other international research foundations, all eager to recruit the best international next-generation scientists. Over the next year, four of us would regularly meet for breakfast prior to each meeting to discuss the agenda and our strategy: Gerry Wrixon, President of UCC, Don Thornhill, Chairman of the HEA, Maurice Bric and myself. Not being a scientist, my role at these foresight meetings was to ask seemingly naive questions to help steer discussion led by the other three to what were in our view the key issues. Together with the subsequent philanthropically funded Programme for Third-level Institutions (PRTLI), the SFI and the Research Councils have proved to be milestones in the modernization of the Irish research landscape, with very significant spin-offs for the Irish economy.

---

* Basic or 'curiosity-driven' research, whose material benefits may not be immediately evident, but which can produce unexpected and immensely valuable results. Professor Frühwald in his 1995 address to the Royal Irish Academy reminded his listeners that, on average, only 20 per cent of investment in such research will prove 'successful'.

Coincidentally with these developments I found myself involved in a new area of activity already briefly referred to, and one which would continue for some fifteen years or more. The 1990s and the following decade saw a Europe-wide demand for institutional assessment of the university sector, research councils and other such organizations supported by state funding agencies. By far the most wide-ranging was the Federal- and State Commission to examine the functioning of the German research system, with special reference to the German Research Council (DFG) and the Max-Planck-Gesellschaft (Max-Planck-Foundation).* We were a group of eight under the chairmanship of the head of the British Science and Engineering Council, professor of material science/ceramics at Oxford University; five were colleagues from Germany, Austria and Switzerland. The other anglophone member was the president of Stanford University, who had emigrated from Germany some thirty years earlier. Thankfully, I was for once not the sole woman: our social scientist member was a colleague from the renowned Zurich Polytechnic Helga Novotny, originally from Vienna. The amount of documentation we received prior to our numerous site visits across Germany during the two years of our investigations across the state was impressive in its bulk and detail. On these visits, among them to Bonn (at the time still the Federal capital), Munich and Dresden, we met university and research council personnel, heads of state government, ministers and senior civil servants, the German education and research sector being within State rather than Federal competence. During the many weeks we spent together working for the Commission, our Stanford colleague and I continually found common ground, for the Anglo/Hibernian–American tradition is more student-oriented than it is in the German university system, represented by our six other colleagues. We were concerned that the German university requirement of a second major doctorate, the *Habilitationsschrift*, as a mandatory

---

* *Bund-Länder-Kommission zur Evaluierung des deutschen Forschungssystems*. The Max-Planck-Society for the Advancement of Science is a formally independent non-governmental and non-profit association of German research institutes dedicated to basic research and the promotion of the careers of outstanding young scientists.

qualification for appointment to tenured university posts was disad-
vantageous to women, and indeed could force them to have to choose
between university career and having a family. Our arguments, although
carefully considered, were not in the end accepted.

Yet the atmosphere among those we met was always impressively
open and reflective. This was indeed the new, Europe-focused Germany,
conscious of its obligations to the international community. Following
receipt of our final report, we were given extensive feedback by the
various parties, all in all an enlightening and enriching experience.

Probably in consequence of membership of that review group, I
found myself over the next decade involved increasingly in commissions charged with assessments for national research systems and grant-
awarding bodies, among them the Danish, Norwegian, Swiss and Israeli
research councils. Sometimes I was asked to take part in assessments
of departments of German, as in the universities of the Federal State
of Saxony and of individual universities such as Berne and Lucerne in
Switzerland, and of the humanities faculty at Salzburg, which I chaired.

The last decade of the old millennium ushered in a memorable
milestone, which brought me back memories of my father's stories of
his long and unfruitful attempts to promote reconciliation between the
two jurisdictions on the island of Ireland. With the historic signing of
the so-called Good Friday or Belfast Agreement of 1998, the 1990s peace
process was finally brought to fruition. Brokered by Taoiseach Bertie
Ahern and the British Prime Minister Tony Blair with the tireless assistance of US Senator George Mitchell, it became law following referenda
in both parts of Ireland on the eve of 2 December 1999. Recognizing the
legitimacy of the wish of the majority of people in the north of Ireland
to remain part of the United Kingdom and of the substantial proportion
of the citizenry there and of the Republic of Ireland to aspire to a united
Ireland, the Agreement brought to an end much of the thirty-year-old
violence. However, to most citizens of the Republic, the 'North' was
a foreign country, more foreign in a sense than England, since relatively few people ever travelled there, apart from Christmas shoppers
taking train trips to Newry and Belfast when currency differentials were

favourable. For, as one of my father's closest friends, the long-serving Stormont MP Cahir Healy had bitterly observed back in 1925, '… the Free State leaders … launched us [the northern nationalists], rudderless, into the hurricane, without guarantee or security, even for our ordinary civic rights'.* For all the anti-partition talk of Irish politicians and governments thereafter, we, Irish citizens and our governments, had effectively turned our backs on Northern Ireland until the first two women Presidents of Ireland, Mary Robinson and the Co. Down-born Mary McAleese (1997–2011), courageously began to challenge hidebound mentalities on both sides of the border. As in the case of the fall of the Berlin Wall, I deemed myself very fortunate to have lived to see the Good Friday Agreement.

I retired on 30 September 1998. Now at last I was able to spend more time and do things together with Albert who had been so supportive over these previous twenty-three years at Trinity, never once making me feel guilty at spending so much time away from him and the family. Initially it was something of a shock to have me around the house and start interfering as I inevitably did with the way he ran the house, as my golfing friend Anne O'Riordan wittily observed when her husband retired: 'For better or for worse, for richer or for poorer, in sickness and in health – but not for lunch.' In September 1998, following my retirement my departmental colleagues put on a wonderful send-off in the form of a symposium on 'Germany's challenging nineteenth-century'† attended by virtually all my Irish, German and British friends/colleagues and accompanied by a memorable dinner in the Dining Hall with countless numbers of former students and speeches which made me weep in gratitude and ache with laughter. Sheila Watts was responsible for coordinating my Trinity colleagues' parting gift, a portrait by Andrew Festing, following five days sitting in his London studio. (I was a highly self-conscious sitter – at one stage the artist called to Albert, 'Will you stop her talking and fidgeting!') My vanity was injured when

---

* In an open letter to the *Irish Statesman* 17, 354 (18 December 1926).

† Published under the editorship of Jürgen Barkhoff, Gilbert Carr and Roger Paulin. (Tübingen: Niemeyer, 2000).

I saw the penultimate result with a protruding vein on my neck to which he replied, 'I paint what I see.' An accommodation was reached and thanks to my Trinity colleagues' generosity I joined the handful of Trinity women and the many male academics hanging on the walls of the Provost's House and Common Room.[*]

---

[*] Since then, many fine portraits of Trinity women have been added to the collection, most notable that of Corinna Lonergan by Carey Clarke.

# — TEN —

## *The 2010s: towards the finish?*

In the years following Albert's death and the loss of the caring role I had had for nearly a decade, voluntary work helped fill an emotional need in my new life as a gregarious person now living alone. Thus, when I saw a stocky, elderly man with a crutch limping along with his shopping bag near the local supermarket, I stopped to offer him a lift home; he was having none of it. The crutch, I later learnt, was the result of a couple of failed hip operations. As a labourer on construction sites in Britain, he told me later, he had regularly carried up to fourteen tons of cement in bags on his shoulder weekly. The following week I encountered him again, and this time he grudgingly accepted. That was the beginning of a thoroughly eccentric friendship, and as far as I was concerned a privileged insight into quite another side of life in mid-twentieth-century Ireland from the one I had known. Paddy Maugham, a couple of years younger than myself, was a Mayo man, born, he believed, into a Traveller family. At four years of age, probably on the death of his mother in childbirth,* he was arrested for begging and sent to one of the

---

\* Towards the end of his life he was contacted via the social services by a woman four years his junior who alleged she was his sister; he showed me her photograph – the

more notorious industrial schools, Letterfrack in Galway. 'I remember a man coming to see me now and then,' he recalled, 'but then he didn't come any more. Oh yes, and I once got to share a bar of chocolate at Christmas with another boy, just the once.' The regime was evidently both harsh and soulless, long hours working on the bogs or the potato fields, punishment for every misdemeanour, while the universal use of the leather strap in the classroom had the effect, he once said, that none of them really ever learnt to read or write. But Paddy was a survivor and, having been sent at sixteen from Letterfrack to work for a local farmer with no pay and minimal food, he ran away and managed to get himself to England where for twenty years and more he built motorways, hospitals and schools:

> McAlpine went by motor-car
> And Wimpey went by train.
> And Paddy tramped the Great North Road,
> And got there just the same.[*]


My Saturdays with Paddy led in due course to my being absorbed into his 'network'. Years after his death I am still invited every month or so to visit a family who had befriended him. Although they themselves had few worldly goods, they generously re-filled his whiskey glass when we went there for tea. It all started with his friend and regular sparring partner Brendan, whom we would meet on Saturdays at the nearby Sundrive supermarket. Paddy was usually grumpy and dismissive of Brendan, a bachelor and retired parks attendant who lived in a local council flat. Brendan irritated Paddy with his invariable good humour ('What has

---

dead spit of him, I felt. She had been put into care on the death of her mother and was now a grandmother. They arranged to meet and 'she was nice enough'. To prove relationship, he would need to do a DNA test, costing €660. Paddy, living on an old-age pension, was careful though never mean with money. But I don't think that was the real reason why he refused to take it any further: he just didn't have the emotional energy.

[*] Cit. in John O'Donoghue. *In a Strange Land.* (London, 1958), 202.

he to be cheerful about?'), as he exchanged pleasantries with a group of elderly men and women outside the post office, for whom the Saturday morning shop was an event in their social calendar. Our ritual was always the same. For the first few months of our acquaintance, I would collect Paddy at his small house at 8.45 am (I got a lash of his tongue if I was even a minute late), take him to the supermarket, carry his bag to the car now heavy with potatoes, a turnip and a head of cabbage, loaves of bread etc., wait while he had his argument with Brendan, then across to the butcher for his week's supply of steak, sausages and bacon. We would then go back for a cup of tea and a chat about life and politics in his sitting room, always grubby but well-ordered for his needs. He had his sack of coal on one side of the fire, his armchair on the other and on the mantelpiece the photographic record of his annual visits to the diocesan pilgrimages to Lourdes. Pride of place was the framed picture of an unusually benign-looking Paddy alongside Dublin's Archbishop Diarmuid Martin, well over a foot taller than he.

The story of Paddy's life as he told it to me over the five or six years of our friendship is a vignette of Irish social history of our generation for those born poor. I learnt of his early years, his work 'on the lump' in Britain, where he virtually never had contact with any but his fellow countrymen, his return to Ireland, again working on roads and building bridges, his thirty-year-long marriage to 'a nice quiet woman' whom he had met aged forty at a dance hall, the monthly visits to Cappagh Hospital to see his wife's sister who had been born with severe encephalitis. I would drive him there and was always treated to a solid three-course lunch (at the generously subsidized cost of three euro). Then there was the redress process: 'I got a whole set of solid windows with the money,' he would say proudly. And then there was the visit to his wife's grave, and finally his funeral. When he first asked me to drive him to the grave, I naturally said yes, presuming it was in some Dublin churchyard. 'I'll treat you to a B&B and your dinner,' he told me grandly. 'But where is her grave?' 'Oh, in West Clare.' A promise was a promise, but the idea of me and Paddy overnight in a B&B was not a prospect I relished, so, as we were both early risers, I proposed starting out at six o'clock in the morning. The four-hour journey each way could be well managed in a day. I arrived a few minutes early to find Paddy looking impatiently at his watch and already arguing with Brendan, whom to my relief he had asked to 'come along for the ride' and who as usual took no notice of Paddy's remarks. It was pouring cats and dogs as we bumped along the country roads between Ennis, where Paddy stopped at a newsagent's shop to buy flowers, and the cemetery out on a promontory over the Atlantic. His duty done, Paddy invited us both to a slap-up dinner at the local hotel in Ennistymon, and I felt a right snob as I ate my share with eyes averted as the two elderly men left part of the menu on their grubby pullover fronts.

The best was yet to come. As we arrived back that evening, tired but with a sense of achievement, Paddy turned to Brendan: 'You know,' he said, 'Eda is not a bad driver.' He paused and added: 'For a woman.' But I never lost my admiration for him, for what he had made of his life after such a dreadful start, and though he never expressed it, his readiness to accept whatever good came his way. When he had to go into the hospice at Harold's Cross towards the end of his life and I visited him in the shabby old ward, he declared contentedly that they looked after him well and the 'grub is good'. One or two years into our friendship he told me he had decided to learn to read properly (he could manage the headlines in the *Mirror* and the *Evening Herald*) and to do sums. This surely was an amazing example of his doggedness in making a success of his life where others would have gone under. Through *Alone,* that wonderful organization founded by Willie Bermingham, the fireman who had become familiar with some of the appalling conditions Dublin's old and poor had to endure, he got himself a tutor and even bought a computer. He would tell me of his progress on our Saturday outings and of the social events the organization now provided him with. Such was the stimulus these gave him, a naturally gregarious man, that he started going on bus tour holidays for the first time since his wife's death. I wish he could have been at his own funeral in the local church, with a harpist, attended by some twenty people who had helped him, his social worker in the redress process, his adult literacy and computer tutors and several neighbours, the bin man and even the newsagent from Ennistymon. A group of them subsequently accompanied his coffin all the way across Ireland to join his wife in Clare. These are the kind of stories that do not get into the media, but which give a glimpse into the contribution that the voluntary sector gives to Irish society.

There was a nice sequel for me a few years later, in 2019. I got a phone call one lunchtime from the McGowan family Brendan had introduced me to when I used to drive himself and Paddy on visits to their home in Harristown. The family was from Co. Leitrim, neighbours of Brendan's in their early days. Now he had suffered a stroke and was in hospital in St James's. When I got to the ward, I found the father on one side of the bed talking to him, on the other Louise, one of his three pretty daughters, holding the unconscious Brendan's hand, calling his name and from time to time kissing him on the forehead. Both had taken time off work at their own expense to be there. During the next week they came every day and phoned me to tell me how he was getting on. Brendan never recovered consciousness and one day Louise rang to say he had died and that he was lying in a Crumlin funeral home. He had no family anyone knew of. When I went to join them, I found his open coffin surrounded by mourners, the neighbours and other fellow Leitrim friends, at its feet a pile of Leitrim regional newspapers with the racing news prominent. Leitrim figured prominently next day at the cremation, the ceremony concluding with rousing Leitrim songs.

IRELAND'S SOCIAL EVOLUTION

I felt myself fortunate to have lived to witness some of the remarkable developments in Ireland's social history which took place in the 2010s, notably the introduction of civil marriage between two persons regardless of their sexual orientation, and the Thirty-fourth Amendment to the Constitution (2015) to permit abortion in certain circumstances, carried in the event by a large majority. Surprisingly, the vote had not split along religious vs secular lines. There were also notable divisions between the different confessions. Within the Protestant community, the Church of Ireland was generally, Methodists broadly supportive, while Presbyterians were vigorously opposed. The Catholic Church was forthright in its opposition, but unexpected was the statement issued by the Islamic Centre at Clonskeagh's mosque on 17 April, a month before the vote, expressing the belief that 'as Muslims we must believe in equality and inclusiveness. The Constitution guarantees all Irish citizens freedom of conscience and Muslims must exercise that right when voting on 22 May 2015.' The broad consensus obtaining across the generations, if much less evident among older citizens, was expressed by the Labour leader Brendan Howlin: 'The one issue at the core of this referendum is equality under the Constitution, and anything else is extraneous.' Further evidence of how Irish society was changing, particularly at its younger end, was the positive public reaction to the succession to Enda Kenny of Dr Leo Varadkar in 2017 as the first openly gay Taoiseach in the history of our state. His status as a gay man and the fact that he was half Indian by birth probably attracted more global media attention abroad than at home. Irish citizens in the interim years were far more focused on events affecting their personal lives, notably the bank crash of 2008/9, the consequences of which continued to put a question mark over their future and the Irish state's capacity to survive. And then there was the great unknown: the impact on Ireland of the Brexit vote in June 2016, the full consequences of which, I believe, are yet to be felt.

## MY FRIEND MARYANNE

Up until 2012 almost all my voluntary work with the bereaved and those in hospital had been among people I had never previously met. Although over time some became good friends, I was not emotionally involved. In the next year or two that pattern changed: my oldest friend Maryanne started, very gradually, to forget arrangements we had made. When one of us called to collect her, she was never ready. She would constantly lose her wallet or forget her keys, creating problems on her return. It took us years to recognize what would turn out to be the seven-year saga of her Alzheimer's. Four of us cared for her in those years:

Maeve McRedmond, her other close friend from College days, and her next-door neighbours, the two Harte sisters, Marie, a cardiologist, and Michelle, a social worker, both nearly twenty years younger than Maeve and me. I had had little experience with dementia. My mother, our elderly relations and Albert had suffered a degree of memory loss in their final years, but no more than was a predictable part of ageing. And yet what astonishes me in hindsight is how I could have failed to realize that what was happening to my dear friend, that it was not just her legendary unpunctuality and tendency to sit back and let others take the initiative, but something far more serious.

I record our experience over the next years to help us empathize with those going through the process, whether as subject or carer, of what is in fact the horrible disintegration of a personality. I really should have been quicker on the uptake, especially considering that in the winter of 2011–12 I had taken a lecture course on '21st Century Brain Research' given by a combined team of leading researchers in their discipline at Trinity College: in psychology, neuroscience, chemistry, physics, biology, physiology and sociology.* Most of the lecturers on the eighteen-week course were collaborating on their special area on research into two diseases, Parkinson's and Alzheimer's. At one of our first sessions, the physiology lecturer showed slides of a contrasting cross-section of two human brains. To my amusement one was of a healthy seventeen-year-old male, the other, much-diminished, that of a 77-year old female, recently widowed: whatever about the brain size, the 'further particulars' matched my then situation precisely. I was reassured by the point made by the professor of psychology and at the time current Dean of Research at Trinity, Ian Robertson, when he listed the more useful strategies in delaying the onset of memory loss (and worse) in older people. These were, he suggested, staying usefully involved in other people's lives, identifying with their needs and supporting them

* Wolfgang Frühwald said to me on a visit to their Augsburg home in 2006 following his lengthy stints as President of the German Research Council and the Max Planck Foundation that just as the discovery of the human genome had been the great achievement of twentieth-century research, the human brain would be the key topic for the new century.

to the best of one's abilities, learning new skills (the most effective on account of the combination of cognitive and motor skills being learning to play a new musical instrument – alas, not for me) and taking plenty of exercise. But as my friends and I learnt from our extended networks of acquaintances over the following years, dementia in its various forms is harshly democratic: you could do all these things and many more, and still become its victim.

It was doubly odd that I still didn't face the fact that Maryanne was ill, considering that we both had some experience with a parish neighbour, Angela, with whom we both regularly played bridge. She, like Maryanne, was unmarried without close family ties, had never left home except for annual holidays, looked after elderly parents till their death and since then had lived alone with and for her dog. As Angela was a keen gardener, in the summer of 2014 I suggested a short trip to the National Trust gardens of Northern Ireland. Having collected Maryanne we arrived for Angela, who evidently still needed to pack: her dog, whom she had assured us would go to kennels for the duration, was sitting expectantly on the doorstep. And the arrangements? 'I didn't get around to them, so we'll have to take her with us.' I'm not keen on domestic pets and the need to stop every half hour on our circuitous journey to our Enniskillen B&B via the rhododendron gardens of Rowallane in Co. Down to 'meet the dog's needs' only confirmed my prejudices. But otherwise, it was a happy memory of the beautiful Fermanagh gardens of Florence Court, Crom and Castle Coole and of northern hospitality, the various excursions enlivened by constantly having to re-trace our steps to retrieve forgotten handbags and wallets, which invariably turned up in the car. That winter Angela's condition deteriorated rapidly: she was taken into hospital after a fall and a night lying alone on the floor, discovered only by accident by a friend who happened to call; she had virtually no food in the house and her clothes, normally so spick and span, had evidently been long unwashed. Her oldest friend, now wheel-chair-bound, phoned to tell me, reminding me that Angela was a very private person. I visited her weekly but while she was glad to see me, the subject of why she was in hospital was carefully avoided by both of us.

After six months of her VHI insurance footing the bill of some €110,500, she was transferred to a ward with three utterly demented women, with nowhere to store her clothes. These were just stacked in a holdall under the bed in a corner from which I had to poke to retrieve her weekly washing; it became evident there was no one else doing it. She died several months later shortly after her eightieth birthday, just when her wardship of court finally came through. Fear of what lay ahead had evidently prevented her from seeking medical aid from her local family doctor or making any arrangements. Angela's story is yet another harsh example of how even many reasonably well-off citizens can slip through the net of Irish society and face illness and death alone.

Maryanne's situation was similar but different, since she had always been a sociable and generous person with many friends who loved her company and knew to look out for her. My active and at times bossy involvement began when she started having problems with her finances. She had worked almost all her life for the Irish lighthouse service, first as a shorthand typist and later in the lower rungs of middle management, Irish Lights being a patriarchal and thoroughly male-dominated organization. I felt she must have a reasonably decent pension, as she had never had to pay rent or, as some parents might have insisted, contribute to her keep. At first things just got 'stolen', mainly her wallet, and she would ring to ask me to take her to the bank. Or she would run out of money, and again we were off to the bank. Soon when I went to sit down while she transacted her business, she would ask me to queue with her, and when I stood back as her turn at the counter came, she would ask me to help her write her cheque or, more particularly, lodge a share dividend. The first was temporarily dealt with when she was introduced to the ATM machine and, oddly enough, never forgot her pin number. She insisted I memorize it and I resisted until she got distressed, fortunately, as it turned out. The following year she started ringing me up a couple of times a week. With her 'small' pension she was, she said, having to scrimp on food. I was reluctant to interfere. Eventually she got so distressed that she insisted I look at her bank statement. To my amazement the pension was quadruple the supposed amount, and her current account was some

€44,000 in credit. Even then, the phone calls continued, and each time I simply took out her bank statement from its place and reassured her. My problem, and it is the same for everyone in my situation, was and is respect for the other person's dignity. To take over responsibility for significant activities in another person's life, even in what you believe is their best interest, is to deprive them of their liberty.

The bank file in her neat finances folder was not her doing, but a consequence of a court summons for non-payment of tax on her shares over several years. This was sorted out by her nephew, a very busy GP living some twenty miles away. He engaged an accountant, who spent several sessions in her home, put her finances in order and organized a file for her various documents, which had been retrieved from various locations around the house. Meanwhile, whenever I called twice or three times a week to drive her to friends or have a meal in my house and waited for her to get ready, I noticed piles of unopened post on her table. If I mentioned it Maryanne's answer was always, 'They can wait.' Then she rang to say the accountant hadn't received her annual tax form and was pressing her to make the returns or get a friend to help her. Would I do it? Of course. What a mountain! Firstly, the unopened envelopes contained repeat demands for unpaid bills, house insurance, utilities, bin service etc. Where was the folder? She brought it down from her study as I still wasn't allowed upstairs. It was a complete mess. Several key papers had disappeared. Eventually, if I was going to take charge of her affairs, bad conscience or not, I had to resort to deceit. I took advantage of her neighbour Michelle's visit to ask her to keep Maryanne engaged as I slipped upstairs to the study.

It was an unbelievable sight, later described by Michelle with her social worker experience as 'senile squalor'. To get into the study you had to climb over rolls of old carpet on the narrow landing to find inside the door boxes of purchases never used: garden furniture, printers, television sets, curtain materials, unopened packets of medicines. Papers were scattered everywhere. The chairs and a sofa bed were piled high with tea sets, cooking equipment, vases, trays and a variety of objects, some not yet out of their packets. It was not much different in the other rooms. The smallest of the four upstairs rooms had been occupied for a time by a former junior colleague of Maryanne's at Irish Lights, who had fallen ill and become homeless. In the kindness of her heart, she had taken him in to stay with her for a few weeks, much against the advice of Maeve McRedmond's husband Louis, who as an experienced lawyer and old College friend was anxious that she should not be exploited. The man stayed for years but eventually moved into a nursing home, leaving many of his possessions in her house. They overflowed the wardrobe and chest of drawers, the residue piled on his former bed, with several more items in the large spare bedroom. How he and she between them had amassed so many boxes and bottles of medicines, again many unopened, we could not understand: at one stage I filled fifteen black sacks and carted them off to her reluctant but obliging chemist for disposal. Maryanne's own bedroom was merely full of clothes and several office-type large plastic containers, overflowing with papers. Only in hindsight did we come to understand our friend's almost manic passion over the years for retail therapy as a sort of sad compensation for what she felt was her life's failure. If I was to take charge of her affairs, I had to confess, which I did, making little of the 'bit of untidiness'. Her reaction made me feel thoroughly guilty: 'You know, Eda, I'd trust you with my life. I was afraid you would think less of me if you saw the mess I am in.'

Over the next few months, with Michelle's always surreptitious help, I gradually made inroads, in the process making some unexpected discoveries. I sorted the finance folder, which I then hid from her 'investigations'. With the professional assistance of her empathic accountant Thérèse Bermingham we got her tax affairs into routine order. I would assemble the necessary information each year while Thérèse submitted the returns. The bills were paid as they came in. Initially she resisted the idea of direct debits: 'I need to keep control,' she would say. It was only when the overflowing bins were not collected, the heating oil ran out and penalties were impending from unpaid property tax that I overrode her objections. With her permission I lodged dividend cheques, but she seemed uninterested now that she had shed responsibility. When I asked her bank's advice about transferring the greater part of her current account balance to a deposit account, I discovered that she had over €100,000 in a separate savings account, but in another branch. Again, she wasn't interested. The last bastion to be tackled were the plastic boxes in her large bedroom. They were so packed with papers that with her permission I simply took them home to sort at leisure: papers and bills going back over sixty years had never been thrown out. Over the winter of 2015 to 2016 I went through the six boxes plus piles of papers from the study, sorting each category into their separate box, in consultation with her nephew who alas was now seriously ill with cancer. I shredded, tore up and disposed of some twenty-five sacks of ancient bills, bank statements and other yellowing papers. It was not much different with the clothes, many never worn. Her four wardrobes were so full that it was hard to hang up any of the garments lying around. The seventeen jumpers retrieved from her bed and the ten pairs of slacks were sorted and put in drawers. On my next visit, a couple of days later, they were all back in the bed, perhaps like some comforting teddy bears. Among the papers I discovered uncashed dividend cheques going back years to the value of over €18,000 (later, when we were clearing the house after she eventually went into care in November 2017, Michelle and I discovered another €12,000 worth).

It was a simple task to sort out the domestic disorder compared with the problems of her physical health. Always slim, she was visibly losing weight and would eat voraciously whenever she came over for a meal with me. She would complain of being sick, until we took to checking her fridge, and often found her food long past its sell-by date. Maeve, Marie and Michelle and I organized a rota to have her fed most days, but she had stoutly resisted having anyone in the house. 'Are you saying there's something wrong with me?' she would ask suspiciously. When Maeve's husband Louis died and Maeve no longer needed her Filipino cleaner Janet for several hours, she cleverly appealed to Maryanne's soft heart: 'I find I can't afford Janet, but she needs the money: you couldn't take a few hours?' She would, of course. It was also thanks to Maeve's strategy that two years earlier before her cognitive deterioration set in, we had successfully arranged to have Maryanne's nephew and myself given power of attorney: Angela's wretched last months had made me all too aware of the problems of failing to make viable financial arrangements. But how to persuade Maryanne? Then one day, having rung her nephew for his permission (only too gladly given in view of his own illness), I asked her to do me the favour of giving me moral support while I organized it for myself. 'Most of my relations, you'll remember, Maryanne, got a bit gaga in old age,' I reminded her. While we were waiting in the solicitor's office she suddenly piped up, as we had hoped: 'And I might as well do the same.'

How thankful we and her nephew and his wife were that this had been done in time, as in the course of 2015 her problems became more and more time-consuming. She would refuse to eat what Janet cooked for her while insisting she had already eaten. I brought her lunch, or she came over to me. Maeve took her out twice a week for a meal and had the same experience, as did her neighbours who cooked for her at the weekend. There were ever more minor crises and phone calls for help. I would ring several times a week, only to find I couldn't get through, would drive over and find the telephone was off the hook, the mobile lost. Over the next two more difficult years, I found myself falling into the lamentable tendency to regard Maryanne as 'a problem' rather than as a person. The same had happened to me a few times in the last months of Albert's illness, making me feel guilty but unable to stop my thoughts. She clearly needed full-time care but there was no way she would give her consent. I can never forgive myself for the abortive relief I felt on the day a phone call came through on a bad line to the effect '... MacDonald has died'. *Poor Maryanne, at last*, I thought. But no, it was her nephew. In the end she had an accident in November 2017 and was brought to hospital to be discharged into the care of Highfield Healthcare in the north Dublin suburb of Whitehall, which specialized in patients suffering from Alzheimer's and other forms of dementia. The Hartes and I, usually with Maeve, took turns to visit her each week, distressed to see her soon reduced to skin and bone, her warm and witty former self transformed into a poor soul who would either piteously beg to be taken home or physically attack you. And yet the care philosophy and practice of that wonderful institution, which had been founded by a doctor from his private means and was now under the direction of his son as a public hospital, was such that, though we invariably went in with dread, we always left feeling full of admiration at the sheer kindness and imaginative care with which all the staff treated their patients, as if they were their own mothers or grandmothers. The saga of Maryanne's illness brought home to me how fragile each individual life is, what an immense amount of care is involved in supporting someone with dementia, who is unmarried, lives alone and either has no family or whose few relatives are not at hand to deal with minor crises. Maryanne had a genius for friendship but what we did had never been enough.

And what of those without close friends, the many who for reasons of self-respect, have kept themselves to themselves? On 1 June 2019, just as my companions on our *Via Francigena* pilgrimage to Rome had reached the top of a Tuscan hill, and stopped bathed in perspiration, my mobile rang: Maryanne had died. I managed to get a plane home next morning and arrived in time for her funeral, organized by her nephew's widow and their children only months after their own father's death. Seventy-eight years of friendship, a good part of it shared with Albert who loved her company and wit, and whose affection for her was mutual.*

When Maryanne had gone into care in 2017, an immediate issue was what to do about her house in the sought-after suburb of Donnybrook and which was needed to help fund her long-term care. Her nephew and niece were all too happy to have Michelle and me look after it. We contacted an agent who agreed to take over responsibility for finding tenants for the house, once we had cleared the contents. And what a marathon it was, physically extremely hard work and emotionally taxing, as, after checking every piece to be disposed of with her heirs, we found ourselves carting off to an auctioneer innumerable objects

---

* On a lighter note: one night in 1970 I couldn't sleep. I had found a small lump on my breast. I was clearly going to die: two-year-old Mireia would somehow be fine, but, I feverishly thought, what about Albert? And then the solution came to me: I would write to Maryanne, ask her to wait a year after my death and then propose to Albert: he'd never do it himself, but they would be ideal for each other. Years later I told Maryanne who immediately said with a grin, 'What a pity. I'd have jumped at it!'

which had once meant something to Maryanne (such as her three or four tea sets, most never used) and guiltily dumping so many others. Just as the last of the endless black sacks had been squeezed into the bins or paid to be taken to the city dump, we remembered the attic, which proved to be brim-full of possessions of sixty years, including ancient Christmas decorations.

Looking back at the time of writing two years after her death, it feels as though I had done nothing else for the previous seven years. This wasn't so. I had just allowed myself to become obsessed with it all, partly no doubt from feelings of survivor guilt. Those years were also a further part of constructing my new life, of having to learn after almost half a century of marriage to be and to do things differently: how to put petrol into the car (I had never done it in forty-seven years), fill out my tax returns and create new daily and weekly routines as a single person where for so long we had done them as a couple.

In August 2013 I turned eighty. Later that year the Provost, Patrick Prendergast, graciously allowed me to hold the launch of my father's biography in the wonderful salon of Provost's House. (I had spent the previous ten years reading myself into the vast mass of secondary literature of the period and familiarizing myself with the primary sources via evening courses.) The book was launched with an eloquent speech by Liam Cosgrave, former Taoiseach and son of my father's first 'boss', W.T. Cosgrave, as head of the first Free State government. * I planned it as a first volume on the lives of the early Free State civil servants, to be followed by one on Ireland's first minister to Washington, T.A. Smiddy, and then one on the brilliant Paddy McGilligan, who among other things had been Minister for Industry and Commerce, External Affairs, and Finance, Professor of Law at UCD and who for some surprising reason has hitherto eluded the biographer. My biography of Tim Smiddy, my mother's father, based on an unexpectedly rich archive of official documents (mainly in the NAI) and substantial family papers, including over

---

* Eamon Phoenix officiated at the Northern Ireland launch in Dungannon, attended, to my great pleasure, among others by my former student, Rev. Dr Charles McMullen of West Church, Bangor, and his wife Barbara.

400 letters, appeared in the autumn of 2018. The McGilligan project will have to wait for someone else. His papers in UCDA I found to contain few personal documents and would have to be read via often poor-quality microfiches demanding on elderly eyes.

Mireia and John, with the help of their friend and restaurant chef Áine Maguire, had marked my transition into old age by a terrific party in the house for all my family and friends from my department, golf and various other activities. Áine's memorable supper included among other delights an entire wild salmon and three whole fillet steaks. But, whether I liked it or not, I had to face the fact: at eighty, one is old and *die Wehwehchen des Alters,* the little aches and pains of ancient-hood, make themselves felt and threaten, if you let them, to take over one's life. I had planned to mark the occasion of entry to my ninth decade in imitation of my colleague, the classicist and Trinity's renowned Public Orator, John Luce, by climbing Croagh Patrick, the great former volcanic mountain commanding spectacular views over Clew Bay across from our son-in-law John's parental home in Rosbeg, Westport. Alas, arthritic knees soon put paid to the idea. At that point a much more attractive offer came up: I was invited to join a group of four people, almost twenty years my junior, on the current section of their annual pilgrimage walk to Santiago de Compostela. It was their second time doing the entire 1550-km stretch of the Camino Frances from Puy de Dôme in France; the previous year they had come over the Pyrenees in temperatures of 40°C. This time they were to start their annual 200-km section in the cooler autumn, at the stage called Puerto de Reina in the province of Navarra, named after its magnificent Romanesque bridge. May Redmond was a golfing friend to whom I had been giving occasional German lessons so that she could talk to her daughter-in-law's family from East Germany, who had no English. The party consisted of herself and her husband Aidan, their brother-in-law Kieran, an Augustinian friar, biblical scholar and art historian, and his Italo–English confrère Paul Graham, who at the time was Provincial of the Order in England. Would I manage it? Wouldn't I be a drag on the others, seasoned hill-walkers as they all were? For three of them even had had experience of walking in the mountains of Nepal. It is not a race, May assured me, and everyone goes at their own pace and even some of the way by bus or taxi.

So I said yes and that September started on what would prove to be one of the most enjoyable experiences of my later life. May provided me with a detailed list of necessities, from blister packs for toes and heels and Vaseline for tender foot soles and a two-litre plastic bag for water to a minimalist number of clothes, and a map showing the heights (and troughs) of each day's walk. We would set out each morning as near to 6 am as possible in order to get as much of the daily 20 km done before it got hot. I was awakened on the first day by church bells outside our Puerto de Reina hostel and spent some ten minutes on instructions 'preparing' my feet before setting out. After a snack breakfast on that first day, we stopped briefly in the pitch dark at the Puerto to fill our water containers at the fountain. Shod in the prescribed leaden-heavy walking boots and thick woollen socks and with my two adjustable sticks (which kept slipping), I plodded after the others, who with the help of a mobile's small torch identified the yellow Camino shell sign on the roadside to show us our path. Living in a city I had forgotten what it was like to be in the complete blackness of the countryside, beautiful but eerie. The very first uphill slope saw me puffing and panting. I opened my mouth to moan but something reminded me of the stern advice given me some years earlier. On my visit to Rome where he was then living as Secretary to the Abbot General of his order, a former doctoral student of mine from Glenstal Abbey, Dom Henry O'Shea OSB, had invited me to climb up to Subiaco to see the celebrated cave where the sixth-century St Benedict had allegedly received his call to establish the first of Europe's medieval religious orders. I was recovering from a chest infection at the time and began to complain as soon as the going got tough when I heard Henry's voice murmur, 'Our abbot always says, you lose merit if you complain.' Stoicism was called for then as it was now and rewarded after a few kilometres by the sight of a village and café. Never have coffee and croissants tasted better.

Every day we met pilgrims or travellers from different countries, besides the many Spaniards, several perfectly equipped and garbed

Koreans, with whom to their great surprise and delight Paul, who had spent eight years in their country, chatted in their own language. We met young and old from Italy, France, the Low Countries, Sweden, Germany, Britain, Ireland and even a couple of former 'boat people' from Vietnam, and the occasional Hungarian on whom I could try out the remaining few words of my hard-won Hungarian from student days. Just one elderly lady we met on the Camino was a true medieval pilgrim: she had a few words of German and told me she came from Bulgaria and had walked all the way across Europe, pulling a little cart behind her with her clothes and provisions for the whole journey to her Santiago destination and back, supplemented with what she could beg on her way. She seemed to have no money and (presumably) slept in the open.

While Kieran moved with admirable ease between all west and south European languages, including some Italian dialects (he never found occasion to practise his Hebrew, Greek or Aramaic), I took a few days to learn to move from one tongue to the next. My smattering of Spanish, acquired from attempts to read *Don Quixote* in the original, plus a year's course in the Dublin Instituto Cervantes, improved rapidly, particularly in central Spain where I could engage elderly local villagers in polemical challenges to their *encomia* or extravagant tributes to 'El Caudillo' (Franco, the 'Spanish *Führer*') for all he had 'achieved' for Spain. No one bothers about grammar and syntax on the road; the need for any form of communication banishes lingering inhibitions in no time. But it was relaxing now and then to be able to have proper conversations with Catalan pilgrims, and with their neighbours from Valencia and the Balearic Islands, whose dialects are closely related, and to hear from all we met on the way what had led them to the Camino.

Each year thereafter we spent ten days or so on the Camino, reaching the marvellous Cathedral of Santiago four years later in May 2016 after 770 km (in my case and attested in a colourful certificate). The special attraction of the 'French' Camino to distinguish it from the more arduous northern coastal Camino is that it goes through poor country, so that most of the splendid Romanesque churches have survived in their pristine simplicity. Some, alas, had had side altars with all-too-graphic baroque statues of Christ or the saints suffering agonies of martyrdom. Our pilgrimage was *très Catholique* in the sense that we would sightsee at our destination after we had washed our shirts and socks and had a rest, then attend mass and normally have the frugal €10 pilgrimage dinners, but then once or twice would indulge ourselves in a proper *cena* (supper), much enhanced thanks to Aidan's professional expertise in wines. The following year, 2017, was to be the Italian *Via Francigena* to Lucca, but the others had to go without me as I was ill. In subsequent years we have walked through Savoy in the spring, the plains of Lombardy (unending, but enlivened by some six or seven species of heron enjoying the wet rice fields and a flight of yellow wagtails) and Tuscany. The more urbanized Italian version is neither as well organized nor as unique as the Spanish Camino, which apart from the beautiful cities of Burgos and Leon, takes one through a landscape seemingly forgotten by time. The pandemic year of 2020 was to have seen our arrival in Rome, to be greeted by Paul, who now lives there, but the coronavirus put it on the long finger. *Aufgehoben ist nicht aufgeschoben* as the phrase has it (postponement doesn't mean cancellation). Instead, we went on a less pious gastronomic pilgrimage to the West of Ireland in the autumn of 2020.

Meanwhile, there was plenty to do at home. Apart from the work of the School of Ecumenics there were the preparations for our annual Trinity second-hand book sale, started by the Trinity Women Graduates Association and others, which for over twenty-five years I chaired and, not least thanks to Ann Budd, our incomparable secretary, Richard Haworth of Geography, Mary Carson of Chemistry and senior members of the library staff and many others, had raised well over a quarter of a million euro for the Trinity Library's research collections. The department remained, as ever, an abiding interest and the 'old guard' met socially at regular intervals, especially when Sheila Watts returned on a visit to her family in Dublin. The close of the decade was marked by some memorable events for us all. After an interim of three years, permission was given in 2018 to fill the vacant chair of German, a complex process prepared with her usual focus and flair by the then head of department, Dr Caitríona Leahy. To the delight of his past and present colleagues, the external assessors recommended our former student and later colleague Jürgen Barkhoff to Board and Council as the successful candidate, and he was duly appointed in 2018 as the eighth incumbent of the 242-year-old chair of German at Trinity. We were most fortunate in securing as replacement for his associate professorship an outstanding candidate from Hugh Ridley's UCD department, Mary Cosgrove, who came to us via Warwick and Edinburgh. Shortly after, an alumna of the Trinity department, Caitríona Ní Dhúill, was appointed to the chair of German in University College Cork, following her years of research and teaching in Vienna and in Durham University's German department. In the spring of 2019 Gilbert Carr's life's work in the form of the immensely learned study of the early works of the Viennese satirist Karl Kraus, the 885-page *Demolierung – Gründung – Ursprung. Zu Karl Kraus' frühen Schriften und zur frühen Fackel* was published and received the very rare tribute of a page-long review in Germany's globally read *Frankfurter Allgemeine Zeitung*.

## — ELEVEN —

# *The 2020s: looking back – and forward*

'*Although many may not think so, I believe being a woman can be quite an advantage.*' – Thekla Beere

Time, they say, goes so fast for the old. Yet the first almost two years of the 2020s seem to have been with us for many years. Not on account of politics, at once alarming and seemingly all-absorbing (Trump, Boris, Brexit, etc), but rather the pandemic, which has dislocated our perception of time. Will it never end?

But I, writing just one year before entering my ninetieth decade, must now draw this account of my life to an end. I do so with a look across the decades and one or two reflections on the three main themes of this memoir – women, the academic world, and the faith I was brought up in and have endeavoured to practise all my life.

If I look back at when my generation was young, it is at an Ireland so profoundly different from what we know today. But not to reiterate those things we know: that today most Irish people are physically healthier (including the elderly), better educated, more mobile, with far greater opportunities than ever before, and that children are better protected. Nor shall I have anything to say on the issues that moralists worry about: those on the margins of society, the problems of drug-taking, alcohol, the harmful effects of social media, mental health issues (particularly in the young), that childhood is now much too short, or that the moral compass provided for the majority in our former authoritarian society by the Catholic Church is now no more and has yet to find an accepted replacement.

Instead, an observation and three reflections on selected aspects of '… the larger questions that draw us to [auto]biography in the first place: questions between life and writing, between self and other, between individual lives and collective histories',* that is, the three themes of this book, women, the academic world and the faith I was brought up in and have endeavoured to practise all my life.

The first is no doubt a trivial observation – though trivialities can be indicators of general trends. When I was an adolescent and a young adult, we all wanted to be different, to dress and look as different as we could from the next girl. Whereas today, in the so-called age of individualism, young women all appear to me to want to look the same, their appearance seemingly not an expression of their personality but a conformity to what is seen as 'the thing to be'. Or indeed that almost all Irish women (and a lot of children) feel the need to change the hair colour they were born with and that practically everyone parts her hair down the middle, regardless as to whether it suits them or not. (I am told by artists that central parting only suits those with a rare symmetrical face, some 5 per cent or less of the population.)

## WOMEN IN THE WORLD OF WORK

Here indeed a great deal has changed, and, on the whole, for the better. That Irish people are immeasurably better educated today than when I was young, that is, in the sense of second- and third-level qualifications, is well known. I have been heartened to learn that the gender pay gap

* Caitríona Ní Dhúill. *Metabiography, Reflecting on Biography*, London: Palgrave Macmillan, 2020, 3.

narrowed, from 46 per cent in 1938 for industrial workers to 34 per cent by the end of the twentieth century. Yet how slow progress continues to be even today is striking, and will not surprise women in the Irish workforce, especially in the private sector, as evidenced in the pay gap for all employees. I can't help feeling concerned that women who now constitute 46 per cent of those employed gainfully in the Irish economy, up from 40 per cent in 1998, and who, while in the late 1990s they were paid on average 27 per cent less than their male counterparts for the same work, twenty years later, in 2018, still experience a differential as high as 25 per cent. Today, for every 100 individuals working, there are twenty-four retired, as recorded in the 2016 Census. In the context of very much increased life expectancy and Irish voters' unwillingness to accept a longer working life, and the fact that by 2050, now less than thirty years away, the ratio will rise to at least 40, and possibly as high as 48, if Ireland fails to attract enough migrants, women are right to feel angered that certain things have *not* changed. From my younger friends, who are generally highly qualified women, I hear depressing statistics: of men and women who graduated in 2010 and enjoyed the same starting salary, seven years later the 'typical woman' was earning almost 10 per cent less than her male counterpart.* In other words, it seems evident that while Irish society in theory favours gender equality and a greater balance between the age cohorts, we are not prepared to pay for either. In the political sphere, women continue to be under-represented. Between 1919 and 1922, when Constance Markiewicz was Minister for Labour – the first in Ireland or the UK – and 1979, when Máire Geoghegan-Quinn was appointed Minister for the Gaeltacht, no woman held a ministerial post. The ratio has since improved, but not significantly. The need for gender balance is the more important today, given the often-contradictory attitudes among the Irish public: never in my lifetime have governments and politicians been the focus of such sustained criticism, yet never have public expectations of what the state is expected to do for them been higher. Until adequate childcare supports

---

* CSO Statbank, EHA50–51; CSO Statbank, QLF01; CSO Statbank, NEA04; CSO Statbank, PEC15.

for those who want or need to combine career and family are in place, Irish women will not achieve true parity with their male colleagues. As instance of how deeply entrenched prejudicial attitudes have been in the past, I recall a discussion some forty years ago, when I was a member of the Board of Trinity College and at the time the only female professorial member. The issue was paid maternal leave: the majority were evidently strongly opposed to the idea as 'impractical'. I remember asking: 'If women don't have children, who will fund your pensions?' Change, as the poet says, comes dropping slow.


## THE UNIVERSITY: WHERE DO WE GO FROM HERE?

What is the future of our universities and what does society expect, or, much more importantly, require from them? We academics, especially in view of the kind of bureaucratic and time-wasting controls imposed on us by muddled thinking on the part of government and media as to what universities are about, often lose sight of an essential aspect of our position: we are privileged, and we need to earn our privileges. One of the irritating features of many academics to the outsider is a misplaced sense of entitlement, which is only true in individual cases. Generally, however, most of us work extremely hard but often forget that we are where we are thanks to the gifts we were born with and the opportunities we were offered, and that circumstances permitted us to make use of.

When Micheál Martin became Minister for Education and Science in 1997, among other initiatives he helped put academic research in all disciplines on a sound basis by instituting, for the first time in the state's history, research councils for the humanities and social sciences and for the natural sciences. In 1998 Mary Harney as Tánaiste oversaw the setting up of Science Foundation Ireland. These key institutions proved of immense benefit to the research community in our universities and elsewhere, as did the twelve-year Programme for Research in Third-Level Institutions (PRTLI), funded mainly by the extraordinary generosity of the Irish-American philanthropist Chuck Feeney. A notable feature of these initiatives in the present context has been the success of women applicants for their generous funding.

Yet what is missing today, in my view, is *a considered policy* by government for the university as a national institution, parallel with what was done for scientific research. For decades government attitudes to the university seemed to vary between resentment, neglect, ignorance and unfounded expectations, such as using the third-level sector to mask unemployment statistics in bad times or as today assuming you could pack more and more students into the same buildings with the same funding in the era of the knowledge economy and expect the same results. Modern universities are extremely complex organizations and defy simplistic solutions. With so many demands on the public purse it is unrealistic of university staff to demand special treatment. But the Irish public and its governments need to consider what society needs from the university (society in the broadest sense of the term, to include culture, the polity, the economy), and determine how it must be funded. *Essentially the university exists to educate and train the next generation for the multiplicity of tasks that lie ahead of them in an ever more rapidly changing world and to extend the boundaries of knowledge.* There is no point in wasting money to doing these vital things badly. If the present student numbers cannot be adequately funded, the state will have to make the electorally unpopular decision to reduce the numbers of those attending in order to educate them properly, though not in the transactional on-line manner that the COVID crisis has made necessary, as a temporary emergency measure. *Bildung ist Umgang*, wrote Austria's great novelist and educator, Adalbert Stifter (1805–1868): education is through mutual meeting of minds, of the learned and experienced with the imagination, originality and dynamism of the young. This is not utopianism: in the past decades, the international reputation and success of Irish graduates worldwide has shown that it can and has been done.

~

In conclusion then: it is hard, if not impossible, for the young and middle-aged to understand that very many old people don't necessarily feel old. Even if my body creaks and often aches, I continue to feel as I always have done and tend to be surprised when people want to treat me differently, just because I am part of the 'elderly age cohort'. So – though I don't intend this to be my last word – here are just a few 'pearls of wisdom' from the perspective of some eighty years of conscious experience, to the young, who today, for all the restrictions and often unsurmountable obstacles my generation faced, have it a lot tougher than we did:

- Believe in yourself and know that every single person in the world is unique.

- Don't cod yourself, nor allow yourself to have a false image of what you think you would like to be.

- Always, especially in times when you feel low, love yourself (though not at the expense of those around you).

- Try to think yourself into the mindset of other people, especially those who have different values from you and / or you don't like, or who appear not to like or respect you. Ask yourself: why do they think / act like that?

- Empathy is a great virtue, both for its own sake and as a source of personal happiness to those who acquire and cultivate it.

St Teresa of Avila, who was as wily as she was saintly, provides me with a constant corrective: as we grow older, she suggests, we notice the faults of our friends much more than our own. It is a helpful exercise in life to imagine what *they* think of *us*. I have had the good fortune to have been born a happy person. That I have generally remained one through the ups and downs of life, I believe I owe to the essence of the Christian gospel message, however imperfectly lived.

'*I believe that I may understand.*' (St Anselm)

# Select Bibliography

Akenson, D. *Small Differences: Irish Catholics and Irish Protestants, 1815–1922*. Dublin: Gill and Macmillan, 1990.

Bartlett, Thomas. *Ireland. A History*. Cambridge: CUP, 2010.

Biaghini, Eugene and Mary E. Daly (eds). *A Social History of Modern Ireland*. Cambridge: CUP 2017.

—and Dan Mulhall. *The Shaping of Modern Ireland: a centenary assessment*. Cambridge: CUP, 2016.

Brown, Terence. *Ireland: a social and cultural history 1922–2002*. London: Harper Perennial, 2004.

Bryson, Anna. *No Coward Soul: a biography of Thekla Beere*. Dublin: IPA, 2002.

Carbery, Mary. *The Farm by Lough Gur*. Dublin: Lilliput Press, 2018 (1937).

Clancy, Patrick, Sheila Drudy et al. *Ireland: sociological perspectives*. Dublin: IPA in association with the Sociological Society of Ireland, 1995.

Clear, Caitríona. *Nuns in Nineteenth-Century Ireland*. Dublin: Gill and Macmillan, 1987.

—*Women of the House. Women's Household Work in Ireland 1922–1961: discourses, experiences, memories*. Dublin: Irish Academic Press, 2000.

Cockshut, A.O.J. *Man & Woman: a study of love in the novel 1740–1940*. New York: OUP, 1978.

—*True to Life: the art of biography in the nineteenth century*. London: Collins, 1974.

—*The Art of Autobiography in the Nineteenth and Twentieth Century*. New Haven: Yale UP, 1984.

Coleman, Marie. *The Irish Sweep: a history of the Irish Hospitals Sweepstake, 1930–87*. Dublin: UCD Press, 2009.

Connolly, S.J. *The Oxford Companion to Irish History*. New ed. Oxford: OUP, 2002.

Coolahan, John. *Irish Education*. Dublin: Institute of Public Administration, 1981.

Cullen, Mary. 'Women, emancipation, and politics, 1860–1984'. *A New History of Ireland* 7, 826–91.

D'Alton, Ian and Ida Milne (eds). *Protestant and Irish: the minority's search for a place in independent Ireland*. Cork: University Press, 2019.

Daly, Mary E. *Women and Work in Ireland*. Dublin: Economic and Social History Society of Ireland (ESRI), 1997.

—*The Slow Failure: population decline and independent Ireland, 1920–1973*. Madison Wisconsin: The University of Wisconsin Press, 2006 (History of Ireland and the Irish Diaspora).

—*Sixties Ireland: re-shaping the economy, state and society 1957–73*. Cambridge: CUP, 2016.

Delaney, Enda. *Demography, State and Society: Irish migration to Britain, 1921–1971*. Liverpool: Liverpool UP, 2000.

—*The Irish in Post-War Britain*. Oxford: OUP, 2013.

*Dictionary of Irish Biography. From the Earliest Times to the Year 2002*, ed. James Maguire and James Quinn. Nine vols + 2. Royal Irish Academy and Cambridge: CUP, 2009 + 2018 (on-line www.dib.ie).

Earner-Byrne, Lindsey. *Letters of the Catholic Poor: poverty in independent Ireland, 1922–1940*. London: Blackwell, 2017.

Farmar, Tony. *Privileged Lives: a social history of middle-class Ireland 1882–1989*. Dublin: A&A Farmar, 2010.

Ferriter, Diarmaid. *Mothers, Maidens and Myths: a history of the ICA*. Dublin: FÁS, 1995.

—*Occasions of Sin: sex and society in modern Ireland*. London: Profile Books, 2009.

—*Ambiguous Republic: Ireland in the seventies*. London: Profile Books, 2012.

—*The Transformation of Ireland, 1900–2000*. London: Profile Books, 2014.

Fischer, Clara and Mary McAuliffe (eds). *Irish Feminisms, Past, Present and Future: essays in honour of Mary Cullen and Margaret MacCurtain*. Dublin: Arlen House, 2015.

Fitzpatrick, David. *Irish Emigration 1801–1921*. Dublin, 1984.

–'"A Peculiar Tramping People": the Irish in Britain, 1801–1870'. *A New History of Ireland* 5, 623–60.

Foster, R.F. *Modern Ireland 1600–1972*. London: Allen Lane / Penguin, 1988.

Frühwald, Wolfgang. *Zeit der Wissenschaft: Forschungskultur an der Schwelle zum 21. Jahrhundert* (Science Today: research culture on the eve of the twenty-first century). Cologne: Dumont, 1997.

Hayden, Mary. *The Diaries of Mary Hayden*. 5 vols. Edited and annotated by Conan Kennedy. Killala: Morigan, 2005.

Healy, John. *The Death of an Irish Town*. Cork: Cork UP, 1968.

Hennessy, Peter. *Never Again: Britain 1945–51*. London: Penguin, 2006.

—*Having It So Good: Britain in the fifties*. London: Allen Lane, 2006.

—*Winds of Change: Britain in the early sixties*. London: Penguin Random, 2019.

Hopkins, Gerard Manley. *Poems and Prose*. Selected and with an introduction by W.H. Gardner. London: Penguin, 1985.

Howlin, Niamh and Kevin Costello (eds). *Law and the Family in Ireland, 1750–1950*. London: Palgrave, 2017.

Hume, Basil. *Searching for God*. London: Hodder and Stoughton, 1977.

Jackson, Alvin. *Ireland 1798–1998: politics and war*. Oxford: Blackwell 1999.

Jackson, John A. *The Irish in Britain*. London: Routledge, 1963.

à Kempes, Thomas. *Imitation de Jésus-Christ*. Lille (Nord), 1911.

Kennedy, Finola. *From Cottage to Crèche: family change in Ireland.* Dublin: Institute of Public Administration, 2001.

Kennedy, Kieran A., Thomas Giblin and Deirdre McHugh. *The Economic Development of Ireland in the Twentieth Century.* London: Routledge, 1988.

Keogh, Dermot, F. O'Shea and Carmel Quinlan (eds). *The Lost Decade: Ireland in the 1950s.* Dublin: Mercier Press, 2004.

Lee, J.J. *The Modernisation of Irish Society, 1848–1918.* Dublin: Gill, 1973.

—*Ireland 1912–1985. Politics and Society.* Cambridge: CUP 1989.

Lloyd Praeger, Robert. *The Way That I Went.* London: Collins 1937.

Lynch, Patrick. 'The economist and public policy', *Studies* 42 (1953), 241–60.

McMahon, Deirdre. 'John Charles McQuaid. Archbishop of Dublin, 1940–1972'. *History of the Catholic Diocese of Dublin*, ed. James Kelly and Daire Keogh. Dublin: Four Courts Press, 2000, 355–61.

MacCurtain, Margaret. *Ariadne's Thread: writing women into Irish history.* Dublin: Arlen House, 2008.

—*Metaphors for Change: essays on state and society.* Dublin: Arlen House, 2019.

MacCurtain, Margaret and D. Ó Corráin (eds). *Women in Irish history: the historical dimension.* Dublin: Arlen House, 1978.

Meenan, James. *The Irish Economy since 1922.* Liverpool: Liverpool UP, 1970.

*National Programme of Primary Instruction.* Issued by the National Programme Conference. Dublin: Educational Company of Ireland, 1922.

Ní Dhúill, Caitríona. *Metabiography: reflecting on biography.* London: Palgrave Macmillan, 2020.

Nowlan, Kevin B. and T.D. Williams. *Ireland in the War Years and After, 1939–1951.* Dublin: Gill and Macmillan, 1969.

O'Brien, Sorcha. *Electric Irish Homes: rural electrification, domestic products and Irish housewives in the 1950s and 1960s.* e-prints. Kingston.ac.uk, 2018.

O'Faolain, Julia and Lauro Martines (eds). *Not in God's Image.* London: Fontana, 1974.

Ó Gráda, Cormac. *A Rocky Road: the Irish economy since the 1920s.* Manchester: Manchester UP, 1997.

Parkes, Susan. *A Danger to the Men? A history of women in Trinity College Dublin 1904–2004*. Dublin: Lilliput Press, 2004.

*Report and Programme presented by the National Programme Conference for the Minister for Education*. Dublin: Stationery Office, 1926.

*Revised Programme of Primary Instruction in National Schools*. Appendix to the Annual Report of the Commissioners of Education. Dublin: Stationery Office, 1903.

*Revised Programme of Primary Instruction*. Dublin: Roinn Oideachais. Oideachas Náisiunta, 1934.

Robinson, Lennox (ed.). *A Golden Treasury of Irish Verse*. London: Macmillan, 1935.

Sagarra, Eda. *Kevin O'Shiel: Northern nationalist and Irish state-builder*. Dublin: Irish Academic Press, 2013.

—*Envoy Extraordinary. Professor Smiddy of Cork*. Dublin: Institute of Public Administration, 2018.

Scally, Derek. *The Best Catholics in the World. The Irish, the Church and the End of a Special Relationship*. London: Penguin Random House, 2021.

Shiel, Michael J. *The Quiet Revolution: the electrification of rural Ireland 1946–1976*. Dublin: O'Brien Press, 1984.

Totah, Sister Mary David. *The Joy of God: collected writings*. London: Bloomsbury, 2019.

Tyrrell, Peter. *Founded on Fear: Letterfrack Industrial School: war and exile*, Diarmuid Whelan (ed.). Dublin: Irish Academic Press, 2006.

Valiulis, M.G. and Mary O'Dowd (eds). *Women and Irish history. Essays in honour of Margaret MacCurtain*. Dublin: Wolfhound Press, 1997.

Varden, Erik. *The Shattering of Loneliness: on Christian remembrance*. London: Bloomsbury, 2018.

Vaughan, W.E. (ed.). *A New History of Ireland*, vols 5 and 6. Oxford: OUP, 1996.

Whyte, John H. *Church and State in Modern Ireland, 1923–1970*. Dublin: Gill and Macmillan, 1971.

# *Index*

Grosz, Georg, 135

Guards Regiments, 5

Guinness, 176

*Guinness Book of Records,* 92

Gwynn, Fr Aubrey, SJ, 43, 46

Habsburg armies, 66

Halpin, Attracta, 155

Hamburg, 172

Hammerstein-Robinson, Helga, 144

Hampshire, 125. *see also* Farnborough Hill

Hanson, Rev Richard, bishop of Clogher, 125, 147n

Hantsch, Hugo, 60, 61, 62

Härle, Gertrud, 52, 84

Harms, Wolfgang, 172, 178

Harney, Mary, 193n, 203n, 208, 236

Harold's Cross Hospice, Dublin, 101n, 216

Harrison, George, 88

Harristown, Dublin, 217

Harte, Marie, 219, 224, 225

Harte, Michelle, 219, 222, 223, 224, 225, 226

Harvard University, 175

Haughey, Charles J., 136–137, 161n, 180, 183, 205

Haworth, Richard, 231

Health (Family Planning) Bill 1979, 180

Healy, Cahir, 211

Heath, Edward, 113

Hederman, Mark, OSB, *Underground Cathedrals,* 185n

Hedin, Sven, 53

Hegel, George W.F., 117

Heidelberg University, 77, 166

Heiligenkreuz, 63

Heine, Heinrich, 151, 162, 176, 187, 197

Heliopolis, 55

Heller, Erich, 68, 106n

*Hello Dolly* (film), 88n

Hely-Hutchinson, John, 135

Henkel, Arthur, 77

*Hermathena: A Dublin University Review,* 135

Hertford College, Oxford, xiin

Herzmanovsky-Orlando, Fritz, 58

Hessen (Germany), 47

Heuss, Theodor, 48

Higgins, Michael D., 205

High Court, 65n

Higher Education Authority (HEA), 207, 208

Highfield, Omagh, 10, 11

Highfield Healthcare, 225–226

Hignett, Dorothy, 73

Hill, Derek, 134

Hilliard, Alan, 185n

Hitler, Adolf, 47, 48, 53n, 59, 65, 107, 108, 177–178, 200

Hitler Diaries, 46n

Hoek of Holland, 49

Hofmannsthal, Hugo von, 60
*Der Schwierige,* 59

Holland, Charles, 138

Holland, Mary, 34

Holocaust, 167, 178

Holy Ghost Fathers (*now* Spiritans), 101

Holyhead, 9, 28, 114

Holy Roman Empire, 195n

Home Office (London), 107

O'Flanagan, Brian, 25

O'Flanagan, Dr Harry, 25

O'Flanagan, Ita (Eda's aunt), 25

Ogilvie, Lady, 70

O'Hagan, John, 161

O'Hanlon, Gerry, SJ, 132n, 181

oil crises (1973 and 1979), 113, 158

Oireachtas, 116

O'Kane, Aisling, 160

Omagh, Co. Tyrone, 10–11, 16, 44

Omagh bombing (1998), 115

Omagh Tennis Club, 2

O'Mahony, Kieran, OSA, 228, 230

O'Malley, Donough, 90

O'Malley, John (Eda's son-in-law), 228

O'Malley, Mireia (Eda's daughter).
  see Sagarra, Mireia

O'Meara, Patrick, 149

Ó Murchú, Máirtín, 188, 205

O'Neills, 2

O'Rahilly, Alfred, 26, 98

O'Reilly, Dr Frank, 196

O'Reilly, Joan, 44n

O'Riordan, Anne, 211

O'Rourke, Mary, 153

Orwell, George, *Animal Farm* and
  *1984*, 34

Orwell House, Dublin, 189

O'Shea, Dom Henry, OSB, 229

O'Shiel, Cecil (née Smiddy) (Eda's
  mother), xiii, 1, 9, 21, 23, 25, 27–28,
  28n, 31n, 33, 67, 68, 69, 77, 94,
  97–98, 100, 101, 115, 125, 127, 141
    family, 3, 5; marriage to Kevin, 2,
      191; sister Pearl, 190–191
    financial flair, 191–192
    golf playing, 38–39, 188, 192

illness and death, 187–189,
  189–190, 219

O'Shiel, Clodagh (Eda's sister). *see*
  Forshaw, Clodagh

O'Shiel, Elizabeth (Mitty) (née
  Roantree) (Eda's grandmother),
  2–3, 6, 10
    sisters of, in religious orders, 5, 6–8

O'Shiel, Frank (Eda's uncle), 3

O'Shiel, Kevin (Eda's father), 1–2, 3,
  4, 11, 14, 16, 23, 26, 64, 70, 95, 98,
  106, 124, 192, 210, 211,
    charitable work, 22
    close friends, 22, 26
    Eda's biography of, 2–3, 227
    family, 2, 3; first marriage, 1–2;
      marriage to Cecil, 2, 191;
      maternal aunts, 6–7
    illness and death, 114–115
    investments, 191
    love of nature, 18–19
    writings: letters, xii; memoirs,
      114–115

O'Shiel, Syra (Eda's aunt), 2, 3, 8

O'Shiel family (Tyrone), 2, 3, 29n. *see
  also* Shields

Otto, *Deutsche Grammatik*, 39

Otway-Ruthven, Jocelyn, 124, 126,
  134, 135–137

Outer Mongolia, 53

Owens College, Manchester, 86

Oxbridge, 46, 67n, 135

Oxford, xii, 37, 68–70, 74, 77, 92,
  95n, 106n, 107, 121, 122, 123, 147,
  152, 160, 167, 169n, 173, 209
    Benet Hall, 140

*Oxford Junior Encyclopaedia*, 29

# Issued

EM(S)                                  DUE DATI

ving with my century : a. 20 Nov 202
PL8000104229
em Value: €1.00

tal value of item(s): €1.00
ur current loan(s): 1
ur current reservation(s): 2
ur current active request(s): 0

 renew your items please log onto My
count at https://dublincity.spydus.i

nk you for using your local library

faith, 8–10, 51, 69, 93, 101, 234, 238; and Catholic Church, 180–187; clerical abuse scandals, 183–186

family, 1–10. *see also* O'Shiel, Cecil (mother); O'Shiel, Kevin (father); aunts in religious orders, 5–8; father's illness and death, 114–115; mother's decline and death, 187, 188–189, 190; sister. *see* Forshaw, Clodagh

language studies, 35–36, 39

leisure pursuits, 19–20, 22–25, 27, 38–40. *see also* golf

marriage and family, 91–110. *see also* Sagarra, Albert (husband); earlier romances, 67–68, 92–93; courtship and engagement to Albert, 93–95; meets Sagarra family in Barcelona, 95–97; wedding and honeymoon, 97–99; childlessness, 100–101; adoption of Mireia, 101–106; family life in Manchester, 118–124; new life in Dublin, 126–131; family home, 127–128

political interests and views, 31–32, 34, 47–48, 67, 177–178. *see also* German unification; women's rights

portrait of, 211–212

professional career: schoolteacher, 65–66, 68; job interviews, 68–70; German department, Manchester, 70–78, 84–89, 91–92, 102–103, 106–110, 117–118, 122–124;

Chair of German at Trinity, 124–128, 132–153, 157–171, 188, 197–198; Registrar of Trinity, 137–142; NCEA, 154–156; European project, 165–173; RIA Secretary. *see* Royal Irish Academy (RIA); retirement symposium and portrait, 211–212

publications and writings, 108–109, 117–118, 128, 201–202; biographies, 227–228; daily routine, ix–x, 109; diaries, xi–xii; Festschrift articles, 187; memoir, ix–xi

research interests and advocacy, 79, 84, 90, 93, 102, 106, 109–110, 171–174, 192–193, 199, 204–210. *see also* academic research; German language and literature; German Research Council; Irish Research Council; Fontane studies, 174–176, 197–199

retirement, life following, 212–231; voluntary work, 212–227, 231–232; friend's dementia, 219–227; 80th birthday, 227, 228; pilgrimage walks, 226, 228–231; fundraising, 231; 'pearls of wisdom,' 238

Sagarra, Eduard (Eda's father-in-law), 95, 96, 97, 98, 99

Sagarra, Eduard (son of Ramon), 98

Sagarra, Guadelupe, 96

Sagarra, Isabel, 97

Witherby's *British Birds,* 20
Wolff, Theodor, 78
women in the workplace, xiii, 6,
234–236
    equality/equal pay. *see* gender
        equality
    'female academy' at Trinity,
        132–156
women's movement, 117, 182
women's rights, 81, 82–83, 115–117,
    180–181, 182, 236. *see also* gender
    equality
Woolworths, Dublin, 30
Workers' Educational Association,
    86–87
World War I, 61, 62
World War II, 11, 12, 24–25, 47, 115.
    *see also* 'Emergency' period
Wright, Barbara, 142, 145
Wright, Bill, 134
Wright, Jane (*later* Grimson), 142

Wrixon, Gerry, 208
Wroclaw/Breslau (Poland), 53
Wruck, Peter, 174
Württemberg, 108
Würzburg, 162
Wyse-Jackson, Vanessa, 150

*X* Case (1992), 183

Yates, W.E. (Gar), 117, 169n
*Yes, Minister* (TV series), 137n
Yiddish, 85
Yorkshire, 114, 188
Young, George Macaulay, *Portrait of
    an Age,* 108

Zurich, 57
Zurich Polytechnic (*Eidgenössiche
    Technische Hochschule*/ETH), 209
Zurich University, 55–57
Zussman, Jack, 86n, 92–93, 94